INTRODUCTION
TO
MYTH

HAYDEN SERIES IN LITERATURE

Robert W. Boynton, Consulting Editor

*Former Principal, Senior High School
and Chairman, English Department
Germantown Friends School*

INTRODUCTION
TO
MYTH

PETER R. STILLMAN

Charlotte Valley Central School
New York

HAYDEN BOOK COMPANY, INC.
Rochelle Park, New Jersey

ACKNOWLEDGMENTS

The author wishes to thank the proprietors for permission to quote copyrighted works, as follows:

JAMES THURBER. "The Unicorn in the Garden." Copyright © 1940 by James Thurber. Copyright © 1968 by Helen Thurber. From *Fables for Our Time,* published by Harper & Row. Originally printed in *The New Yorker.*

JACOB and WILHELM GRIMM. "The Water of Life." Reprinted with permission of Macmillan Publishing Co., Inc., from *Household Stories* by the Grimm Brothers. Translated by Lucy Crane. Copyright © 1954 by Macmillan Publishing Co., Inc.

Sir Gawain and the Green Knight. Translated by Theodore Howard Banks, Jr. Copyright © (1929) 1957. Reprinted by permission of Prentice-Hall, Inc., Englewood Cliffs, N.J.

EDWIN ARLINGTON ROBINSON. "Miniver Cheevy." Copyright © 1907 by Charles Scribner's Sons. Reprinted by permission of Charles Scribner's Sons from *The Town Down the River* by Edwin Arlington Robinson.

KENNETH PATCHEN. "In Order To" from *Collected Poems* by Kenneth Patchen. Copyright © 1954 by New Directions Publishing Corporation. Reprinted by permisson of New Directions Publishing Corporation.

RICHARD CHASE. *Jack and King Marock.* Copyright © 1943 by Richard Chase and renewed 1971. Reprinted by permission of the publisher, Houghton Mifflin Company.

THOMAS HARDY. "Neutral Tones" reprinted with permission of Macmillan Publishing Co., Inc., from *Collected Poems* by Thomas Hardy. Copyright © 1925 by Macmillan Publishing Co., Inc.

(ACKNOWLEDGMENTS continued on page 212.)

Library of Congress Cataloging in Publication Data

Stillman, Peter R
   Introduction to myth.

   (Hayden series in literature)
    1. Myth in literature. 2. Literature—
Collections. I. Title.
PN56.M94S8   809'.933'7   77-2904
ISBN 0-8104-5890-X

3	4	5	6	7	8	9	PRINTING
80	81	82	83	84	85		YEAR

PREFACE

This book is not a collection of myths. These abound, in anthologies, ethnic collections, and anthropological studies. Nor is this a sociological, archaeological, psychological, or historical examination of the forces of mythology in human affairs. Advanced works dealing with the relationships of myth to the social and behavioral sciences are very complex and presume the reader's fascination with whatever field of scholarship they represent.

To interested students—and teachers—mythology can pose vital questions about human visions of the universe: the spiritual and intellectual strands that bind us together through time and across deep and alien seas; the unexplainable creative urges that fuel us even in the bleakest of times; and the twin presences of good and evil, joy and sorrow, birth and death that we all must grapple with and reconcile.

While myth collections may provide the raw materials for such question-raisings, they inevitably lead to mistaken assumptions. Instead of providing insights into the universality of the human response to the world, they tend to suggest the opposite: that the Greeks, for instance, believed absolutely in a swarm of preposterous gods, despite their otherwise high level of civilization; or that Eskimo mythology is no more than a simple reflection of a harsh and primitive life style. Most of these collections, furthermore, make only scant connections between mythology and literature, often mistaking one for the other or, at best, blurring the two.

The premise of this book is that the gap between such anthologies and the high-level scholarly examinations of mythology is worth filling.

Myths are not merely localized, primitive responses to natural or cultural phenomena. Nowhere on earth has a society developed a cosmology that did not involve itself with fundamental truths about all humankind. In all places, in all times, a society's myths have formed what mythologist Joseph Campbell refers to as "the magic ring of truth." While this is a complex idea, it is demonstrable and vitally important. Students, once they have been introduced to it and guided through some of its proofs, should find electrifying applications to the study of the self, both their own and those of others. This book attempts such an introduction.

Without mythology there could be no literature. All literature, consciously or unconsciously, is based in mythology. If this thesis seems an overstatement, consider that poetry and fiction are at heart metaphorized attempts to state truths about the human condition, and that even the shabbiest examples of either, regardless of their subject, must at least be believable to be read by an intelligent audience. What we reject as unacceptable in literature is not bad style so much as what we cannot reconcile with what we know to be metaphorically true. A Western, for example, may be written in wooden prose, but if the hero story is faithfully told, reflecting the archetypal heroic quest of mythological origin, we will accept it.

This book offers numerous pieces of prose and poetry, along with comments and questions, chosen to demonstrate the bond between myth and literature. A few works represent conscious borrowings by modern authors from classical myths. Tennyson's *Ulysses* is an obvious example. Most, however, owe their origins not to any learned legend, but to truths which, mirrored in countless myths, have been with us forever.

Although no attempt is made to demonstrate the evolution of a particular myth into a consciously artistic work we would classify as "literature," I have included some selections that pre-date prose fiction and have also paraphrased a few actual myths. These provide necessary links not so much between ancient and modern times but between mythology and literature.

If all literature springs from mythological roots, then much of this text will pose an irony, for if students grasp this truth about literature's origins, the need for carefully selected prose and poetry disappears; *any* work will reveal vastly more of itself than before. No magic pedagogical formula underlies this assumption. It simply makes sense that when students begin to comprehend their own involvement in the mythological scheme of things, what they read cannot be seen as alien matter. Hence, their responses and perceptions will become deeper and less contrived.

The structure of this book is uncomplicated. Although the introduction is a long one, it is as simple and straightforward as the subject allows. It is followed by short, fairly specific chapters that offer many opportunities for discussion. Each chapter includes closely structured reading assignments that exemplify the main ideas of the text. The last section of the book contains selections which student and teacher may apply in whatever ways seem interesting. The readings were selected not only for their obvious application to the subject at hand, but also for their excellence.

This is not a difficult book. Indeed, the difficulty lay in avoiding the fascinating byways in the dozens of scholarly works on the subject of myth in order to keep matters simple and direct. It is, I hope, a worthwhile, even a necessary, book—if it succeeds, that is, in leading readers to some important understandings about the awesome truths implicit in myth-making and its role in our lives.

CONTENTS

I

INTRODUCTION

But often, in the world's most crowded streets,
But often, in the din of strife,
There rises an unspeakable desire
After the knowledge of our buried life;
A thirst to spend our fire and restless force
In tracking out our true, original course;
A longing to inquire
Into the mystery of this heart which beats
So wild, so deep in us—to know
Whence our lives come and where they go.

—Matthew Arnold, from *The Buried Life*

I

INTRODUCTION

*. . . every form of literature has a pedigree, and we
can trace its descent back to the earliest times.*

— Northrop Frye

Much of the confusion and contradiction regarding
mythology has to do with the term itself. *Myth*, like numberless
other words in our language, has grown muddy and imprecise.
Taken from the Greek *mythos*, in that language it simply meant
plot. But today in English it is rubbery enough to cover anything
we look upon as untrue or antiquated. "That's a myth," we say,
meaning that an idea, an observation, or a belief is foolish or based
on wrong information. Closer to the truth but still misleading is the
notion that a myth is an exotic, long-ago tale suitable only for
young children.

Myths somehow do seem to belong to another time,
another place. They have an alien flavor and are most often judged
to be "what someone else believes." Many of the myths we have
been exposed to—in children's books, movies, even literature texts—
reinforce cherished, misbegotten ideas about one's own racial and
societal superiority; for we have been led to understand that myth
reflects an attempt by primitive societies to unravel through fanciful tales the nature of human beings and the cosmos. One has only to
examine from this point of view a sampling of creation myths from
around the world to sense that their makers and tellers must have
been hopelessly baffled about how man originated.

It is not a far leap from that conclusion to the assumption
that societies who base their religion—and hence their deepest values—on quaint and colorful myths are out of step with the modern

3

world, and therefore backward. Just such thinking can, of course, be found at the root of some of the most enduring human prejudices and behind the countless conquests and exploitations of one society by another. To place a misunderstanding of mythology at the center of the world's woes would be an oversimplification. Yet, it is a factor. We have always found it convenient to view others with eyes so shuttered by our own values, our own world view, that those of another people appear "primitive" and foolish by comparison.

A clearer view of mythology should aid each of us in better understanding our place in the human family, and this is a hoped-for byproduct of your experience with this book. It's main purpose, however, will be to take a fairly definitive look at myth as a shaper of human artistic responses to a puzzling, often terrifying universe.

Each person who tells a story molds the story to his tongue and to his mouth, and each listener molds the story to his ear. Thus, the same story, told over and over, is never quite the same.

—Julius Lester

In this book mythology finds a place in what is essentially a literature text. Is mythology itself then literature? Yes, in that it is *voiced* as such; that is, its stories (or tales or legends) are forms familiar to those found in literature. But no, mythology is not literature, at least in a technical sense. Myths do not originate, to our knowledge, with any one person, nor were they at first written down. Commonly, centuries passed between the earliest expression of a myth and the time it was first recorded. Myths are produced by groups or societies, usually over a long period. Furthermore, they change with time, adding and subtracting characters and events, shifting emphases, even completely changing the identity of a central figure. Finally, while myths are artistic, they are not conscious works of art. Generally, none of these observations applies to literature.

It is impossible, however, to make entirely satisfactory distinctions between the two. Myth and literature both use the narrative form. Both entertain. Despite the high purposes they serve, myths are at heart good stories. If they weren't, they would not have survived. Myths, like any assortment of modern short stories, novels, or movies, can be funny, sad, sentimental, or terrifying.

Quite often myths are based on real persons and events. Furthermore, they often reveal a moral. Even the idea that a myth has evolved over centuries, in contrast to a work of literature, which keeps its original form, has a weakness. Print freezes literature. If a century ago Herman Melville had simply told his great story about Moby Dick to members of his community instead of writing it down, the white whale by now might be an evil computer (like HAL in *2001: A Space Odyssey*).

A simple way of beginning to understand what a myth is would be to see it as an attempt to say something important in story form—something that would be too awkward or difficult to explain literally, like death, for example. It would originate as a fragment, not as a full-blown story. It would eventually be expanded and changed, for a variety of reasons. Its message would be made consistent with other important messages embodied in other kinds of stories spawned by the same society. An unconscious weaving process would take place, as that society's significant concerns gradually became organized in mythic form.

Without mythology there could be no literature. Critic and scholar Northrop Frye writes, "Every society has a verbal culture, which includes ballads, folk songs, folk tales, work songs, legends, and the like. As it develops, a special group of stories, the stories we call myths, begins to crystallize in the center of this verbal culture. These stories are taken with particular seriousness by their society, because they express something deep in that society's beliefs or vision of its situation and destiny. Myths, unlike other types of stories, stick together to form a mythology. . . . Literature as we know it, as a body of writing, always develops out of a mythical framework of this kind."

As Frye states, mythology is at the very center of things in any society, deeply bound up in, and growing out of, the ways that people have perceived their world. Seemingly, myth-making and myth-telling are at the same level of essentials as shelter and warmth. This is not to suggest, however—as some textbooks do—that a society baffled by some natural phenomenon such as thunder and lightning would feel an urgent need to concoct a tale about it for themselves and future generations to swallow without question. Because myths are taken *seriously*, we should not conclude that they are taken *literally*. We do not believe that a stork brings babies, although the tale has been told millions of times. Nor should we assume that the Netsilik Eskimo believes that the fox created night and the hare created day. Both tales are the stuff of myth; both are literally unbelievable but also true, as we shall see.

Myth can be defined in many ways, but in the literary context it is the distilled essence of human experience, expressed as metaphoric narrative.

—John Alexander Allen

Myths are metaphors which stand for things other and greater than themselves. A metaphor is a figurative expression as opposed to a literal (or factual) one. Technically, the metaphor is distinguished from the simile. Both are figures of speech used to compare essentially dissimilar things. In the metaphor, one thing actually becomes the other: "Homework is garbage." Similes, however, involve the use of *like* or *as*, maintaining both a connection and a distinction between the things being compared. "Homework is like garbage. It stinks."

Some literature texts make much of the differences between these two figurative devices, as you may already know. They are distinguished here only to avoid future confusion. Our concern with metaphor is not a closely critical one. We are using *metaphor* in a wider and more general sense as a way to point out how myths are figurative ways of stating great and otherwise unknowable truths about life.

We live in a society in which facts are seen as synonymous with truth. Centuries ago, those who dabbled in the sciences were considered eccentric, sacrilegious, and/or dangerous. Today we have developed a nearly opposite point of view. We place our faith in science and technology, relying on the observable "truths" they have revealed to us. The problem with this attitude is that it has led us to demand narrow kinds of proofs on which to base our thoughts and actions. Even our language reflects this narrowness. Alan Watts comments in *The Two Hands of God*, "Factual language obviously represents the view of nature which is held to be normal, practical, and sane—the world of science and industry, business and bureaucracy, of hard facts and cold calculations. It is a world that is rather flat, dry, and dusty—like a city parking lot—but which many of us find enormously reassuring and to which we cling as to sanity itself." Such a near-total reliance on the rational and technological aspects of life is described by the renowned psychiatrist Carl Jung as a worship of "the goddess Reason," in his view "our greatest and most tragic illusion." Jung was not saying thereby that there is anything wrong with rationality as such, but that we have let it take us over, at great cost. He, like many other great modern thinkers, believed that its influence has created a world of short-sighted particulars in the place of larger, unifying ideas; that it has caused society to abandon its age-old ties with mythology, leaving us individually isolated from the powerful truths that myths embody.

The distinctions between factual and figurative kinds of truths are not easy to deal with, particularly because most of us have grown up to believe that *literal* truth (or rational or factual truth) is the real goods, while figurative statements are simply fanciful. When we say that myths are to be understood figuratively (or metaphorically), it implies that we mean *only* or *merely* figuratively. We tend to be stuck with the idea that if something cannot be taken literally (the stork story, for example), it cannot be taken as any kind of truth at all.

Facts provide information. They are the necessary ingredients of reasoning. They do not, however, provide all the answers. They do not tell us where we came from or what we are destined for. They do not point a path through life. They do not give us the courage to go on when we feel most like quitting. They do not, and never will, explain the forces of good and evil, or soften the fear of death, or solve any other riddle of life. Unless we are able to recognize and participate in the kinds of truths that present themselves in the metaphorical images of mythology, the answers to these riddles are unknowable. "Myth," observes Ananda Coomaraswamy, "embodies the nearest approach to absolute truth that can be stated in words."

At this point it would be quite possible to read through a collection of myths without discovering anything that approaches an "absolute truth." Not only possible but likely. It is one thing for a textbook to tell its reader that the truths are there, disguised in metaphors. It is another thing to offer some tangible evidence that will make this idea discoverable.

When the poet Gerard Manley Hopkins described the grandeur of God as ". . . like shining from shook foil," he provided a concrete image to express an idea that cannot be put literally, that is, in the language of facts. The image is knowable. Furthermore, it is a vivid, satisfying metaphor. Through it, we can form a strong association with the other, greater thing that "shook foil" represents. Hopkins's metaphor provides a bridge between the sayable and the unsayable, between the knowable and the unknowable.

Myths do the same thing, even a seemingly silly one like the centuries-old stork story. Some psychologists believe that our first experience with terror comes at birth, and also, very possibly, our first intuition about death. The image of this gentle bird plucking us from a garden (or, in another version, finding us floating in a container on the water) and delivering us into the loving arms of our parents is pleasant and comforting. It offsets the trauma of birth which lodges in the young. It also puts temporarily to rest early childhood concerns about another complex business, human reproduction.

Both the garden and water metaphors symbolize our endlessness in a way that is easy and comforting for a child. The garden is a universal symbol for the constant renewal of life and the eternal birth and death cycle of nature that makes renewal possible. Water, too, is symbolic of birth and regeneration. Consider the story of the infant Moses, which has hundreds of counterparts in mythology, or Noah's story, in which the flood stands for both death and the regeneration of life and which also is repeated in countless myths. Part of one Christian baptismal rite includes the words, "O God, who by water didst wash away the crimes of the evil world, and in the overflowing of the Flood didst give a figure of regeneration. . . ."

The bird metaphor itself is interesting. Jung interpreted the bird in myth as a symbol of transcendence, that is, of a passing beyond the seemingly impossible. This isn't hard to understand. Birds are earthbound when they are first born. Eventually, however, they develop the power to rise above their ties to earth, figuratively to transcend earth and move into a higher sphere. Both Jung and mythologist Joseph Campbell comment on the fact that shamans (medicine men) often dressed in bird costumes when they prepared to enter into a trance. Upon being released from the trance, they commonly reported that they had visited other spheres —that they had died and been reborn.

Thus, the lowly legend of the stork takes on, if you let it, powerful meanings. Its metaphoric images express ideas about life that would otherwise be extremely difficult or awkward or impossible to explain. With this simple nursery tale of birth, we are pointed toward the very other end of life with some kind of reassurance that the journey will not end in the misery and terror of death.

In myth the problems and solutions are valid for all mankind.

—Joseph Campbell

Our examination of the stork legend may have planted the idea that for myths to reveal their secrets one must indulge in laborious research. This isn't true. We are attempting here to forge some important critical understandings about mythology as a subject, and to reach such understandings does take serious study. But myths were not developed to provide material for analysis. They were meant to be understood and used by everybody. What is beautiful about mythology is not its appeal for the scholar, but its universal applications to all of us.

Most beginning students of our subject are impressed by the differences between the mythologies of various societies rather than by their similarities. That textbooks tend to stress these differences makes it extremely difficult to understand myth's universal applications. (The same tendency also makes it easy to believe that other societies had some pretty foolish notions about life.) On the surface, myths *do* differ from place to place. That they do so is only reasonable. A people whose geographical environment is dominated by the seashore is going to incorporate fish into its myths, not mountain lions. An Eskimo culture will have no monkey symbols. If one contents himself with this level of comparison, there is nothing at all universal about myths.

Remember the story of Brer Rabbit and the Tar Baby? Ananda Coomaraswamy classifies more than 260 versions of this story from around the world! There are only three possible ways to account for this proliferation: The story kept getting repeated until it eventually worked its way around the world, coming to rest in the tales of Joel Chandler Harris; or the many versions may be taken as simply a remarkable coincidence; or the "Stickfast" image was buried somewhere in the minds of many different people and worked its way to the surface in roughly similar form the world over.

This last explanation is the one many modern scholars see as being the most plausible, although agreement is far from unanimous. A now famous experiment was once conducted with newly hatched chicks. A model of a hawk was pulled over their pen moments after they were hatched. All of them scurried for shelter. When the model was pulled backwards—that is, in a way contrary to natural flight—they showed no fear, nor did they react in any way when models of nonpredatory birds were passed overhead. The obvious conclusion is that their fear of the hawk is not learned; it is built in. By analogy, human beings may be thought to have built-in images and responses too.

This is not to say that we are programmed like chickens or that our behavior is wholly instinctive rather than learned. There is much evidence, however, to indicate that from birth we are all psychologically responsive to certain basic images. To what degree this is true no one knows, although modern psychology has turned up increasing proofs of the theory's validity.

Jung established the concept of the "collective unconscious" to explain this idea. He relied heavily on mythology to verify his reasoning. What the collective unconscious is cannot be described in physiological terms or even fully explained using the language of psychology. Evidence of its existence is found in the universal application of certain kinds of symbols (or images) to which we attach much importance. These symbols are not consciously manufactured. Seemingly they dwell in each of us, expressing themselves in rites and stories strikingly similar from place to place and throughout various periods of history. Jung called these images and stories *archetypes*.

We rely on these images both as individuals and as members of a society. The sharing of common symbols assures individuals that they are not alone, that their membership in the group is secure. It is not necessary to know these things consciously; it is enough to sense them somehow beneath the conscious level.

Earlier, Jung was quoted as deploring our abandonment of nonliteral kinds of truth in favor of "the goddess Reason." As a psychiatrist he had ample opportunity to observe the effects on his patients of such a mistake. Over and over he found proof that when we lose contact with the collective unconscious, we spontaneously generate mythlike visions in our dreams, employing the same archetypes found throughout mythology. Jung saw this as an unconscious struggle to reunite ourselves with the images that provide security and order in an otherwise chaotic, menacing world.

The idea of a collective unconscious represents a mighty assumption, even though there is strong evidence to support it. Mythic dreams offer one kind of proof and myths themselves offer another. There seems to be no entirely satisfactory alternative way to explain why it is that societies with no possible way of communicating with one another have created and passed down for centuries stories that touch upon the same vital questions and employ closely similar motifs (themes) and archetypes. All of us, through all time and across the seas, share in this symbolic way the life experience.

It is not known how many archetypal images there are. Some of the easily observable ones are water (with distinctly separate meanings for seas and rivers); the sun (with the related images of fire and sky); wind; the earth (as a source of life); the garden (cyclical regeneration); the desert (death, infertility); certain colors, such as black (mystery, death), red (violence, passion), and green (life, growth); the circle (wholeness, unity, God); and the serpent (evil, chaos, wisdom).

Common archetypal motifs are creation (in which the world and man were created by supernatural beings); immortality (the idea that we are part of a natural cycle without a final death); and the hero's quest (which depicts life as a long and hazardous journey involving distinct phases such as initiation, battles with demons, riddle-solving, achievement of an impossible goal, and return).

A well-known Greek myth, the subject of much art, poetry, and music, deals with the love of Orpheus and Eurydice. Orpheus's skill with the lyre was beyond description. When he played it, trees and stones moved with its sound, rivers flowed in its direction, and raging beasts became gentle. All nature was charmed. His brief marriage to the nymph Eurydice ended when she was bitten by a serpent and her spirit was carried to the underworld, known to the Greeks as Hades.

Orpheus traveled to Hades and, with the aid of his lyre, convinced Pluto and Persephone, King and Queen of Hades, to restore his beloved wife. They agreed, but with a condition: In their trip away from the underworld, Orpheus was not to look back at Eurydice until they reached the upper world. Nearly to their goal, Orpheus dared a look. As he did, Eurydice faded to a shadow, doomed to wander Hades forever. By breaking his pledge, probably because it was beyond him to keep it, Orpheus lost what mattered to him most.

Northrop Frye has made reference to a tale originating with a tribe of California Indians. In it, a man also sought his dead wife in the afterworld and was told that he might bring her back to the land of the living if he did not touch her on the way. He, too, was unable to keep to the condition and lost her forever.

Not only are these two examples strikingly similar as stories; they also seem to be saying the same thing—that to return from a life beyond this one in the same human state is impossible and futile to attempt. Mary Shelley's novel *Frankenstein* is a restatement of this idea. There are many other similar examples in mythology and literature.

Compare these two versions of creation, the first from Greek mythology, the second from Genesis:

Before earth and heaven were created, all things were one aspect, to which we gave the name of Chaos—a confused and shapeless mass, nothing but deadweight, in which, however, slumbered the seeds of things. Earth, sea, air were all mixed up together; so the earth was not solid, the sea was not fluid, and the air was not transparent. God and Nature at last interposed, and put an end to this discord, separating earth from sea, and heaven from both. The fiery part, being the lightest, sprang up, and formed the skies; the air was next in weight and place. The earth, being heavier, sank below; and the water took the lowest place, and buoyed up the earth.

In the beginning, God created the heaven and the earth. And the earth was without form, and void; and darkness was upon the face of the deep. And the Spirit of God moved upon the face of the waters. And God said, Let there be light; and there was light. And God saw the light, that it was good; and God called the light Day, and the darkness he called Night. And the evening and the morning were the first day.

And God said, Let there be a firmament in the midst of the waters, and let it divide the waters from the waters. And God made the firmament, and divided the waters which were under the firmament from the waters which were above the firmament: and it was so. And God called the firmament Heaven. . . . And God said, Let the earth bring forth grass, the herb yielding seed, and the fruit tree yielding fruit after his kind, whose seed is in itself, upon the earth: and it was so.

It is not that these versions are exactly the same; it is that they use the same kinds of images—light and dark; earth, sea, and air; formlessness and form; sleeping, buried seeds.

In Greek mythology, the Titan Prometheus made the first man, fashioning him from clay. In The Bible, God formed Adam from dust. In Greek mythology, Pandora, the first mortal woman, unleashed all the plagues and problems of mankind by opening the box given her by Zeus. In The Bible, Eve doomed all future generations to suffering by eating the fruit of the Tree of the Knowledge of Good and Evil and convincing Adam to do the same.

Just as the textile or pottery designs of "primitive" peoples may often seem to us as sophisticated as our own, and sometimes much more tasteful, so "primitive" myths and folk tales can be on at least the same imaginative level as our own stories.

—Northrop Frye

It is not at all surprising to find such close and obvious similarities between Greek mythology and The Bible. There are many such similarities, and most of them come from direct cross-cultural influences, unlike the two stories dealing with the attempted return of a dead mate from the underworld. What follows cannot be explained as either the result of one culture influencing another or as a single random coincidence.

The Yanomamo are a South American Indian tribe living in scattered villages in the jungles of southern Venezuela and northern Brazil. We would classify them as "primitive"; that is, they are without a written language, no sense of community extending beyond their own villages, no comprehension of a history beyond their own, and almost no contact with the outside world. They are a Stone Age people.

Napoleon Chagnon, an anthropologist who lived with the tribe for a year and a half, labeled them "the fierce people" because of their dedication to many forms of violence, mostly directed against other Yanomamo. Some of his observations about them follow, along with some comments concerning their implications:

> [Their] comparative poverty is more than compensated for by the richness and complexity of their . . . myths and legends. . . . Individuals can and do modify concepts, embellish them, improve on them and, in general, use their imaginations when trafficking in myths or concepts of the soul and afterlife.

Excerpts from Chagnon's description of their cosmology (description of the universe) provide evidence of a strong mythological connection between these remote and illiterate Indians and some of the most advanced civilizations:

> The Yanomamo conceive of the external world as having an origin, boundaries, supernatural beings, and a specific nature. The cosmos is comprised of four parallel layers, lying horizontally and located one on top of the other. They are like inverted platters: gently curved, thin, circular, rigid, and having two surfaces, top and bottom.
>
> The uppermost layer . . . is empty or void, but some things had their origin there in the distant past. These moved down to other layers. Today, the uppermost layer is sometimes described as being "an old woman," a phrase used to describe an abandoned garden or a female who is no longer capable of producing offspring. This layer does not figure prominently in the everyday life of the Yanomamo; it is merely something that is there and once had a function.

This level may clearly be looked upon as the pre-creation Chaos described in the two creation versions in the previous section. The old woman–garden image may also be seen as a fertility symbol since the female and the garden are universally conceived of as such. (Look up, for example, the story of Demeter in Greek mythology.)

The next layer is called *hedu ka misi*: sky layer. It is made of earth on the top surface and provides the eternal home for the souls of the departed. A complete replica of life on earth is to be found on top of *hedu*, except that its inhabitants are the spirits of men, not real men. . . . Everything that exists on earth has a counterpart on *hedu*, a sort of mirror image, although the activities of the two groups of objects and beings are independent of each other. The bottom surface of *hedu* is the visible portion of the sky.

This celestial replica of earth should not be mistaken for the Judeo-Christian concept of Heaven. Here, one's spirit does not dwell in eternal bliss; life continues much as before. Numerous American Indian legends refer to such a state, where one's spirit follows more or less the life one led on earth. But the idea of another place beyond death is fundamental to all mythology. So too are its earthlike features. The great scholar of world religions, Mircea Eliade, observes: "The world that surrounds us . . . the world in which the presence and the work of man are felt—the mountains that he climbs, populated and cultivated regions, navigable rivers, cities, sanctuaries—all these have an extraterrestrial archetype. . . ."

Man dwells below the sky on "this layer": *hei ka misi*. It originated when a piece of *hedu* broke off and fell to a lower level. This layer is a vast jungle, sprinkled with innumerable Yanomamo villages. These are conceived to be located on earth. . . . Even foreigners are thought to live in a type of house that resembles the Yanomamo dwelling; after all, foreigners derived from the Yanomamo by a process of degeneration.

Finally, the plane underneath this layer is almost barren. A single village of spirit-men is found here, the Amahiri-teri. A long time ago, after the earth layer was formed by a piece of *hedu*, another chunk of *hedu* fell down and crashed through earth. It hit earth at a place where the Amahiri-teri lived, carrying their village down to the bottom layer. Unfortunately, only their *shabono* (dwellings) and gardens were carried with the piece of *hedu*. Hence, the Amahiri-teri have no neighborhood in which to hunt for game, and so they send their spirits up to earth to capture the souls of living children and eat them. There is a constant struggle between the evil spirits of Amahiri-teri shamans and the evil spirits of shamans on this layer, earth: They send malevolent demons against each other and preoccupy themselves with defending their respective villages from evil spirits. . . .

Here, in loose form, is an acknowledgment of the evil forces which plague us all. The Amahiri-teri spirits terrorize the earth-dwelling Yanomamo by threatening their children's souls, but tribal shamans offer protection with spirits to counter the threat.

Evil and misery are parts of the human condition, as much so for us as for the Yanomamo. To make these forces sufferable, societies organize some kind of mythological response. One of the most popular recurring motifs in art and literature is man's struggle with the potential for evil in himself, personified in The Bible by Satan and elsewhere depicted as a vast array of monsters, spirits, fiends, ghouls, or dark forces. Evil is usually rebuffed, however, through religious faith, magic, some symbolic form of goodness, a hero or heroine, or some combination of these elements.

At death, the soul of a Yanomamo (called the *no borebo*) travels to *hedu* in the following manner:

> The trail along which the *no borebo* travel forks after it reaches *hedu*. . . . After the soul reaches the fork in the trail, a spirit, the son of Thunder, Wadawadariwa, asks the *no borebo* if it had been generous during its life on earth. If it had been stingy, Wadawadariwa directs the soul along the path that leads to . . . a place on *hedu* where the souls of stingy Yanomamo burn eternally. . . .

The similarity between the hot spot in *hedu* and our Biblical Hell are obvious enough; and certainly Wadawadariwa bears a resemblance to Satan. In Greek mythology, the path to Hades has no fork, but the departed must cross a river. In Norse myth, the dead enter a whirlpool (the Maelstrom). Crossings, turnings, and other obstacles the soul must confront are not only typical ways to depict the difficulties of spiritual transcendence, but necessary ingredients in all hero myths.

Yanomamo who die as children do not reach *hedu*. This is because their wills are believed to be too immature and innocent. Instead, their spirits walk the earth. Many of us will recognize the similarity between this idea and the Limbo of Christianity, where the souls of children too young to have been cleansed of Original Sin through the sacrament of Baptism, and not yet old enough to have consciously sinned, are consigned.

Yanomamo mythology is rich in ancestor tales. The first beings are considered to be the spirits of plants and animals essential to survival. Because of this they figure importantly in Yanomamo mythology. Chagnon narrates the tale of Iwa (alligator), one of the first beings. Unlike the others, Iwa knew the secret of fire and kept some hidden in his mouth. He refused to share it, keeping it only for himself. The others played pranks to make Iwa open his mouth in laughter so that they might snatch the fire. When finally Dohomamoriwa succeeded in making Iwa laugh, Kanaboriwa, a bird, flew into Iwa's mouth and fled with the fire. From that time on, everyone had fire.

The Yanomamo are therefore indebted to the cleverness of Dohomamoriwa and to the courage and swiftness of Kanaboriwa, for without the gift of fire even their rudimentary level of civilization would have been impossible. So too were the Greeks indebted to the god Prometheus, who, by trickery, stole fire from heaven and carried it to earth. In a Navaho legend, Coyote was the fire stealer. Raven performed the same feat for the Pacific Northwest Indian.

Another aspect of Yanomamo legend that relates to Greek mythology concerns Kanaboroma, a descendant of the moon spirit. Kanaboroma's legs became pregnant; women were born from the left leg and men from the right. Dionysus, the Greek god of wine and vegetation, was snatched from his dead mother's womb by Zeus, who sewed the unborn baby into his thigh until he was ready to be born.

Omauwa and Yoawa, two of the first Yanomamo beings, once dug a hole in search of water. It became so deep that the entire jungle was flooded and most of the first beings drowned. Only generally does this myth correspond to the story of Noah, but they have the same symbolic meaning. Each is a statement about the death and rebirth cycle of nature. There are other flood tales in mythology, hundreds of them. In a Sioux Indian legend, a buffalo holds back the waters, losing a single hair every year and a leg at the end of each of four epochs. With the loss of his fourth leg, the waters are released and the world is flooded, only to be reborn when the waters recede. Zeus, the supreme god of the Greek pantheon, once flooded the earth, and there is an all-consuming flood connected with the ancient Babylonian myth of the hero Gilgamesh.

Any comparison of mythologies will yield striking similarities. Yanomamo mythology is no more exemplary of this fact than that of any other culture. It was chosen for examination because it supports some critically important truths about all mythology:

1. That people respond in imaginative ways to the universe.
2. That the relative technological level of a society has little bearing on the complexity and sophistication of that society's myths.

3. That there must be some common needs and concerns about life in all of us that are better conveyed in myth than in any other form.
4. That these common needs and concerns are invariably metaphorized in common archetypal images.

The unicorn is a mythical beast.

—James Thurber

By now you should be able to begin to understand the vital place of myth in anyone's life, including your own. Mostly for fun, but also because important truths are often packaged in frivolous looking containers, read the late American humorist James Thurber's "The Unicorn in the Garden." You'll see what happens when one fails to allow for the kind of truth we have discussed.

THE UNICORN IN THE GARDEN
James Thurber (1894–1961)

Once upon a sunny morning a man who sat in a breakfast nook looked up from his scrambled eggs to see a white unicorn with a golden horn quietly cropping roses in the garden. The man went up to the bedroom where his wife was still asleep and woke her. "There's a unicorn in the garden," he said. "Eating roses." She opened one unfriendly eye and looked at him. "The unicorn is a mythical beast," she said, and turned her back on him. The man walked slowly downstairs and out into the garden. The unicorn was still there; he was now browsing among the tulips. "Here, unicorn," said the man, and he pulled up a lily and gave it to him. The unicorn ate it gravely. With a high heart, because there was a unicorn in his garden, the man went upstairs and roused his wife again. "The unicorn ate a lily," he said. His wife sat up in bed and looked at him coldly. "You are a booby," she said, "and I am going to have you put in the booby hatch." The man, who had never liked the words "booby" and "booby hatch," and who liked them even less on a shining morning when there was a unicorn in the garden, thought for a moment. "We'll see about that," he said. He walked over to the door. "He has a golden horn in the middle of his forehead," he told her.

Then he went back to the garden to watch the unicorn, but the unicorn had gone away. The man sat down among the roses and went to sleep.

As soon as the husband had gone out of the house, the wife got up and dressed as fast as she could. She was very excited and there was a gloat in her eye. She telephoned the police and she telephoned a psychiatrist; she told them to hurry to her house and bring a strait jacket. When the police and the psychiatrist arrived, they sat down in chairs and looked at her with great interest. "My husband," she said, "saw a unicorn this morning." The police looked at the psychiatrist and the psychiatrist looked at the police. "He told me it ate a lily," she said. The psychiatrist looked at the police and the police looked at the psychiatrist. "He told me it had a golden horn in the middle of its forehead," she said. At a solemn signal from the psychiatrist, the police leaped from their chairs and seized the wife. They had a hard time subduing her, for she put up a terrific struggle, but they finally subdued her. Just as they got her into the strait jacket, her husband came back into the house. "Did you tell your wife you saw a unicorn?" asked the psychiatrist. "Of course not," said the husband. "The unicorn is a mythical beast." "That's all I wanted to know," said the psychiatrist. "Take her away. I'm sorry, sir, but your wife is as crazy as a jay bird." So they took her away, cursing and screaming, and shut her up in an institution. The husband lived happily ever after.

Moral: Don't count your boobies until they are hatched.

II

THE HERO'S QUEST

Why is mythology everywhere the same, beneath its varieties of costume?

—Joseph Campbell

II

THE HERO'S QUEST

The bullfighter, the Grand Prix driver, the rodeo rider on the bucking horse—each is a crowd pleaser, a star. Why is it that spectators single out such daredevils for special attention, devotion, near-worship? Why is it that the casual baseball fan has no difficulty ticking off the names of six good pitchers but probably can't recall three great second basemen? Why are quarterbacks enshrined in the public memory while the names of linesmen quickly fade? (The reason for speaking almost exclusively of males is explained at the close of this section.)

Most of us don't wonder about these matters, either because they aren't really important or, more likely, because we grew up accepting them without question. What makes a hero *is* a fascinating question, however, with profound implications. The types of heroes mentioned share common characteristics which suggest much about how we see ourselves, determine our goals, and view our passage through life. To honor an individual, either real or legendary, with the exalted title of hero, we must be satisfied that he has ably performed certain ritualized tasks and feats. Furthermore, his character must be essentially noble. (Even great athletes often suffer public condemnation for unsuitable behavior off the field of play, regardless of how well they perform while in uniform.)

A hero must leave behind him, or overcome, the weaknesses and temptations we give in to; must be totally committed to his heroic role; and must suffer dangers and agonies beyond those we are able to endure—even if he suffers them in a basically meaningless contest. Furthermore, he must act out his role alone. That he may at times be surrounded by others has no bearing on this solitude. Most importantly, the hero must have a difficult goal, which he will reach on his own.

We honor running backs over receivers because the former are subjected to enormous physical punishment; bronc riders over calf ropers because their feat is more nakedly dangerous than the other; pitchers over second basemen because the former are cast in a lonely and harrowing role; and bullfighters over tennis players because of their ritual acting-out of the drama of the single warrior pitted against the savage forces of nature. While it can be argued that all athletes have difficult goals, we tend to admire, even stand in awe of, those who accomplish the most nearly impossible or most perilous ones.

To these characteristics—all necessary to the conception of the hero—should be added one more: The hero figure must, despite his superhuman achievements, have something in common with even the meekest of people. It is essential that we see in the hero many of the same qualities—the raw stuff of heroism—we find in ourselves. Within each of us dwells the hero image, although most of us are reluctant or afraid to act it out. Some of our fondest fantasies picture us in various familiar heroic roles modeled on characters and situations we have read about or seen.

Not all of our heroes are athletes, of course, or famous warriors, or flinty-eyed, tall-in-the-saddle saviors of the pretty schoolmarm. These are obvious examples and perhaps a bit corny. They are, however, quite legitimate representatives of mythological heroes through the ages. They are also useful in pointing the way toward deeper considerations about the important function of the hero myth and its relationship to literary themes.

Identification with heroes has always provided a strong, guiding influence for both the individual and society. Because the hero's achievements and high purpose establish positive, believable, and possibly attainable goals for everyone, the individual tends to direct the better part of himself or herself toward the same goals. Courage, nobility, sacrifice, fortitude, and grit are highly prized in nearly all societies. They help to assure the rightness of a society's values, institutions, and actions. If a society's heroes personify these qualities, that society's members will aspire to them. Furthermore, on a personal level, the hero figure points a way through life's most baffling and fearsome obstacle—death. No mortal quite understands it. It remains beyond the reach of any philosophy. Its biological explanation offers cold comfort and fails to unlock its spiritual and intellectual secrets. Science offers one kind of truth—a bleak one. But mythology offers another, metaphorical truth, reassuring and humane.

The hero endures. He has confronted death, as well as the agonies leading to it. He has crossed alone into unknown territory, suffered, and returned. So will we, his experience tells us. Thus, the hero tale brings back to us what we could otherwise not know: that we are not simply trapped, doomed; that while we are often foolish, petty, selfish, we are also made of immortal stuff and are meant for more than a "brief candle" length of life.

Many scholars in fields dealing with myth see the hero story as the central motif of all mythology. Certainly it is the dominant one; the hero myth is universally a powerful shaper of beliefs, rituals, and arts. Yet, despite its countless variations, there is only one hero story. And we have all grown up with it, enjoying it a thousand times over in fairy tales, legends, and folk ballads; and in modern poems, stories, novels, movies, and plays. Right now, without further reading, you would be capable of spinning a hero tale that would accurately follow the ancient lines of this keystone myth. Instead, read the following version of it. It may seem strange to say, but even if you haven't heard this story before, you will recognize it.

THESEUS AND THE MINOTAUR

No one knows whether Theseus was fathered by a god or a mortal. Aegeus, king of Athens, spent a drunken evening in the arms of Aethra, daughter of King Pittheus. The next morning he left to return to his homeland but first wedged a sword and a pair of sandals under an enormous rock, telling Aethra that if she bore a son who grew strong enough to move the rock and recover the objects, she should send him to Athens with the tokens so that the king would recognize him.

What Aegeus did not know was that the god Poseidon, ruler of the seas, had that same night also slept with Aethra. A son, Theseus, was born. When the lad was but sixteen he was already prodigiously strong. Aethra told him of the tokens Aegeus had left, and Theseus easily moved the rock aside, claimed the sword and sandals, and left for Athens. On the way he met and conquered a number of menacing adversaries: Corynetes, whom Theseus slew with the brute's own cudgel; the robber Sinis, whom he destroyed in a manner which Sinis had used to kill countless victims; Scieron, another fierce robber who received at Theseus's hands the same fate he had dealt to others; and Damastes (Procrustes), who made a practice of stretching the limbs of his short

guests and severing those of his tall ones to fit his infamous
bed. Theseus again triumphed, slaying Damastes in his bed.

Theseus finally arrived in Athens, long after Aegeus had
forgotten his union with Aethra. At this time Athens was in
dire straits, and Aegeus was sorely troubled. For one thing,
the sorceress Medea, by preying on the king's fears, had won
a firm grip on his will. For another, Athens was threatened
from without, on the one hand by the king's brother Pallas
and his fifty sons, and on the other by King Minos of Knossos on the island of Crete, whose son Aegeus had had a hand
in killing not long before Theseus's birth. Minos had attacked
the then-plague-ridden Athens and as a victory tribute had
demanded that every nine years Athens send to Knossos
seven youths and seven maidens. These unfortunates were
fed to the Minotaur, a monster with a bull's head and a
man's body, which was kept in the Labyrinth, a vast maze
beneath Minos's palace.

When Theseus arrived in Athens he was greeted with
honor, for word of his conquests had preceded him. Aegeus
held a banquet for him, but because of the rules of hospitality, did not ask about Theseus's descent or his homeland.
Nor, for the same reason, did Theseus volunteer any information.

Medea, however, quickly divined Theseus's true identity
and, sensing that he presented a threat to her eventual control of the kingdom, convinced Aegeus to poison him. As
Theseus raised the cup of poisoned wine to his lips, Aegeus
noticed the youth's handsome ivory-handled sword and recognized it as the one he had wedged beneath the rock. Just
in time he dashed the cup from Theseus's hand and embraced
him as his son.

All Athens rejoiced when Aegeus acknowledged Theseus.
Medea fled, and Theseus quickly put down the rebellious
Pallas and his sons. Notwithstanding, a pall hung over the
kingdom, for the time of paying tribute to Minos was draw-
ing near when the seven youths and seven maidens had to
be chosen by lot and sent to Crete.

When Theseus learned of the tribute, he volunteered to
be one of the fourteen victims. Although Aegeus was opposed, his son insisted. In the faint hope that his mighty
offspring might defeat the monster and escape Crete, Aegeus
asked him to fly a white sail on his return home as the
earliest possible indication that he was safe. Otherwise, the
ship was to carry its traditional black sails.

Shortly after their arrival at Knossos, Theseus was asked to participate in the annual games. He wrestled and defeated the great champion Taurus. Minos's daughter Ariadne witnessed the event and was taken by the Athenian's beauty and courage. She knew that even if he succeeded in conquering the terrible Minotaur as well, he would never find his way out of the Labyrinth without help. Therefore she sought out its designer, Daedalus, who gave her instructions on how to do so.

Ariadne approached Theseus in secret and told him how to find the center of the maze. She also gave him back his sword and a ball of thread which he was to fasten at the entrance and unwind as he worked his way through the tunnels.

Theseus entered the Labyrinth alone. Moving deeper and deeper into the dark, twisting passages, he grew fearful. Still he pressed on until finally he entered the very center —the Minotaur's lair.

Although the Minotaur was by far the most terrifying and powerful adversary Theseus had ever met in combat, he fought with great courage and finally slew the monster with his sword. Following the trail of the thread, Theseus, sore and exhausted from battle, eventually made his way back to the entrance.

Ariadne was overjoyed that the brave Theseus had returned safely. She knew that she could no longer stay in her father's palace, however, for she had betrayed him. Taking Ariadne, Theseus gathered the young Athenians and fled for the harbor and the black-sailed ship.

It was not fated that Theseus and Ariadne would reach Athens together. One version of the tale is that when the ship reached the island of Naxos word arrived from Knossos that Minos would call an end to his tributes from Athens if Ariadne were returned and that Theseus gave her up with little protest. Other versions have it that she died of grief on the island of Cyprus when Theseus's ship was blown away in a storm; that she was captured by the god Dionysus; and that Theseus simply abandoned her, because, according to one teller of the tale, "More strange than dear did Theseus hold Ariadne."

At any rate, when Theseus finally approached his home port he forgot to raise the white sail. Aegeus spotted the black one far out at sea and was so overcome with grief and disappointment that he leaped to his death.

Despite this tragedy of his homecoming, Theseus returned to Athens a hero and became a wise and powerful ruler.

We can safely label the Theseus story a myth—a narrative without known origins, which grew from some historical roots and evolved into a metaphorical tale not by the intent of any author or storyteller, but because of the blending of mythological motifs with a handful of real events and persons. There was a Theseus who ruled over Athens; and Knossos and Athens did fight a war. Furthermore, the ruins of an actual labyrinth continue to intrigue visitors to Crete.

What makes Theseus a mythical hero is not what he did in real life, however, or that the historian is able to locate the ground on which he walked. Quite the opposite. The tale of Theseus comes down to us not because of the so-called facts, but despite them. His mother clearly did not mate with a god; he almost certainly did not lift up a rock to claim the tokens of his manhood°; he very probably did not slay infamous highwaymen who blocked his way to Athens, for it is equally likely that they never existed; and as for his battle with the Minotaur—this is simply the stuff of a rip-snorting story.

Theseus is a hero because his story grew from a few fragments of fact into the mythological story of stories—the Heroic Quest. It goes under various other names too—the adventure tale, the epic, the search, the exploration, the escape, the wandering, even the love story. An examination of their common characteristics will lead to an obvious conclusion, however: Each is a retelling of one key story, although the variations in the stories may mask this fact.

Huckleberry Finn and *Pinocchio,* for example, essentially relate the same quest story as the myth of Theseus, although the three tales differ in so many particulars that most readers will at first miss the overriding similarities. It is these similarities that are important to our examination of the hero and the quest.

Heroes are often of obscure or mysterious origin. Huckleberry Finn is a waif who drifts in and out of the community. He is without roots, a real family, or definite origin. Pinocchio's background is unique enough; he has been carved from a block of wood. And Theseus may or may not be the son of the god Poseidon. There are countless proofs in literature and mythology of this general

---

°King Arthur was a boy of fifteen when he succeeded in pulling a sword from a stone and thereby passed the initiatory test for leadership. Sigmund, the great Teutonic hero, passed a similar test by pulling a sword from a tree.

truth. Other familiar examples are Superman, who came from another planet; the Lone Ranger, who was orphaned by killers and, after serving as a Ranger, became a wanderer; and Robin Hood, an outlaw whose origins are hotly disputed by historians who have attempted to verify his actual existence. Occasionally, a hero will be the type who might have grown up in the house next door. Most often, however, he is not a fixed member of any community and therefore has a freedom of movement denied to most of us, as well as a detachment from the petty concerns which distract and weigh us down.

This seeming freedom is not without its drawbacks. When the hero is summoned, he cannot simply slip into the crowd and merge with the rest of us. He stands out. He must go. *Most heroes are called upon to make a journey (quest) by urgent necessity* (although some come to it by accident). Even though they may dread the summons, it is their response to the fateful call that sets them apart from Everyman (you and me), who might respond with, "Really, it'd be great, but I've got a tennis lesson. . . ."

Throughout *Huckleberry Finn*, Huck thinks constantly upon cowardly ways to avoid his mission but nevertheless sees the journey through. Theseus must have been divided in his feelings about volunteering to be among the fourteen victims. And had he not felt fear when he ventured alone into the Labyrinth, he would have been either a fool or absolutely sure of his invincibility.

Heroes are neither fools nor invincible. Even the nearly invincible heroes have weaknesses. Superman can be laid low by exposure to the element kryptonite; Achilles's heel was the one vulnerable place on his body; and the Teutonic hero Siegfried had a similar spot on his back. If a hero has no reason to feel fear, his quest cannot be considered heroic.

The hero's way is not always direct or clear to him. Sir Gawain, hero of an Arthurian tale that lies before you in this book, wandered for months before he came upon the place of his dreaded rendezvous with the Green Knight. Odysseus's journey homeward took ten years, for the way was filled with detainings and detours. Theseus did not know the real reason why he was drawn to Athens and later found himself in a maze—a confusion of passageways. Life's ways are puzzling, these tales suggest. The path is never clear.

The hero has a goal. King Arthur's knights dedicated their lives to the quest for the Holy Grail (a sacred vessel used by Christ at the Last Supper). Pinocchio's goal was to become fully human. Huckleberry Finn wanted to reach Cairo, where Jim could step ashore a free man. Theseus vowed to free Athens of the symbol of its troubles, the Minotaur; and Jason's goal was to capture the

Golden Fleece. Not all goals are as noble or ambitious as these—at least on the surface. Dorothy in *The Wizard of Oz* simply wanted to find a way home.

The hero's way is beset with dangers, loneliness, and temptation. That heroes face physical danger needs little comment. The perils of the life journey are symbolized in the quest story by evil, death-dealing adversaries; seas and rivers too broad or storm-tossed to cross; mountains too high to climb; and countless other dangers and obstacles. Seldom does a hero confront only one threat to himself. Most often the way is strewn with them.

The perils Odysseus faced are too numerous to recount here, but they include such familiar ones as his ordeal in the cave of Polyphemus, the Cyclops; his encounter with the giant Laestrygonians; and the twin terrors of Scylla and Charybdis.

Ashore and afloat, both Odysseus and Huckleberry Finn must repeatedly rely on wit, grit, and good fortune to survive the hazards of the way. The same is true of Jason and his quest for the Golden Fleece and of Frodo in Tolkien's *Lord of the Rings* trilogy. Theseus's journey from his birthplace to Athens was marked by one do-or-die battle after another.

Loneliness is not as obvious a threat to the hero as blood-thirsty monsters, yet it is possibly more discouraging to the successful completion of the mission. To follow the way of the quest, a hero must isolate himself from the familiar, reassuring roads we travel and plunge alone into alien, hostile country. It takes a great heart to do this. It is not the romantic call of the open road to which the hero responds; it is the chilling call of the dark, lonely way.

Many quest tales supply friends, servants, or disciples as company for the hero. These companions do little to offset the hero's loneliness nor do they share in his high sense of mission. They do not fully comprehend the goal and are most often motivated by simple devotion. Odysseus, Jason, and Frodo had such companions. So did Don Quixote. Jesus's disciples never fully understood their leader or His purpose. Spiritually, the hero is always alone.

Because he is lonely and often afraid, the hero is especially vulnerable to temptations that would end his misery or at least interrupt it. Huckleberry very nearly turned Jim in, a move which would have ended his own pain. Pinocchio, we recall, was readily swayed from his goal a number of times, and even the gallant Gawain compromised himself in an attempt to avoid his fate. Hamlet's famous "To be or not to be . . ." soliloquy similarly reflects his irresolution about going on. Temptations appear in many forms. The hero is usually warned at some point in his journey about what he must avoid. Of course, they turn out to be the very things that he will desire most.

Temptations tend to appeal to the senses rather than to the intellect. The hero may be exhausted but has been warned against sleep under certain conditions. When he is hungriest he knows that he must not eat certain foods, and when he is thirstiest he must not drink from certain springs or goblets or taste the wine offered by certain hands. Women often appear as the most dangerous temptation of all (although they have an opposite, beneficent function, too). They promise more than food, drink, and rest. They offer sexual pleasures, bliss . . . the satisfaction of every sensual craving. Women were very nearly Odysseus's and Jason's downfall, and if Lois Lane ever gets her way, Superman will be permanently reduced to being Clark Kent. Until recent film makers shattered the Code of the West, the cowboy hero avoided the dancehall girl and stuck to the trail.

The hero has a guide or guides. Although the hero is alone, he is seldom without guidance and protection of some sort. At some point after he has been singled out by passing an initiatory test—the moving of a rock, a victory in combat, or some similar show of strength and valor—he crosses a threshold and leaves behind him the familiar world of everyday. At or near this point, however, the hero meets a guide who provides information, magic weapons, or charms. This guide may be ugly—hags and odd little men are typical —although beautiful maidens and fairy godmothers also serve in this role. The hero does not receive a literal spelling-out of the hazards and the way. Guides may leave important questions unanswered or use riddles and other confusions.

These guides are among the most fascinating characters in myth and literature, probably because of the forms they take, the powers they possess, their air of mystery, or their links to forces that oppose the hero's quest. Rarely are they completely free to act in the hero's behalf. While they provide help vital to the completion of his mission, their aid is limited by enchantments or powers stronger than their own. Ariadne may not openly oppose her father the king to help Theseus. Her aid must take the form of a ball of fragile thread. Similarly, Medea must act behind her father's back to work in Jason's favor in his quest for the Golden Fleece. The token given to Gawain by the Lady of the Castle is in one way his salvation but in another his undoing. Dorothy journeys toward Oz armed with charms, instructions, and companions, yet still must face terrible ordeals.

The hero descends into darkness. At some point, the hero must go alone to the dreaded place. This is the ultimate test, and the hero will feel fear and despair when it approaches. He senses that it will hurt; that it will be bloody; that it may kill him. Typically, this experience happens in darkness. Huckleberry Finn travels only by night and in a dense fog experiences total isolation and fear. The hero may journey to Hades or some other Hell-like place symbolizing everlasting night and suffering (as Orpheus did). Some form of underworld is also found in *Alice in Wonderland,* Tolkien's *Lord of the Rings* trilogy, *Pinocchio,* the story of Theseus, Virgil's *Aeneid,* Homer's *Odyssey,* and countless other quest tales. The hero may even be swallowed by a great fish, as were Jonah, Heracles, Raven (an American Indian hero), and Blood-clot boy (page 172).

The darkness and descent needn't be literal. It is enough for the hero to experience the terrible loneliness and fear that come with darkness. In the Western *High Noon,* for example, the hero goes through this experience at midday on a sun-drenched street. Gawain's confrontation with the Green Knight occurs in daylight, which does not take away from the personal sense of darkness he feels. Darkness, both literal and figurative, is also the setting for Christ's ordeal. His cry from the cross, "Why hast thou forsaken me?" is a profoundly powerful expression of loneliness and despair. The descent is the most complex of the quest stages. It is seen as a metaphorical explanation of death and rebirth; as a sacrificial rite in which the hero's suffering will renew the vigor of his society; as a purification rite in which one is cleansed of his own sins; as a self-annihilating act, after which one will transcend one state of life and enter a higher, better state; or, simply, as a growing-up, leaving one's innocent childhood behind. These are not necessarily distinct or contradictory interpretations. The passage—the labyrinth which is life—can hold all these meanings.

This is the important point. Seen as metaphor, the descent into darkness takes on powerful meaning. It leads to a deeper appreciation of man's endless and somehow beautiful struggle to project himself beyond the limits of his lifespan and to involve himself in eternity. Virtually all good literature is symbolic of this struggle.

The hero is not the same after emerging from the darkness of his descent. The change takes many forms, depending on the nature of his quest and the degree of suffering he has undergone. Theseus was a brave but innocent youngster when he entered the Labyrinth. When he emerged he was a man. The same is true of Gawain. Wisdom, maturity, and spiritual enlightenment are commonly granted the hero after his ordeal. Significantly, these are not the things the hero set out to find.

What the hero seeks is usually no more than a symbol of what he really finds. The hero's goal is most often tangible—to slay a dragon, to bring back a sacred object, or to fulfill a dark promise. But what he really accomplishes is the attainment of a higher state of being. One is not a hero because he slays a dragon but because in the process he grows greater in ways only he will eventually come to understand.

The hero suffers a wound. Neither Gawain nor Theseus was badly wounded. Some heroes, however, go through worse ordeals, even to the point of death. Odin, a Teutonic god, willingly sacrificed an eye to gain wisdom (in effect, losing an eye so that he might see more clearly) °; and then, in a later episode, he sacrificed himself again: "For nine nights, wounded by my own spear, consecrated to Odin, myself consecrated to myself, I remained hanging from the tree shaken by the wind, from the mighty tree whose roots men know not." Christ's wounds killed Him, but His mission as savior demanded that He die. Campbell observes that this kind of ultimate heroic experience serves to ". . . release again . . . the flow of life into the body of the world."

Heroes die as saviors or because their powers wane. King Arthur's death is an example of the latter, as are the deaths of the Irish warrior hero, Cuchulainn, and the great Teutonic hero, Siegfried. Although they dread death, they do not resist it. It is necessary. Only through such total sacrifice can a society be assured of a renewal of its highest aspirations and ideals, as embodied in its greatest heroes. Through his death will come the hero's resurrection, a convincing proof that we are destined to continue in ever-stronger ways.

With few exceptions, mythological heroes are male. Keep in mind that *hero* is being used in this chapter in a narrowly specific way. The hero is not so labeled just because he is brave. He is a hero because he has been assigned a special archetypal role and has succeeded in filling it. Females in mythology exhibit bravery and fortitude in high degree. Ariadne is one example from many that might be mentioned. Yet, females are not generally cast in the archetypal hero role outlined here. Why? Because they have other important functions. Not because, as many are quick to say, myths were made up by males. If this were entirely true, it could equally well follow that the woman's role in myth would be a universally inferior one, which is not the case. Quite the opposite is closer to the truth.

Campbell states that in myth, woman is "the life of everything that lives." All being springs from her. (Did not Ariadne provide Theseus with the thread of life?) She is the hero's progenitor

---

°Tiresias, the renowned seer of Greek mythology, was blind; and King Oedipus blinded himself when he was confronted with truths that he had been too "blind" to see.

and often his protector and guide. She knows vastly more than he does. In fact, says Campbell, she "... represents the totality of what can be known." If the hero attempts to understand her rather than treat her as a sex object or an inferior, she will unlock her secrets for him and will ultimately allow him to become king in a world where she reigns as queen.

Where the female hero does appear in myth and legend, the archetype is somewhat different from that of the male. She is always a maiden. She is innocent, virtuous, and beautiful. In other words, the perfect mortal female. Her perfection works both against her and for her, in that order. At first, she will be hounded from society by jealous rivals and locked away (Cinderella), driven into a perilous country to die (Psyche, Snow White), and/or placed under a spell of sleep (Sleeping Beauty, Snow White). Word of her beauty will have reached a god or prince, however, and sooner or later such a personage will appear. If her suitor is a god, he may disguise himself; if he is a prince, he may be under a spell of ugliness, which only she can break. These are forms of a test, basically to determine whether or not she has the wisdom to see beyond the surface of things. She will experience fear or revulsion but will stick it through until the god decides to reveal himself in his own immortal beauty, or until she stumbles across the secret which will free the prince from his ugly form. At this point, having passed the test, she will be granted immortal life with her mate. (In fairy tales this is known as living "happily ever after.")

As with the male hero, it isn't necessary that all these elements appear in any one story. If you are familiar with the myth of Psyche and Cupid, the story of "Beauty and the Beast," "The Frog Prince," or any of the tales above, you will recognize this motif.

THE WATER OF LIFE

Jacob Grimm (1785–1863)
Wilhelm Grimm (1786–1859)

Once there was a king who was so ill that it was thought impossible to save his life. He had three sons, and they were all in great distress on his account. They went into the castle gardens and wept at the thought of his dying. An old man came up to them and asked the cause of their grief. They told him that their father was dying, and nothing could save him.

The old man said, "There is only one remedy which I know. It is the Water of Life. If he drinks of it he will recover, but it is very difficult to find."

The eldest son said, "I will soon find it." And he went to the sick King to ask permission to go in search of the Water of Life, since that was the only thing to cure him.

"No," said the King. "The danger is too great. I would rather die." But he persisted so long that at last the King gave his permission.

The Prince thought, "If I bring this water I shall be the favorite, and I shall inherit the kingdom." So he set off, and when he had ridden some distance he came upon a dwarf standing in the road, who cried, "Whither away so fast?"

"Stupid little fellow," said the Prince proudly, "what business is it of yours?" And he rode on.

The little man was very angry and made an evil vow.

Soon afterwards, the Prince came to a gorge in the mountains, and the farther he rode the narrower it became, till he could go no farther. His horse could not go forward, nor even turn round for him to dismount. So there he sat, jammed in.

The sick King waited a long time for him, but he never came back. Then the second son said, "Father, let me go and find the Water of Life." He was thinking, "If my brother is dead I shall have the kingdom."

The King at first refused to let him go, but at last he gave his consent. So the Prince started on the same road as his brother. He met the same dwarf, who stopped him and asked where he was going in such a hurry.

"Little snippet, what does it matter to you?" he said, and rode away without looking back.

The dwarf cast a spell over him, and he, too, got into a narrow gorge like his brother, and he could neither go backwards nor forwards. That is what happens to the haughty.

As the second son also stayed away, the youngest one offered to go and fetch the Water of Life, and at last the King was obliged to let him go.

When he met the dwarf, and the dwarf asked him where he was hurrying to, he stopped and said, "I am searching for the Water of Life, because my father is dying."

"Do you know where it is to be found?"

"No," said the Prince.

"As you have spoken pleasantly to me, and not been haughty like your false brothers, I will help you and tell you how to find the Water of Life. It flows from a fountain in the courtyard of an enchanted castle. But you will never get in unless I give you an iron rod and two loaves of bread. With the rod strike three times on the iron gate of the castle and it will spring open. Inside you will find two lions with jaws wide open. If you throw a loaf to each they will be quiet. Then you must make haste to fetch the Water of Life before it strikes twelve, or the gates of the castle will close and you will be shut in."

The Prince thanked him, took the rod and the loaves, and set off. When he reached the castle all was just as the dwarf had said. At the third knock the gate flew open, and when he had pacified the lions with the loaves, he walked into the castle. In the great hall he found several enchanted princes, and he took the rings from their fingers. He also took a sword and a loaf which were lying by them.

On passing into the next room he found a beautiful maiden, who rejoiced at his coming. She embraced him and said that he had saved her, and should have the whole of her kingdom. And if he would come back in a year, she would marry him. She also told him where to find the fountain with the enchanted water. But she said, "You must make haste to get out of the castle before the clock strikes twelve."

He went on and came to a room where there was a beautiful bed freshly made, and as he was very tired he thought he would take a little rest. He lay down and fell asleep. When he woke it was striking a quarter to twelve. He sprang up in a fright, and ran to the fountain and took some of the water in a cup which was lying near, and then hurried away. The clock struck just as he reached the iron gate. The gate banged so quickly that it took off a bit of his heel.

He rejoiced at having got some of the Water of Life, and hastened on his homeward journey. He again passed the dwarf, who said when he saw the sword and the loaf, "Those things will be of much service to you. You will be able to strike down whole armies with the sword, and the loaf will never come to an end."

The Prince did not want to go home without his brothers, and he said, "Good dwarf, can you tell me where my brothers are? They went in search of the Water of Life before I did, but they never came back."

"They are both stuck fast in a narrow mountain gorge. I cast a spell over them because of their pride."

The Prince begged so hard for their release that at last the dwarf yielded. But he warned him against them and said, "Beware of them! They have bad hearts."

He was delighted to see his brothers when they came back, and told them all that had happened to him: how he had found the Water of Life and brought a gobletful with him; how he had released a beautiful princess, who would wait a year for him and then marry him; and how he would then become a great prince.

They rode away together and came to a land where famine and war were raging. The King of this land thought he would be utterly ruined, so great was the destitution.

The Prince went to him and gave him the loaf, and with it he fed and satisfied his whole kingdom. The Prince also gave him his sword, and he smote the whole army of his enemies with it, and then he was able to live in peace and quiet again. The Prince took back his sword and his loaf, and the three brothers rode on.

Later on they had to pass through two more countries where war and famine were raging, and each time the Prince gave his sword and his loaf to the King and in this way he saved three kingdoms.

After that they took a ship and crossed the sea. During the passage the two elder brothers said to each other, "Our youngest brother found the Water of Life, and we did not. So our father will give him the kingdom which we ought to have, and he will take away our fortune from us."

This thought made them very vindictive and they made up their minds to get rid of him. They waited till he was asleep, and then they emptied the Water of Life from his goblet and took it themselves, and filled up his cup with salt sea water.

As soon as they got home the youngest Prince took his goblet to the King so that he might drink of the water which was to make him well. But after drinking only a few drops of the sea water he became more ill than ever. As he was bewailing himself, his two elder sons came to him and accused the youngest of trying to poison him. They said that they had the real Water of Life, and gave him some. No sooner had he drunk it than he felt better, and he soon became as strong and well as he had been in his youth.

The two went to the youngest brother and mocked him, saying, "It was you who found the Water of Life. You had all the trouble, while we have the reward. You should have been wiser and kept your eyes open. We stole it from you while you were asleep on the ship. When the end of the year comes, one of us will go and bring away the beautiful Princess. But don't dare to betray us. Our father will certainly not believe you, and if you say a single word you will surely lose your life. Your only chance is to keep silence."

The old King was very angry with his youngest son, for he thought that he had tried to take his life. He had the court assembled to give judgment upon him, and it was decided that he must be secretly killed.

One day when the Prince was innocently going out hunting, the King's huntsman was ordered to go with him. Seeing the huntsman look sad, the Prince said to him, "My good huntsman, what is the matter with you?"

The huntsman answered, "I can't bear to tell you, and yet I must."

The Prince said, "Say it out. Whatever it is I will forgive you."

"Alas!" said the huntsman, "I am to shoot you dead. It is the King's command."

The Prince was horror-stricken and said, "Dear huntsman, do not kill me. Give me my life. Let me have your dress, and you shall have my royal robes."

The huntsman said, "I will gladly do so. I could never have shot you." So they changed clothes and the huntsman went home, but the Prince wandered away into the forest.

After a time three wagonloads of gold and precious stones came to the King for his youngest son. They were sent by the kings who had been saved by the Prince's sword and his miraculous loaf, and who now wished to show their gratitude.

Then the old King thought, "What if my son really was innocent?" And he said to his people, "If only he were still alive! How sorry I am that I ordered him to be killed."

"He is still alive," said the huntsman. "I could not find it in my heart to carry out your commands." And he told the King what had taken place.

A load fell from the King's heart on hearing the good news. He sent out a proclamation to all parts of his kingdom that his son was to come home, where he would be received with great favor.

In the meantime, the Princess had ordered a pure shining gold road to be made leading to her castle. She told her people that whoever came riding along straight down the middle would be the true bridegroom, and they were to admit him. But anyone who rode on one side of the road or the other would not be the right one. And he was not to be let in.

The year had almost passed, and the eldest Prince thought that he would hurry to the Princess, and by giving himself out as her deliverer would gain a wife and a kingdom as well. So he rode away, and when he saw the beautiful golden road he thought it would be a thousand pities to ride upon it, so he turned aside and rode to the right of it. When he reached the gate the people told him that he was not the true bridegroom, and he had to go away.

Soon after the second Prince came, and when he saw the golden road he thought it would be a thousand pities for his horse to tread upon it. He turned and rode up on the left of it. When he reached the gate he was told that he was not the true bridegroom, and like his brother was turned away.

When the year had quite come to an end, the third Prince came out of the wood to ride to his beloved. Through her he felt he could forget all his past sorrows. So on he went, thinking only of her and wishing to be with her. And he never even saw the golden road. His horse cantered right along the middle of it, and when he reached the gate it was flung open, and the Princess received him joyfully. She called him her deliverer and the lord of her kingdom. Their marriage was celebrated without delay and with much rejoicing. When it was over, she told him that his father had called him back and forgiven him.

He went to his father and told him everything: how his brothers had deceived him, and how they had forced him to keep silence. The old King wanted to punish them, but they had taken a ship and sailed away over the sea, and never came back as long as they lived.

THOMAS RHYMER

Anonymous

True Thomas lay oer yond grassy bank,
    And he beheld a ladie gay,
A ladie that was brisk and bold,
    Come riding oer the fernie brae°

Her skirt was of the grass-green silk,   5
    Her mantel of the velvet fine,
At ilka tett° of her horse's mane
    Hung fifty silver bells and nine.

True Thomas he took off his hat,
    And bowed him low down till his knee: 10
'All hail, thou mighty Queen of Heaven!
    For your peer on earth I never did see.'

'O no, O no, True Thomas,' she says,
    'That name does not belong to me;
I am but the queen of fair Elfland,   15
    And I'm come here for to visit thee.

°*brae*: hillside
°*ilka tett*: every braid

'But ye maun° go wi me now, Thomas,
  True Thomas, ye maun go wi me,
For ye maun serve me seven years,
  Thro weel or wae as may chance to be.'   20

She turned about her milk-white steed,
  And took True Thomas up behind,
And aye wheneer her bridle rang,
  The steed flew swifter than the wind.

For forty days and forty nights   25
  He wade thro red blude to the knee,
And he saw neither sun nor moon,
  But heard the roaring of the sea.

O they rade on, and further on,
  Until they came to a garden green: 30
'Light down, light down, ye ladie free,
  Some of that fruit let me pull to thee.'

'O no, O no, True Thomas,' she says,
  'That fruit maun not be touched by thee,
For a' the plagues that are in hell   35
  Light on the fruit of this countrie.

'But I have a loaf here in my lap,
  Likewise a bottle of claret wine,
And now ere we go farther on,
  We'll rest a while, and ye may dine.'   40

When he had eaten and drunk his fill,
  'Lay down your head upon my knee,'
The lady sayd, 'ere we climb yon hill,
  And I will show you fairlies° three.

'O see not ye yon narrow road,   45
  So thick beset wi thorns and briers?
That is the path of righteousness,
  Tho after it but few enquires.

'And see not ye that braid braid road,

°*maun*: must
°*fairlies*: wonders

That lies across yon lillie leven°?   50
That is the path of wickedness,
    Tho some call it the road to heaven.

'And see not ye that bonny road,
    Which winds about the fernie brae?
That is the road to fair Elfland,   55
    Whe[re] you and I this night maun gae.°

'But Thomas, ye maun hold your tongue,
    Whatever you may hear or see,
For gin° ae word you should chance to speak,
    You will neer get back to your ain countrie.'   60

He has gotten a coat of the even cloth,
    And a pair of shoes of velvet green,
And till seven years were past and gone
    True Thomas on earth was never seen.

Sir Gawain and the Green Knight
Anonymous

In Camelot° Arthur the King lay at Christmas,°
With many a peerless lord princely companioned,
The whole noble number of knights of the Round Table;
Here right royally held his high revels,
Carefree and mirthful. Now much of the company,   5
Knightly born gentlemen, joyously jousted,
Now came to the court to make caroles°; so kept they
For full fifteen days this fashion of feasting,
All meat and all mirth that a man might devise.

Moreover, the King was moved by a custom   10
He once had assumed in a spirit of splendor:
Never to fall to his feast on a festival
Till a strange story of something eventful

°*leven*: lawn
°*gae*: go
°*gin*: if
°*Camelot*: Arthur's capital in southern England
°*lay at Christmas*: sojourned at Christmastime
°*caroles*: dances accompanied by singing

Was told him, some marvel that merited credence
Of kings, or of arms, or all kinds of adventures; 15
Or someone besought him to send a true knight
To join him in proving the perils of jousting,
Life against life, each leaving the other
To have, as fortune would help him, the fairer lot.

And scarcely the music had ceased for a moment, 20
The first course been suitably served in the court,
When a being most dreadful burst through the hall-door,
Among the most mighty of men in his measure.°
From his throat to his thighs so thick were his sinews,
His loins and his limbs so large and so long, 25
That I hold him half-giant, the hugest of men,
And the handsomest, too, in his height, upon horseback.
Though stalwart in breast and in back was his body,
His waist and his belly were worthily small;
Fashioned fairly he was in his form, and in features 30
                        Cut clean.

     All green was the man, and green were his garments:
A coat, straight and close, that clung to his sides,
A bright mantle on top of this, trimmed on the inside
With closely-cut fur, right fair, that showed clearly, 35
The lining with white fur most lovely, and hood too,
Caught back from his locks, and laid on his shoulders,
Neat stockings that clung to his calves, tightly stretched,
Of the same green, and under° them spurs of gold shining
Brightly on bands of fine silk, richly barred;° 40
And everything metal enameled in emerald.
The stirrups he stood on the same way were colored,
His saddle-bows too, and the studded nails splendid,
That all with green gems ever glimmered and glinted.
The horse he bestrode was in hue still the same, 45

     This hero in green was habited gaily,
And likewise the hair on the head of his good horse;
Fair, flowing tresses enfolded his shoulders,
And big as a bush a beard hung on his breast.

     Yet the hero carried nor helmet nor hauberk, 50

°*measure*: height
°*under*: below
°*barred*: striped

But bare was of armor, breastplate or gorget,
Spear-shaft or shield, to thrust or to smite.
But in one hand he bore a bough of bright holly,°
That grows most greenly when bare are the groves,
In the other an ax, gigantic, awful,°   55
A terrible weapon, wondrous to tell of.
Large was the head, in length a whole ell-yard,°
The blade of green steel and beaten gold both;
The bit had a broad edge, and brightly was burnished,
As suitably shaped as sharp razors for shearing.   60

Thus into the hall came the hero, and hastened
Direct to the dais,° fearing no danger.
He gave no one greeting, but haughtily gazed
And his first words were, "Where can I find him who governs
This goodly assemblage? for gladly that man   65
I would see and have speech with." . . . .

. . . the King, ever keen and courageous,
Saw from on high, and saluted the stranger
Suitably, saying, "Sir, you are welcome.
I, the head of this household, am Arthur;   70
In courtesy light,° and linger, I pray you,
And later, my lord, we shall learn your desire."

"Nay, so help me He seated on high," quoth the hero,
"My mission was not to remain here a moment;
Since here, I have heard, is the highest of courtesy—   75
Truly, all these things have brought me at this time.

Sure ye may be by this branch that I bear
That I pass as in peace, proposing no fight.

          "Nay, I ask for no fight; in faith, now I tell thee
But beardless babes° are about on this bench.   80
Were I hasped in my armor, and high on a horse,

°*holly*: to indicate that he came in peace (see lines 77-78)
°*awful*: awesome
°*ell-yard*: forty-five inches
°*dais*: the raised platform on which the most important members of the
          court sat. The rest occupied two long tables along the walls that ran the
          length of the room. The Green Knight rode between the tables to the dais.
°*light*: alight
°*but beardless babes*: i.e., only striplings (see line 49 for comparison)

Here is no man to match me, your might is so feeble.
So I crave but a Christmas game in this court;
Yule and New Year are come, and here men have courage;
If one in this house himself holds so hardy,   85
So bold in his blood, in his brain so unbalanced
To dare stiffly strike one stroke for another,
I give this gisarme, this rich axe, as a gift to him,
Heavy enough, to handle as pleases him;
Bare as I sit, I shall bide the first blow.   90
If a knight be so tough as to try what I tell,
Let him leap to me lightly; I leave him this weapon,
Quitclaim it forever, to keep as his own;
And his stroke here, firm on this floor, I shall suffer
This boon if thou grant'st me, the blow with another   95
                                        To pay;

              Yet let his respite be
              A twelvemonth and a day.
              Come, let us quickly see
              If one here aught° dare say."   100

        If at first he had startled them, stiller then sat there
The whole of the court, low and high, in the hall.
The knight on his steed turned himself in his saddle,
And fiercely his red eyes he rolled all around,
Bent his bristling brows, with green gleaming brightly,   105
And waved his beard, waiting for one there to rise.
And when none of the knights spoke, he coughed right noisily,
Straightened up proudly, and started to speak:
"What!" quoth the hero. "Is this Arthur's household,
The fame of whose fellowship fills many kingdoms?   110
Now where is your vainglory? Where are your victories?
Where is your grimness, your great words, your anger?
For now the Round Table's renown and its revel
Is worsted by one word of one person's speech,
For all shiver with fear before a stroke's shown."   115
Then so loudly he laughed that the lord° was grieved greatly,
And into his fair face his blood shot up fiercely
                                        For shame.

        And said, "Sir, by heaven, strange thy request is;

°*aught*: anything
°*lord*: Arthur

As folly thou soughtest, so shouldest thou find it.   120
I know that not one of the knights is aghast
Of thy great words. Give me thy weapon, for God's sake,
And gladly the boon thou hast begged I shall grant thee."

       Gawain by Guinevere
       Did to the King incline: 125
       "I pray in accents clear
       To let this fray be mine.

       "If you now, honored lord," said this knight to King
           Arthur,
"Would bid me to step from this bench, and to stand there
Beside you—so could I with courtesy quit then   130
The table, unless my liege lady disliked it—
I'd come to your aid before all your great court."

       The King then commanded his kinsman to rise,
And quickly he rose up and came to him courteously,
Kneeled by the King, and caught the weapon,   135
He left it graciously, lifted his hand,
And gave him God's blessing, and gladly bade him
Be sure that his heart and his hand both were hardy.
"Take care," quoth the King, "how you start, coz,° your cutting,
And truly, I think, if rightly you treat him,   140
That blow you'll endure that he deals you after."

       "By God," said the Green Knight, "Sir Gawain, it pleases
           me—
Here, at thy hand, I shall have what I sought."

       With speed then the Green Knight took up his stand,
Inclined his head forward, uncovering the flesh,   145
And laid o'er his crown his locks long and lovely,
And bare left the nape of his neck for the business.
His axe Gawain seized, and swung it on high;
On the floor his left foot he planted before him,
And swiftly the naked flesh smote with his weapon.   150
The sharp edge severed the bones of the stranger,
Cut through the clear flesh and cleft it in twain,
So the blade of the brown steel bit the ground deeply.
The fair head fell from the neck to the floor,

°*coz*: short for cousin, kinsman; Gawain is Arthur's nephew

So that where it rolled forth with their feet many spurned it.   155
The blood on the green glistened, burst from the body;
And yet neither fell nor faltered the hero,
But stoutly he started forth, strong in his stride;
Fiercely he rushed 'mid the ranks of the Round Table,
Seized and uplifted his lovely head straightway;   160
Then back to his horse went, laid hold of the bridle,
Stepped into the stirrup and strode° up aloft,
His head holding fast in his hand by the hair.
And the man as soberly sat in his saddle
As if he unharmed were, although now headless,   165
                                                            Instead.

        For upright he holds the head in his hand,
And confronts with the face the fine folk on the dais.
It lifted its lids, and looked forth directly,
Speaking this much with its mouth, as ye hear: 170
"Gawain, look that to go as agreed you are ready,
And seek for me faithfully, sir, till you find me,
As, heard by these heroes, you vowed in this hall.
To the Green Chapel go you, I charge you, to get
Such a stroke as you struck. You are surely deserving,   175
Sir knight, to be promptly repaid at the New Year.
As Knight of the Green Chapel many men know me;
If therefore to find me you try, you will fail not;
Then come, or be recreant called as befits thee."
With furious wrench of the reins he turned round,   180
And rushed from the hall-door, his head in his hands,
So the fire of the flint flew out from the foal's hoofs.

        Now take heed Gawain lest,
        Fearing the Green Knight's brand,
        Thou shrinkest from the quest   185
        That thou hast ta'en in hand.

II

Full swift flies a year, never yielding the same
The start and the close very seldom according.
So past went this Yule, and the year followed after,
Each season in turn succeeding the other.   190

°*strode*: bestrode

Till the tide of Allhallows° with Arthur he tarried;
The King made ado on that day for his sake
With rich and rare revel of all of the Round Table,
Knights most courteous, comely ladies,
All of them heavy at heart for the hero.   195
Yet nothing but mirth was uttered, though many
Joyless made jests for that gentleman's sake.
After meat, with sorrow he speaks to his uncle,
And openly talks of his travel, saying:
"Liege lord of my life, now I ask of you leave.   200
You know my case and condition, nor care I
To tell of its troubles even a trifle.
I must, for the blow I am bound to, tomorrow
Go seek as God guides me the man in the green."

When in arms he was clasped, his costume was costly;   205
The least of the lacings or loops gleamed with gold.
And armed in this manner, the man heard mass,
At the altar adored and made offering, and afterward
Came to the King and all of his courtiers,
Gently took leave of the ladies and lords;   210
Him they kissed and escorted, to Christ him commending.

He set spurs to his steed, and sprang on his way
So swiftly that sparks from the stone flew behind him.
All who saw him, so seemly, sighed, sad at heart;
The same thing, in sooth, each said to the other,   215
Concerned for that comely man: "Christ, 't is a shame
Thou, sir knight, must be lost whose life is so noble!
To find, faith! his equal on earth is not easy."

Over many cliffs climbed he in foreign countries;°
From friends far sundered, he fared as a stranger;   220
And wondrous it were, at each water or shore
That he passed, if he found not before him a foe,
So foul too and fell that to fight he could fail not.
The marvels he met with amount to so many
Too tedious were it to tell of the tenth part.   225
For sometimes with serpents he struggled and wolves too,

°*tide of Allhallows*: time of All Saints' Day (November 1)
°*foreign countries*: parts of England new and strange to him. The details
    of his travels are not clear, but he goes from Camelot in the south of
    England, up through Wales, and probably as far north as Cumberland.

With wood-trolls sometimes in stony steeps dwelling,
And sometimes with bulls° and with bears and with boars;
And giants from high fells hunted and harassed him.
If he'd been not enduring and doughty, and served God,   230
These doubtless would often have done him to death.
Though warfare was grievous, worse was the winter,
When cold, clear water was shed from the clouds
That froze ere it fell to the earth, all faded.

With sleet nearly slain, he slept in his armor   235
More nights than enough on the naked rocks,
Where splashing the cold stream sprang from the summit,
And hung in hard icicles high o'er his head.
Thus in peril and pain and desperate plights,
Till Christmas Eve wanders this wight through the country   240
                        Alone.

Through many a marsh and many a mire,
Unfriended, fearing to fail in devotion,
And see not His service, that Sire's, on that very night
Born of a Virgin to vanquish our pain.   245
And so sighing he said: "Lord, I beseech Thee,
And Mary, the mildest mother so dear,
For some lodging wherein to hear mass full lowly,
And matins, meekly I ask it, tomorrow;
So promptly I pray my pater° and ave°   250
                      And creed."

    He scarcely had signed himself° thrice, ere he saw
In the wood on a mound a moated mansion,
Above a fair field, enfolded in branches
Of many a huge tree hard by the ditches: 255
The comeliest castle that knight ever kept.

    Gawain gazed at the man who so graciously greeted him;
Doughty he looked, the lord of that dwelling,
A hero indeed huge, hale, in his prime;
His beard broad and bright, its hue all of beaver;°   260

°*bulls:* i.e., wild bulls
°*pater*: the Lord's Prayer, which in Latin begins: *Pater noster*—"Our
    Father"
°*Ave*: the prayers beginning: *Ave Maria*—"Hail, Mary"
°*signed himself*: made the sign of the cross
°*beaver*: reddish-brown

Stern, and on stalwart shanks steadily standing;
Fell° faced as the fire, in speech fair and free.
In sooth, well suited he seemed, thought Gawain,
To govern as prince of a goodly people.

Much mirth was that day and the day after made, 265
And the third followed fast, as full of delight.

Then the man with courteous questions inquired
What dark deed that feast time had driven him forth,
From the King's court to journey alone with such courage,
Ere fully in homes was the festival finished. 270
"In sooth," said the knight, "sir, ye say but the truth;
From these hearths a high and a hasty task took me.
Myself, I am summoned to seek such a place
As to find it I know not whither to fare.

Tell me, in truth, if you ever heard tale 275
Of the Chapel of Green, of the ground where it stands,
And the knight, green colored, who keeps it. By solemn
Agreement a tryst was established between us,
That man at that landmark to meet if I lived."

Then laughing the lord said: "You longer must stay, 280
For I'll point out the way to that place ere the time's end,
The ground of the Green Chapel. Grieve no further;
For, sir, you shall be in your bed at your ease
Until late, and fare forth the first of the year,
To your meeting place come by mid-morning, to do there 285
            Your pleasure.

Tarry till New Year's day,
Then rise and go at leisure.
I'll set you on your way;
Not two miles is the measure." 290

Then was Gawain right glad, and gleefully laughed.
"Now for this more than anything else, sir, I thank you.
I have come to the end of my quest; at your will
I shall bide, and in all things act as you bid me."

"You have toiled," said the lord; "from afar have traveled, 295
And here have caroused, nor are wholly recovered

°*fell*: fierce

In sleep or in nourishment, know I for certain.
In your room you shall linger, and lie at your ease
Tomorrow till mass-time, and go to your meat
When you will, and with you my wife to amuse you   300
With company, till to the court I return.

You stay

        And I shall early rise,
        And hunting go my way."
        Bowing in courteous wise,   305
        Gawain grants all this play.

    "And more," said the man, "let us make an agreement:
Whatever I win in the wood° shall be yours;
And what chance° you shall meet shall be mine in exchange.
Sir, let's so strike our bargain and swear to tell truly   310
Whate'er fortune brings, whether bad, sir, or better."
Quoth Gawain the good: "By God, I do grant it.
What pastime you please appears to me pleasant."
"On the beverage brought us the bargain is made,"
So the lord of the land said. All of them laughed,   315
And drank, and light-heartedly reveled and dallied,
Those ladies and lords, as long as they liked.

    Gawain had arrived on Christmas Eve, planning to leave on the twenty-eighth of December. When the lords and ladies leave on that day, Gawain is also prepared to depart. His host, however, persuades him to stay until New Year's Day, since the Green Chapel is nearby. It is during these three days that Gawain and the host play out the proposed "agreement," whereby he will go hunting and give Gawain whatever game he bags in exchange for "whate'er fortune brings" to Gawain, who is to remain behind in the castle.

    When Gawain awakes on the morning of the twenty-ninth, he finds his host's wife in his chamber. When she makes open advances to him, he fends her off politely, wishing neither to insult her nor to betray his host. She settles for a single kiss. When the host returns he gives Gawain the deer he has killed. Gawain in return gives him a kiss.

    The next morning the lady again attempts to seduce Gawain, and again he fends her off, maintaining knightly courtesy in the face of her open aggression. This time she wins two kisses.

°*in the wood*: out hunting
°*chance*: fortune

When the host that evening gives Gawain the boar he has killed,
Gawain responds by kissing him twice. Now follow what happens
on the third day:

III

      The men there make merry and drink, and once more
The same pact for New Year's Eve is proposed;
But the knight craved permission to mount on the morrow: 320
The appointment approached where he had to appear.
But the lord him persuaded to stay and linger,
And said, "On my word as a knight I assure you
You'll get to the Green Chapel, Gawain, on New Year's,
And far before prime,° to finish your business.   325
Remain in your room then, and take your rest.
I shall hunt in the wood and exchange with you winnings,
As bound by our bargain, when back I return,
For twice I've found you were faithful when tried:
In the morning 'best be the third time,' remember.   330
Let's be mindful of mirth while we may, and make merry,
For care when one wants it is quickly encountered."
At once this was granted, and Gawain is stayed;
                  The host was early dressed.

      After mass a morsel he took with his men.   335
The morning was merry; his mount he demanded.
The knights who'd ride in his train were in readiness,
Dressed and horsed at the door of the hall.
Wondrous fair were the fields, for the frost was clinging;
Fire-red in the cloud-rack° rises the sun,   340
And brightens the skirts of the clouds in the sky.
The hunters unleased all the hounds by a woodside:
The rocks with the blast of their bugles were ringing.
Some dogs there fall on the scent where the fox is,
And trail oft a traitoress° using her tricks.   345

So he° led all astray the lord and his men,
In this manner along through the hills until mid-day.

°*prime*: early morning
°*cloud-rack*: cloud-drift
°*traitoress*: a vixen who confused the dogs by crossing the trail of the male
    fox
°*he*: the fox

At home, the noble knight wholesomely slept
In the cold of the morn within comely curtains.
But the lady, for love, did not let herself sleep,   350
Or fail in the purpose fixed in her heart;
But quickly she roused herself, came there quickly,
Arrayed in a gay robe that reached to the ground,
The skins of the splendid fur skillfully trimmed close.
On her head no colors save jewels, well-cut,   355
That were twined in her hair-fret° in clusters of twenty.
Her fair face was completely exposed, and her throat;
In front her breast too was bare, and her back.
She comes through the chamber-door, closes it after her,
Swings wide a window, speaks to the wight,   360
And rallies him soon in speech full of sport
                                        And good cheer.

The lovely lady came near, sweetly laughing,
Bent down o'er his fair face and daintily kissed him.
And well, in a worthy manner, he welcomed her.   365
Seeing her glorious, gaily attired,
Without fault in her features, most fine in her color,
Deep joy came welling up, warming his heart.
With sweet, gentle smiling they straightway grew merry;
So passed naught between them but pleasure, joy,   370
                                        And delight.

            Goodly was their debate,
            Nor was their gladness slight.
            Their peril had been great
            Had Mary° quit her knight.   375

        For that noble princess pressed him so closely,
Brought him so near the last bound, that her love
He was forced to accept, or, offending, refuse her:
Concerned for his courtesy not to prove caitiff,°
And more for his ruin if wrong he committed,   380
Betraying the hero, the head of that house.
"God forbid," said the knight; "that never shall be";
And lovingly laughing a little, he parried
The words of fondness° that fell from her mouth.

°*hair-fret*: wire headdress for containing her hair
°*Mary*: the Virgin Mary
°*caitiff*: cowardly
°*fondness*: love

His parrying is successful. The lady asks if there is another, and Gawain assures her that there is not. She then asks him for a token to remember him by, but he says he has nothing worthy of her. She offers him a ring, which he politely refuses. Finally, she offers him her silk belt:

"Refuse ye this silk," the lady then said,   385
"As slight in itself? Truly it seems so.
Lo! it is little, and less is its worth;
But one knowing the nature knit up within it,
Would give it a value more great, peradventure;
For no man girt with this girdle of green,   390
And bearing it fairly made fast about him,
Might ever be cut down° by any on earth,
For his life in no way in the world could be taken."
Then mused the man, and it came to his mind
In the peril appointed him precious 't would prove,   395
When he'd found the chapel, to face there his fortune.
The device, might he slaying evade, would be splendid.
Her suit then he suffered, and let her speak;
And the belt she offered him, earnestly urging it
(And Gawain consented), and gave it with good will,   400
And prayed him for her sake ne'er to display it,
But, true, from her husband to hide it. The hero
Agreed that no one should know of it ever.

The lord's in the meadow still, leading his men.
He has slain this fox that he followed so long;   405
As he vaulted a hedge to get view of the villain,
Hearing the hounds that hastened hard after him,
Reynard from out a rough thicket came running,
And right at his heels in a rush all the rabble.°
He seeing that wild thing, wary, awaits him,   410
Unsheathes his bright brand° and strikes at the beast.
And he swerved from its sharpness and back would have started;
A hound, ere he could, came hurrying up to him;
All of them fell on him fast by the horse's feet,
Worried that sly one with wrathful sound.   405
And quickly the lord alights, and catches him,
Takes him in haste from the teeth of the hounds,

°*cut down*: killed
°*rabble*: hounds
°*brand*: sword

And over his head holds him high, loudly shouting,
Where brachets,° many and fierce, at him barked.

 And now, since near was the night, they turned   420
   homeward,
Strongly and sturdily sounding their horns.
At last at his loved home the lord alighted,
A fire on the hearth found, the hero beside it,
Sir Gawain the good, who glad was withal,
For he had 'mong the ladies in love much delight.   425

He, mid-most, met the good man in the hall,
And greeted him gladly, graciously saying:
"Now shall I first fulfill our agreement
We struck to good purpose, when drink was not spared."
Then Gawain embraced him, gave him three kisses,   430
The sweetest and soundest a man could bestow.
"By Christ, you'd great happiness," quoth then the host,
"In getting these wares, if good were your bargains."
"Take no care for the cost," the other said quickly,
"Since plainly the debt that is due I had paid."   435
Said the other, "By Mary, mine's of less worth.
The whole of the day I have hunted, and gotten
The skin of this fox—the fiend take its foulness!—
Right poor to pay for things of such price
As you've pressed on me here so heartily, kisses   440
        So good."

"May God you reward for the welcome you gave me
This high feast, the splendid sojourn I've had here.
I give you myself, if you'd like it, to serve you.
I must, as you know, on the morrow move on;   445
Give me someone to show me the path, as you said,
To the Green Chapel, there, as God will allow me,
On New Year the fate that is fixed to perform."
"With a good will, indeed," said the good man; "whatever
I promised to do I deem myself ready."   450
He a servant assigns on his way to set him,
To take him by hills that no trouble he'd have,
And through grove and wood by the way most direct
        Might repair.

———————

°*brachets*: small female hounds

IV

The New Year draws near, and the nighttime now   455
    passes;
The day, as the Lord bids, drives on to darkness.
Outside, there sprang up wild storms in the world;
The clouds cast keenly the cold to the earth
With enough of the north sting to trouble the naked;
Down shivered the snow, nipping sharply the wild beasts;   460
The wind from the heights, shrilly howling, came rushing,
And heaped up each dale full of drifts right huge.
Full well the man listened who lay in his bed.
Though he shut tight his lids, he slept but a little;
He knew by each cock that crowed 't was the tryst time,   465
And swiftly ere dawn of the day he arose,
For there shone then the light of a lamp in his room;
To his chamberlain called, who answered him quickly,
And bade him his saddle to bring and his mailshirt.

Yet he left not the lace, the gift of the lady: 470
That, Gawain did not, for his own sake, forget.
When the brand on his rounded thighs he had belted,
He twisted his love-token two times about him.
That lord round his waist with delight quickly wound
The girdle of green silk, that seemed very gay   475
Upon royal red cloth that was rich to behold.
But Gawain the girdle wore not for its great price,
Or pride in its pendants although they were polished,
Though glittering gold there gleamed on the ends,
But himself to save when he needs must suffer   480
The death, nor could stroke then of sword or of knife
                        Him defend.

On the moor dripped the mist, on the mountains melted;
Each hill had a hat, a mist-cloak right huge.
The brooks foamed and bubbled on hillsides about them,   485
And brightly broke on their banks as they rushed down.
Full wandering the way was they went through the wood,
Until soon it was time for the sun to be springing.

    "I have led you hither, my lord, at this time,
And not far are you now from that famous place   490
You have sought for, and asked so especially after.

Yet, sir, to you surely I'll say, since I know you,
A man in this world whom I love right well,
If you'd follow my judgment, the better you'd fare.
You make haste to a place that is held full of peril;   495
One dwells, the worst in the world, in that waste,
For he's strong and stern, and takes pleasure in striking.

      "So let him alone, good Sir Gawain, and leave
By a different road, for God's sake, and ride
To some other country where Christ may reward you.   500
And homeward again I will hie me, and promise
To swear by the Lord and all his good saints
(So help me the oaths on God's halidom° sworn)
That I'll guard well your secret, and give out no story
You hastened to flee any hero I've heard of."   505
"Thank you," said Gawain, and grudgingly added,
"Good fortune go with you for wishing me well.
And truly I think you'd not tell; yet though never
So surely you hid it, if hence I should hasten,
Fearful, to fly in the fashion you tell of,   510
A coward I'd prove, and could not be pardoned.
The chapel I'll find whatsoever befalls.
And talk with that wight the way that I want to,
Let weal or woe follow as fate may wish.

      "Of a truth," said Gawain, "the glade here is gloomy;   515
The Green Chapel's ugly, with herbs overgrown.
It greatly becomes° here that hero, green-clad,
To perform in the devil's own fashion his worship.
I feel in my five senses this is the fiend
Who has made me come to this meeting to kill me.   520
Destruction fall on this church of ill-fortune!
The cursedest chapel that ever I came to!"
With helm on his head and lance in his hand
He went right to the rock of that rugged abode.
From that high hill he heard, from a hard rock over   525
The stream, on the hillside, a sound wondrous loud.
Lo! it ground and it grated, grievous to hear.
"By God, this thing, as I think," then said Gawain,
"Is done now for me, since my due turn to meet it
                         Is near,   530

°*halidom*: holiness
°*becomes*: befits

God's will be done! 'Ah woe!'
No whit° doth aid me here.
Though I my life forego
No sound shall make me fear."

And then the man there commenced to call loudly,   535
"Who here is the master, with me to hold tryst?
For Gawain the good now is going right near.
He who craves aught of me let him come hither quickly;
'T is now or never; he needs to make haste."
Said somebody, "Stop," from the slope up above him,   540
"And promptly you'll get what I promised to give you."
Yet he kept up the whirring noise quickly a while,
Turned to finish his sharpening before he'd descend.
Then he came by a crag, from a cavern emerging,
Whirled out of a den with a dreadful weapon,   545
A new Danish axe to answer the blow with:
Its blade right heavy, curved back to the handle,
Sharp filed with the filing tool, four feet in length,
'T was no less, by the reach of that lace gleaming brightly.
The fellow in green was garbed as at first,   550
Both his face and his legs, his locks and his beard,
Save that fast o'er the earth on his feet he went fairly,
The shaft on the stone set, and stalked on beside it.
On reaching the water, he would not wade it;
On his axe he hopped over, and hastily strode,   555
Very fierce, through the broad field filled all about him
                                        With snow.

Said the green man, "Gawain, may God you guard!
You are welcome indeed, sir knight, at my dwelling.
Your travel you've timed as a true man should,   560
And you know the compact we came to between us;
A twelvemonth ago you took what chance gave,
And I promptly at New Year was pledged to repay you.
In truth, we are down in this dale all alone;
Though we fight as we please, here there's no one to part us. 565
Put your helm from your head, and have here your payment;
Debate no further than I did before,
When you slashed off my head with a single stroke."

"Nay," quoth Gawain, "by God who gave me my spirit,
I'll harbor no grudge whatever harm happens.   570

°*no whit*: nothing

Exceed not one stroke and still I shall stand;
You may do as you please, I'll in no way oppose
                                        The blow."

            Then the man in green raiment quickly made ready,
Uplifted his grim tool Sir Gawain to smite;   575
With the whole of his strength he heaved it on high,
As threateningly swung it as though he would slay him.
Had it fallen again with the force he intended
That lord, ever-brave, from the blow had been lifeless.
But Gawain a side glance gave at the weapon   580
As down it came gliding to do him to death;
With his shoulders shrank from the sharp iron a little.
The other with sudden jerk stayed the bright axe,°
And reproved then that prince with proud words in plenty:
"Not Gawain thou art who so good is considered,   585
Ne'er daunted by host° in hill or in dale;
Now in fear, ere thou feelest a hurt, thou art flinching;
Such cowardice never I knew of that knight.
When you swung at me, sir, I fled not nor started;
No cavil I offered in King Arthur's castle.   590
My head at my feet fell, yet never I flinched,
And thy heart is afraid ere a hurt thou feelest,
And therefore thy better I'm bound to be thought
                                        On that score."

            "I shrank once," Gawain said,   595
            "And I will shrink no more;
            Yet cannot I my head,
            If it fall down, restore."

He° mightily swung but struck not the man,
Withheld on a sudden his hand ere it hurt him.   600
And firmly he° waited and flinched in no member,°
But stood there as still as a stone or a stump
In rocky ground held by a hundred roots.

            "Come! lay on, thou dread man; too long thou art
            threatening.

°*stayed . . . axe*: stopped the blow
°*host*: large numbers
°*He*: the Green Knight
°*he*: Gawain
°*member*: part of his body

I think that afraid of your own self you feel."   605
"In sooth," said the other, "thy speech is so savage
No more will I hinder thy mission nor have it
                                        Delayed."

          He lifts his axe lightly, and lets it down deftly,
The blade's edge next to the naked neck.   610
Though he mightily hammered he hurt him no more
Than to give him a slight nick that severed the skin there.
Through fair skin the keen axe so cut to the flesh
That shining blood shot to the earth o'er his shoulders.
As soon as he° saw his blood gleam on the snow   615
He sprang forth in one leap, for more than a spear length;
His helm fiercely caught up and clapped on his head;
With his shoulders his fair shield shot round in front of him,°
Pulled out his bright sword, and said in a passion
(And since he was mortal man born of his mother   620
The hero was never so happy by half),
"Cease thy violence, man; no more to me offer,
For here I've received, unresisting, a stroke.
If a second thou strikest I soon will requite thee,
And swiftly and fiercely, be certain of that,   625
                                        Will repay."

Then gaily the Green Knight spoke in a great voice,
And said to the man in speech that resounded,
"Now be not so savage, bold sir, for towards you
None here has acted unhandsomely, save   630
In accord with the compact arranged in the King's court.
I promised the stroke you've received, so hold you
Well paid. I free you from all duties further.
If brisk I had been, peradventure a buffet°
I'd harshly have dealt that harm would have done you.   635
In mirth, with a feint I menaced you first,
With no direful wound rent you; right was my deed,
By the bargain that bound us both on the first night,
When, faithful and true, you fulfilled our agreement,
And gave me your gain as a good man ought to.   640
The second I struck at you, sir, for the morning

°*he*: Gawain
°*with . . . him*: Gawain's shield was strapped on his back; with a quick flip
    of his shoulders he brings it around to the front
°*buffet*: blow

You kissed my fair wife and the kisses accorded me.
Two mere feints for both times I made at you, man,
                              Without woe.

    True men restore by right,   645
    One fears no danger so;
    You failed the third time, knight,
    And therefore took that blow.

    " 'T is my garment you're wearing, that woven girdle,
Bestowed by my wife, as in truth I know well.   650
I know also your kisses and all of your acts
And my wife's advances; myself, I devised them.
I sent her to try you, and truly you seem
The most faultless of men that e'er fared on his feet.
As a pearl compared to white peas is more precious,   655
So next to the other gay knights is Sir Gawain.
But a little you lacked, and loyalty wanted,
Yet truly 't was not for intrigue or for wooing,
But love of your life; the less do I blame you."
Sir Gawain stood in a study° a great while,   660
So sunk in disgrace that in spirit he groaned;
To his face all the blood in his body was flowing;
For shame, as the other was talking, he shrank.
And these were the first words that fell from his lips:
"Be cowardice cursed, and coveting! In you°   665
Are vice and villainy, virtue destroying."
The lace he then seized, and loosened the strands,
And fiercely the girdle flung at the Green Knight.
"Lo! there is faith-breaking! evil befall it.
To coveting came I, for cowardice caused me   670
From fear of your stroke to forsake in myself
What belongs to a knight: munificence, loyalty.
I'm faulty and false, who've been ever afraid
Of untruth and treachery; sorrow betide both
                              And care!   675

    Here I confess my sin;
    All faulty did I fare.
    Your good will let me win,
    And then I will beware."

°*study*: deep thought on what he had done
°*in you*: in cowardice and coveting

Then the Green Knight laughed, and right graciously 680
    said,
"I am sure that the harm is healed that I suffered.
So clean you're confessed, so cleared of your faults,
Having had the point of my weapon's plain penance,
I hold you now purged of offense, and as perfectly
Spotless as though you'd ne'er sinned in your life. 685
And I give to you, sir, the golden-hemmed girdle,
As green as my gown. Sir Gawain, when going
Forth on your way among famous princes,
Think still of our strife and this token right splendid,
'Mid chivalrous knights, of the chapel's adventure." 690

    "But your girdle," said Gawain, "may God you reward!
With a good will I'll use it, yet not for the gold,
The sash or the silk, or the sweeping pendants,
Or fame, or its workmanship wondrous, or cost,
But in sign of my sin I shall see it oft. 695
When in glory I move, with remorse I'll remember
The frailty and fault of the stubborn flesh,
How soon 't is infected with stains of defilement;
And thus when I'm proud of my prowess in arms,
The sight of this sash shall humble my spirit. 700
But one thing I pray, if it prove not displeasing;
Because you are lord of the land where I stayed
In your house with great worship (may He now reward you
Who sitteth on high and upholdeth the heavens),
What name do you bear? No more would I know." 705
And then "That truly I'll tell," said the other;
"Bercilak de Hautdesert here am I called.

    "I was sent in this way to your splendid hall
To make trial of your pride, and to see if the people's
Tales were true of the Table's great glory. 710

And I, sir, wish thee as well, on my word,
As any on earth for thy high sense of honor."

The men kiss, embrace, and each other commend
To the Prince of Paradise; there they part
                        In the cold. 715

Through the wood now goes Sir Gawain by wild ways
On Gringolet,° given by God's grace his life.
Oft in houses, and oft in the open he lodged,
Met many adventures, won many a victory:
These I intend not to tell in this tale.   720
Now whole was the hurt he had in his neck,
And about it the glimmering belt he was bearing,
Bound to his side like a baldric obliquely,
Tied under his left arm, that lace, with a knot
As a sign that with stain of sin he'd been found.   725
And thus to the court he comes all securely.

The King kissed the lord, and the Queen did likewise,
And next many knights drew near him to greet him
And ask how he'd fared; and he wondrously answered,
Confessed all the hardships that him had befallen,   730
The happenings at chapel, the hero's behavior,
The lady's love, and lastly the lace.
He showed them the nick in his neck all naked
The blow that the Green Knight gave for deceit
                              Him to blame.   735

In torment this he owned;°
Blood in his face did flame;
With wrath and grief he groaned,
When showing it with shame.

Laying hold of the lace, quoth the hero, "Lo! lord!   740
The band of this fault I bear on my neck;
And this is the scathe and damage I've suffered,
For cowardice caught there, and coveting also,
The badge of untruth in which I was taken.
And this for as long as I live I must wear,   745
For his fault none may hide without meeting misfortune,
For once it is fixed, it can ne'er be unfastened."
To the knight then the King gave comfort; the court too
Laughed greatly, and made this gracious agreement:
That ladies and lords to the Table belonging,   750
All of the brotherhood, baldrics should bear
Obliquely about them, bands of bright green,
Thus following suit for the sake of the hero.

°*Gringolet*: Gawain's horse
°*owned*: admitted

For the Round Table's glory was granted that lace,
And he held himself honored who had it thereafter,   755
As told in the book, the best of romances.
In the days of King Arthur this deed was done. . . .

MINIVER CHEEVY

Edwin Arlington Robinson (1869–1935)

Miniver Cheevy, child of scorn,
    Grew lean while he assailed the seasons;
He wept that he was ever born,
    And he had reasons.

Miniver loved the days of old   5
    When swords were bright and steeds were
        prancing;
The vision of a warrior bold
    Would set him dancing.

Miniver sighed for what was not,
    And dreamed, and rested from his labors;   10
He dreamed of Thebes and Camelot,
    And Priam's neighbors.

Miniver mourned the ripe renown
    That made so many a name so fragrant;
He mourned Romance, now on the town,   15
    And Art, a vagrant.

Miniver loved the Medici,
    Albeit he had never seen one;
He would have sinned incessantly
    Could he have been one.   20

Miniver cursed the commonplace
    And eyed a khaki suit with loathing;
He missed the medieval grace
    Of iron clothing.

Miniver scorned the gold he sought,   25
    But sore annoyed was he without it;
Miniver thought, and thought, and thought,
    And thought about it.

Miniver Cheevy, born too late,
   Scratched his head and kept on thinking;   30
Miniver coughed, and called it fate,
   And kept on drinking.

IN ORDER TO

Kenneth Patchen (1911–1972)

Apply for the position (I've forgotten now for what) I had to marry the Second Mayor's daughter by twelve noon. The order arrived three minutes of.

I already had a wife; the Second Mayor was childless: but I did it.

Next they told me to shave off my father's beard. All right. No matter that he'd been a eunuch, and had succumbed in early childhood: I did it, I shaved him.

Then they told me to burn a village; next, a fair-sized town; then, a city; a bigger city; a small, down-at-heels country; then one of "the great powers"; then another (another, another) — In fact, they went right on until they'd told me to burn up every man-made thing on the face of the earth! And I did it, I burned away every last trace, I left nothing, nothing of any kind whatever.

Then they told me to blow it all to hell and gone! And I blew it all to hell and gone (oh, didn't I!). . . .

Now, they said, put it back together again; put it all back the way it was when you started.

Well . . . it was my turn then to tell *them* something. Shucks, I didn't want any job that bad.

JACK AND KING MAROCK

Anonymous

I

One time Jack met up with a stranger said his name was King Marock. King Marock was a roguish kind of feller, liked to play cards, and he was some kind of a witch too, but Jack didn't know that. Jack and King Marock got to talkin', and directly the King bantered Jack for a game of cards. So they started in playin', and Jack got beat seven times, but he had a little money left and kept right on, and then he turned it on King Marock and beat him six times straight, cleaned the old King out of every cent he had. So King Marock told Jack he'd play one more hand and bet Jack's choice of his three girls against the whole pile. Jack said All right, and he won again. But time he laid his cards down, King Marock was gone, and Jack couldn't tell which-a-way he went nor nothin'.

So Jack went to huntin' and inquirin' for King Marock. Couldn't nobody tell him a thing about where the King's house was.

Then Jack met up with Old Man Freezewell, and Jack asked him, "Do you know where King Marock lives at?"

"No," Freezewell told him, "but I'll do ever'thing I can to help ye find him."

Freezewell went and froze ever'thing over real hard that night. Next mornin' he came to Jack, says, "I couldn't find the King, Jack, but I found an old man knows where his girls wash at. Now, this old man keeps beer, and I've frozen all his beer up, and he's mad, but you take this here little rod and go ask him for a drink of beer. He'll tell ye it's all froze, and then you thaw it for him, and that'll please him, and he'll tell ye where King Marock's girls' washin' place is at."

Freezewell told Jack where that old man's house was located, and Jack thanked him, and went on up there and asked the old man for some beer.

The old man says, "Hit won't come. All my beer froze up last night."

Jack took that little rod and tapped all the barrels with it and the beer thawed and the old man was plumb tickled. So him and Jack drawed some beer and sat down and went to drinkin'.

Then Jack asked him, says, "Do you know where King Marock lives at?"

"No," says the old man, "but I know where his girls wash of a Saturday."

So he told Jack where it was, and that Saturday evenin' Jack went down to the river and through the bresh till he came to a deep pool out there one side of a cliff. There was a log there where they went in the water and Jack got over behind it and laid down in the leaves.°

The girls came along pretty soon, took off their greyhound skins and laid 'em on that log. Then they went down in the water and commenced washin' around and washin' around. Jack reached

---

°In mythology it is not unusual for the lady to be caught bathing. Usually she is accompanied by attendants. Actaeon blundered into such a scene, and the offended goddess Diana turned him into a stag. One version of Tiresias's blinding is that he saw the goddess Athena at her bath and that she blinded him on the spot. King David caught a glimpse of Bath-sheba bathing herself, which moved him to treachery and caused the Lord to punish him. Odysseus came upon Nausicaa at a pool, but she was only doing her laundry. Perhaps that is why he did not suffer for his discovery.

up and pulled the youngest 'un's greyhound skin off the log and held on to it. They came out the water directly and the two oldest girls put on their skins and was gone, and Jack couldn't tell which way they went nor nothin'. The youngest looked around for where she'd laid her greyhound skin and couldn't find it and couldn't find it, and fin'ly Jack stood up.

"You give me my skin now."

"Take me home with you and I will."

"Oh, no, daddy would kill me."

"Take me to the gate, then."

"Oh, no, I'd be afraid to do that even, but I'll take you in sight of the house."

Jack gave her the skin and she put it on. Then she got out a solid gold needle and told Jack to take it and prick his finger on the point three times. Jack did that and the girl took him by the hand and they rose right straight up in the air and went flyin' along over the tops of the mountains. Jack had an awful good time doin' that.

Well, he saw a big house directly and the girl says to him, "Yonder it is. You better light now and come in awalkin'."

So she went flyin' on and Jack lit. He walked on up to the gate, and there was King Marock settin' on a bench under a shade bush.

"Good evenin', King Marock."

"Oh, hit's you, is it? How'd you find me?"

"Old man told me."

"Come on in and set down."

Jack went in and he and King Marock sat there and talked till the girls called 'em to supper. They went in the house and pulled up to the table. The girls had the finest kind of supper fixed up. Ever'thing you could think of that was good to eat was there on the boards.

"Just reach now and help yourself," says King Marock, "if you find anything you can eat. Just make yourself right at home."

Jack's mouth was just a-waterin'. He was awful hungry.

"Well, girls," he says, "your supper sure does look good. It sure Lord does!"

Time Jack said that there wasn't a thing on the table but dishwater. King Marock looked right hard at Jack and got up and left.

Then the youngest girl told Jack, says, "You mustn't ever mention the Lord around here, Jack."

Jack said he'd be sure not to do that no more, and then

the girl told him, says, "He aims to kill ye, Jack, if you can't do whatever work he gives ye. Now tomorrow there'll be a thicket to clear and he'll give ye an old axe and a new one and you be sure to take the old axe. You get up before he does tomorrow mornin' and be settin' in front of the fire when he comes in."

II

Well, next mornin' Jack was up real early and had the fire goin' and was settin' there smokin' when King Marock walked in. So they cooked breakfast and eat, and then King Marock took Jack out and showed him a big thorny bresh thicket.

"Now, Jack," he says, "my grannie lost her gold ring in that field there 'fore that bresh growed up. You find that ring by tonight or I'll kill ye and put your head on a spear."

And he handed Jack two axes, an old one and a new one. Jack looked at 'em and took the new one. Then King Marock was gone and Jack went to work on that bresh, but ever' time he cut out a place it growed back twice as thick. He'd go to another place and light into it with the axe, but the same thing 'uld happen. Jack kept on hackin' away first on one side that field, then on another till the sweat just poured, and about twelve o'clock that thicket was twice as big as when he started. Then that girl came out. She had the old axe in her hand.

"How you gettin' on, Jack."

"Only fairly well," says Jack.

"What's the matter?" she asked him.

"Ever' time I cut a lick," Jack says, "hit looks like twice as much grows back up."

"Why didn't ye take the old axe, like I told ye?"

"Hit looked so rusty and brickle I was afraid it 'uld break."

Well, she handed Jack the old axe and he took it and time he'd cut three licks with it that field was plumb cleared, all but one little locust. Jack walked over to it and there was that ring on one of its branches. Jack got it off and laid that old axe there against the little tree.

"Now," the girl told him, "you stay on here till dark and then you come on in and give him the ring. Tomorrow there'll be a well to dreen and he'll give ye an old bucket and a new one, and you be sure to take the old bucket."

Jack came in after dark and handed King Marock the ring.

"You found it, did ye?" says the King. "Surely some of my people are workin' against me."

"Oh, no, there ain't," says Jack.

Next mornin' he led Jack out to an old-fashioned home-dug well, says, "Jack, my grannie's great-grannie lost her thimble in that well and it better come out of there 'fore I get in tonight or I'll cut your head off and put it on a spear."

He handed Jack a new bucket and an old banged-up riddley one. Jack took the old bucket and saw it was full of holes, so he set it to one side and reached for the new one. And King Marock was gone from there and Jack couldn't tell which way he went.

That well-water was 'way down when Jack drawed up the first bucketful, but the more he drawed the more the water rose up, till about twelve o'clock it was runnin' out the top and all over the ground. Jack floundered around slippin' ever' which-a-way in the mud and kept on a-throwin' water till that well got to spoutin'. It liked to washed Jack away from there. Then here came the youngest girl, had the old bucket with her.

"Looks like you ain't doin' so well, Jack."

Jack admitted it.

"Why didn't you take the old bucket, like I told you?"

"That old leaky thing? Why, hit's plumb riddled!"

She handed him that bucket and told him to go on and use it. Jack threw out water with it once and all the water on top of the ground dried up. Then he dipped it in the mouth of the well and it dried up to where it was when he started in. Then he let the bucket down and pulled it up and looked and the well was dry, and there was that thimble layin' on the bottom. Jack set the old bucket there 'side the well and the girl tied a rope on him and let him down. He picked up the thimble and out he came.

"Now," she says, "tomorrow there'll be a big stone house to build out of one rock, and he'll give ye a big sledgehammer and a little rock-axe; and on the peril of your life you take the little rock-axe. You wait here till dark now, 'fore you come to the house with that thimble."

Jack waited and came on to the house about dark.

"Well, Jack, did ye find my great-great-great-grannie's thimble?"

Jack handed it to him.

King Marock he took it and sort of looked around, says, "Surely, surely, some of my people are workin' against me."

"No, there ain't," says Jack.

Next day King Marock took Jack out and showed him a big rock 'side the hill, says, "Jack, you take that rock and bust it and square up the blocks, and by the time I get in tonight you better have me a twelve-story house finished and the stone well dressed, and I want twelve rooms twelve foot square on every story, and if you don't get it all done by the time I get here I'll sure kill ye and put your head on a spear."

He handed Jack a big sledge and a little bitty rock-axe with a sawed-off handle. Jack looked up at that big rock and took the sledge and King Marock was gone.

Jack swung that big hammer and tried to block him out some stone. He hammered and he pounded and he sweated, but ever' lick it seemed like that rock just swelled a little bigger. The sweat got to runnin' off Jack in a stream and he nearly burnt the handle out of that old sledgehammer.

That girl she came out there about twelve o'clock, had the little rock-axe in her hand, says, "Looks like you've not got many stones dressed."

"No," says Jack, "seems like this rock is sort of hard to bust."

"Why didn't you take the little rock-axe, like I told ye?"

"I forgot," says Jack.

"Here," she says, and she handed it to him.

Jack hadn't struck but three licks with it when the rock just r'ared up in the air and there was a twelve-story house.

"Now," the girl told him, "when you see King Marock comin' in this evenin', you go and meet him 'fore he gets here. You take him all through that house and he'll act awful pleased, but when he gets out and turns his back on it, hit'll not be there no more. Then he'll start in cussin' you about it bein' gone, and you tell him he said for you to get it built, but there wasn't a thing in his orders about you makin' it stay built."

Jack said he'd do that, and he went to lay the little rock-axe down somewhere, but he got to lookin' at that house and studyin' about what-all he had to do, and he stuck the rock-axe in his overhall pocket.

So Jack he watched for King Marock and when he saw him comin' he went on out to meet him.

"Well, Jack, did ye get my house built?"

"Yes, sir," says Jack.

"Doors, windows, roof, and everything?"

"Yes, sir."

"How'd you do it?" the old King asked him, and he looked at Jack sort of like he suspected somethin'.

"Let's go on up there and look it over," says Jack, "so you can see does it suit you all right."

He took King Marock up to the house, and they went all through it, looked in all the rooms and how pretty they were, all fixed up just like in a ho-tel, and after a while they came on out.

The old King looked up at it once more, and then he and Jack turned and started on off. Right then somethin' went off like a shot-gun behind 'em and when they looked around that house was gone. Wasn't a thing there but that same old big rock.

King Marock came up to Jack like he wanted to fight, says, "Where's my house?"

"I contracted to build it," says Jack, "not make it stay built."

Well, King Marock looked like he was about to cuss Jack out, but he just sort of shut his mouth to and walked on off a-grumblin' to himself. Jack hung around awhile and directly he went on to the house.

King Marock didn't come to the table for supper, and the youngest girl took Jack out where they wouldn't be heard and told him, says, "He'll make you take your choice of us girls tomorrow mornin', Jack. Which one will you take?"

"Why, I'll take you," says Jack.

"How'll you know us apart standin' side by side with our greyhound skins on?"

"Well, I don't know," says Jack.

"I'll lick my tongue out at ye," she says, "so you'll know that 'un is me."

Next mornin' the King didn't come to breakfast. The girls got the dishes all washed up and directly King Marock hollered for Jack.

Jack came and there stood the three girls with their greyhound skins on. Jack looked and looked, and the old King thought sure he had him that time, hollered, "Choose the youngest 'un, Jack! Pick her out quick or I'll cut your head off!"

Jack stepped back and looked at 'em again. The youngest licked her tongue out right quick, and Jack says, "This is the one, I reckon."

"All right! All right!" says King Marock, "Take her on! Take her on!"

III

And that night, after they'd all gone to bed, that girl came and woke Jack up, says, "He's done found out it was me helped you and he's a-fixin' to kill us both tonight."

"What'll we do?" says Jack.

"We'll run away," she told him. Says, "Now you go to the stable quick and bring down the horse and the mule. You better hurry."

Jack ran to the stable and there stood the sorriest-lookin' old horse and mule you ever saw, nothin' but skin and bones. The old horse's head hung so far down Jack had to prop it up to get the bridle on him. The mule was in the same fix, had his head hung 'way down in the bottom of the feed trough with his ears flopped over, and Jack had to push 'em both out the door; he had to lift their feet over the barn sill. He swarped 'em with a stick and kept on beatin' 'em and fin'ly got 'em to the house. The girl came out with saddles and bridles, a whole new outfit all shined up.

"I'll saddle 'em," says Jack.

"No," she says, "I'll saddle 'em."

She throwed the saddle on the horse and when she pulled the girth, there was as fine a ridin' horse as you'd want, slick as a ribbon and prancin' and a-r'arin' to go. Jack had to hold him down. Then she heaved the saddle on the mule and when she tightened up the belly-band, that old skinny mule filled out just as fat as his hide could hold him. Then she got on the mule and Jack jumped on the horse and they lit out.

"I can't look back now," she told Jack. "If I did he'd be able to witch us. You watch behind ye and tell me when you see him comin'."

They got on a long stretch of road directly; Jack looked back and saw King Marock a-comin'. He and the girl stopped and she handed him a thorn and told him to jump off quick and stick it in the ground behind 'em. Jack did, and all between them and the King was a big thorn thicket, locusts as big as poplars and black-berry briars big as saplin's. It was so thick a rabbit couldn't 'a got through. King Marock had to go back and find that old axe to cut him a way and by that time Jack and the girl got a good gain on him.

Then Jack looked back again, and there was the old King behind 'em, just a-tearin' the road to pieces. Jack told the girl and she stopped and handed him a little bottle of water, told him to pour that on the road behind 'em. Jack did it, and there was a wide river between them and the King. He had to go back after that old rid-dledy bucket to dreen the river off, and by that time they'd gained a right smart on him.

Jack looked over his shoulder again, and here came old King Marock a-r'arin' and a-shoutin' and beatin' his horse somethin' terrible. The girl gave Jack a little handful of gravel and told him to throw them down behind, and when Jack did that all the country between them and the King was one great big rocky mountain. King Marock had to turn around and go back to get that little rock-axe to break a way through, and he hunted and he hunted all over the place for it, but he never did find it 'cause Jack had forgot and stuck it in his pocket.

So Jack and the girl rode on to the settle-ments to get

married. Jack wanted to see his folks first, so they went on to his house.

"Come on," says Jack, "let's go in. They'll sure be surprised when we tell 'em."

"No," she says, "I'll not go in yet. I'll stay here at the gate awhile till you go see 'em first. Now, Jack, when you go in there don't you let any of 'em kiss you till you come out again. Don't let nothin' touch you on your lips, you hear?"

Jack said All right, and went on in. They were all real glad to see him and his mother went to huggin' him and tryin' to kiss him, but he put his hands over his face and laughed and wouldn't let her come anywhere close to his lips. Then he set down in a chair and was just about to tell 'em all about his girl when his little dog came in the door and saw Jack had come back and 'fore Jack knowed it that dog ran to him and jumped up in his lap and licked him right on the mouth. Jack put the dog on the floor, and when he tried to recollect what he was about to tell his folks he just couldn't remember a thing about that girl. She waited out at the gate quite a spell; then she guessed what must 'a happened, so she rode off.

IV

Now there was an old shoemaker in that neighborhood, an old man and his wife and their grown girl. They were ugly as bats, all three of 'em—real homely people. That girl went and cloomb up in a bush right over the spring at this old shoemaker's house, and when his girl came to get water she peeped in the spring and saw that other girl's shadder.

"Well!" she says, "if I'm that pretty, I'll not stay here any longer." And she set her bucket down and left there to hunt her up a sweetheart.

Then the old woman she came out about the water, looked over in the spring, saw that girl's shadder in there, says, "Huh! If I'm that pretty, I'll not live with that ugly old man another minute!" So she left the water bucket standin' there and down the road she put.

Then the old man came out to see what was the matter. He looked in the spring, says, "Surely, surely, I'm not that pretty." He went lookin' around and fin'ly saw that girl up there in the tree, says, "What in the world are you a-doin' up there?"

"Restin'," she told him.

"Come on down," says the old man; "you can rest at the house."

So she came down and filled the bucket and carried it back

to the house for the old man; and his old woman and his girl didn't come back, and didn't come back, so he says to that girl, "I reckon they've done left me. Do you want to hire to do my cookin' and washin' for me?"

"Yes," she says, "I'll hire."

So she stayed on there and did the old man's cookin' and house-keepin' and water-totin'.

Now Jack got to talkin' to an old sweetheart he had there 'fore he left, and pretty soon they fixed up to get married.

All the neighbors wanted new shoes to wear to the weddin' and they got to goin' to that old shoemaker. A young man came there about his shoes, and when he saw that girl he thought she was the prettiest woman he'd ever looked at. So he asked could he stay and talk with her awhile. She told him he could, and he stayed so long she commenced gettin' sleepy; but he didn't leave, and didn't leave, till fin'ly she says to him, "Would you mind coverin' the fire for me?"

He said he would, and when he started shovelin' the ashes up over the logs she slipped up in the loft.

Then she called down to him, says, "You got it covered?"

"Not yet," he told her.

"Well," she says, "your hand stick to the shovel and hit stick to you, and you set there and pat the fire till day."

So that young feller sat there a-hold of the shovel with his shins a-burnin' and kept pattin' in the ashes till daylight.

Then another young man came and—Lord! he thought she was so pretty he just had to stay and talk to her that night. He stayed on and stayed on till she wanted to go to bed.

So she got up and says to him, "Law me! There's a gander to put up. I like to forgot it. Would you put it up for me?"

He said he'd do it, and when he got the gander cornered and caught it, the girl came to the door, says, "You caught it yet?"

"Yes, I got it."

"Then you hold to hit, and hit stick to you till day."

So that boy had to stay out there all night a-holdin' on to that old gander, and it a-hootin' and a-hissin' and floggin' him with its wings, till daylight the next mornin'.

Then Jack came about his shoes, and when he saw the girl he got stuck on her somethin' awful. He kept on hangin' around till 'way up in the night. Then the girl got to gapin' and yawnin' and so she says to Jack all at once, "Oh, law me! There's a calf to pen. I surely like to forgot all about it. Would you mind pennin' it for me?"

Jack said Sure, he'd pen the calf for her, and when he got

out to the calf, she hollered to him, says, "You got hold of the rope?"

"Yes," says Jack.

"Then you hang to hit, and hit hang to you, till day."

So Jack had to hang on to that rope with the calf a-bawlin' and a-pullin' and him a-hoppin' up and down and runnin' all through the mud in the barn lot all night long. Jack was sure a sight to look at when daylight broke. He came to the house and tried to wash up a little and he gave that girl a lot of money not to tell it on him. Hit 'uld not do for such a tale to get out on him and him about to get married; it would 'a ruint him.

Well, the weddin' was that next Sunday and the old man fixed up to go. He asked the girl did she want to go, but she said No, she was a stranger there and she guessed she'd stay at the house; but after the old man left, she slipped out and went on up to the church house.

Jack had just stepped out on the floor to get married when she ran her hand in her pocket and pulled out a little box. She opened it and a banty hen and rooster jumped out. Then she reached in her pocket and took out three grains of barley, threw one of 'em down and the hen got it. The little rooster ran up and pecked the hen, and the girl says, "Take care, my good fellow! You don't know the time I cleared a thicket for ye and stopped Old King Marock with all them thorn trees and briars."

Jack heard her and tried to get a look through the crowd to see what was happenin'. That other girl punched Jack to make him listen to the preacher. The preacher tried to go on, but that girl threw down another grain of barley. The little hen got it and the rooster pecked her again.

"Take care, my good fellow! You don't know the time I dreened a well for ye and stopped Old King Marock with all that water."

Jack wasn't payin' no mind to what the preacher was sayin'. Nearly ever'body quit watchin' the weddin' and crowded around that girl to see what she was doin' with her banty chickens. Then she threw down the other grain of barley for the banty hen and the rooster ran over and pecked the hen. That time even the preacher went over to see what was goin' on.

"Take care, my good fellow! You don't know the time I built a twelve-story house for ye, and stopped Old King Marock with that rocky mountain."

Well, Jack left that other girl standin' there in the middle of the floor, came through the crowd and went up to that girl, says, "Well, I guess I know somethin' about all that."

So he took her by the hand and called the preacher and he married 'em and Jack took the girl on home with him and they lived happy.

Now some folks tell it that King Marock was the Devil. I have heard the tale told that-a-way. Anyhow, even if the old King was mean and roguish, his girl was pretty smart. She made Jack a good wife.

QUESTIONS AND CONSIDERATIONS

The Water of Life

1. Often, the hero turns out to be the younger, or youngest, brother. From what you have read about the hero archetype, why might this be the case? Aside from age, what characteristics make the youngest son different from his brothers? Is it plausible (all literature, even fairy tales, must be somehow believable) that the dwarf would have bestowed his powerful tokens and advice on the youngest brother merely because the youth spoke pleasantly to him? If not, what more substantial reasons might there be?

2. Of what significance, if any, is it that when the youth fled through the iron gate "it took off a bit of his heel"? Relate this to your reading thus far and also to any myth you know of that involves a similar kind of wounding of the hero. Could the wound be considered a necessary experience? An exchange of any kind? Does the wound signify a change in the status of the hero?

3. The two lions that guard the castle are called "threshold guardians." Their function is to keep the hero from entering the dark passage and also to serve as a grim test, always the last one before the plunge into darkness. Interestingly, threshold guardians are still with us. If you live in a fair-sized city, you should be able to find a pair of them somewhere in town. Usually they guard the doors of a large public building, sometimes even a school. See what you can turn up. (Or at least find a photo of New York City's public library.) Consider live threshold guardians too. Where can they be found?

4. More than once in this text you will be directed to the Bible story of Joseph and his brothers. How is *The Water of Life* similar? Consider not only the brothers motif, but also the Water of Life itself.

5. What is the Water of Life anyhow? Look for proofs of the possibility that it is not the Water itself but rather the young prince's successful quest that renewed the king's (and thereby the kingdom's) vigor.

6. To what other Biblical story does *The Water of Life* relate? In what ways?
7. In picking up the sword, the young prince performed a simple act. Theseus, you recall, had to move a huge rock to win his sword; Arthur had to pull his from a stone; and Sigmund had to yank his from a tree. Does this suggest that the prince didn't earn his sword in a heroic way? Why or why not?
8. Who is the hero's guide in this tale, the dwarf or the princess? Why did the prince have to wait until the end of the year to claim the princess?
9. What does this tale suggest about the necessary qualities of a hero? Be particular and specific. Just what is it that he exemplifies?

Thomas Rhymer

1. Thomas Rhymer is quite unlike the young prince of "The Water of Life," yet he too is a hero. For one thing, he is innocent, a requirement for most heroes. How is Thomas's innocence established? (There is more than one indication.) How might his occupation as a rhymer (poet) qualify him for the quest he is drawn into?
2. Why did Thomas go with the queen? Don't be satisfied with the obvious—that she was compellingly attractive. Would most men willingly agree to involve themselves in a mysterious and perhaps perilous adventure, especially with the stipulation that they must serve seven years, "Thro weel or wae" (roughly, *good* or *bad*)?
3. Note the references to color (including claret, a shade of red). Of what significance is it that most of the colors relate to the queen, but that by the conclusion Thomas has taken on the color she wears?
4. What part of the archetypal quest tale compares with Thomas's wading for forty days and nights "thro red blude to the knee"? In The Bible, what happened for the same stretch of time? In that story, what color was the first tangible clue that the ordeal was over?
5. The queen points out three roads to Thomas, but gives him no choice as to which they will take. Will Thomas ever have that choice? Why or why not? Explain how and why the roads are metaphors.
6. Why is Thomas admonished to say nothing about what he may hear or see? (Apparently this is to hold for all his time in Elfland.)
7. Something to speculate on, which can be neither proved nor disproved in the poem, is that quite often earth time and the time in magic places such as an elfland or other unearthly hideaway are not the same. It could be that Thomas's seven years "past and gone" amounted to one night in his experience. Discuss this possibility.

8. Unlike the young prince of *The Water of Life*, whose rewards were too numerous to recount, Thomas came back with nothing more than a coat and shoes. Develop a substantial argument on the thesis that his rewards were nevertheless at least as great as those of the prince. Who was the more "heroic" of the two? Who was probably more altered by his quest?

9. In what ways, if at all, does the queen measure up to Campbell's observation that such a woman is "the life of everything that lives" and that she "represents the totality of what can be known"? (Certainly she knows more than Thomas does.)

Sir Gawain and the Green Knight

1. Here, in this abridged version of the famous Middle English epic poem, is a splendid example of the heroic quest. Virtually all of the classic ingredients are here, and you should by now be able to recognize them. Single out the following and explain briefly how each fulfills its archetypal role, referring to line numbers whenever possible:
    (a) The hero's call
    (b) The goal, as it is first explained to the hero
    (c) The hazardous journey (in what specific way is it hazardous?)
    (d) The temptations (there are more than one)
    (e) The guide (who the guide is may escape you at first reading)
    (f) The charm that will protect the hero
    (g) The winning of the "sword"
    (h) The descent into darkness
    (i) The hero's wound
    (j) The actual prize of the quest, which must be different from what the hero expected it to be.

2. As with *Thomas Rhymer*, color plays an important part in this story. Furthermore, both works have a cyclical theme, the former seven years, *Gawain* a year and a day. Farther along in your reading you will learn more about fertility symbols and myths that deal essentially with fertility themes. At this point, however, you have probably begun to sense that quest stories are somehow bound up with nature themes, growth cycles, and fertility generally. In a paper, analyze the uses of color, seasons, and the year-and-a-day cycle in terms of their possible relationship to fertility.

3. Why didn't Gawain shrink from the quest? Why did he rise to such an apparently meaningless challenge in the first place? Is there a sensible rebuttal to the statement that Gawain's kind of chivalry is downright stupid, or at least that it has no place in today's world?

4. What does Gawain learn from his encounter with the Green Knight? Simply that true grit is rewarded?

5. The Green Knight's blow wounds Gawain superficially. What might have been the outcome, however, had Gawain spurned the green belt? How can the Green Knight call Gawain the "most faultless of men" in view of his having failed to hand the belt over as part of their bargain?

6. In connection with temptation, detail what happens on each day of Gawain's stay at the Green Knight's castle. What two kinds of chivalry is he forced to choose between? Who is actually in more danger during this period, the host pursuing wild animals or Gawain lodged comfortably in the castle? Explain.

7. On each of three days, the Green Knight hunts and kills a different animal. How do the characteristics of each of these animals relate to the goings-on at the castle during the same three days?

8. Discuss why it is that at the conclusion of *Thomas Rymer* and *Gawain* both heroes are wearing green.

9. *Gawain* is rich in fantastic impossibilities, not least of all the Green Knight himself. How, nevertheless, does the author add sufficient realism to his tale to make it not only exciting but somehow believable? Be specific.

10. Why is it that the Green Knight is referred to more than once as the hero?

Miniver Cheevy

1. Not everyone accepts the call. In fact, most of us refuse it. Miniver Cheevy is much closer to being a model for Everyman than are Thomas and Gawain. Miniver is a failed hero, one of a type who can be found in many stories. Failed heroes tend not to get very far, like the two older brothers in *The Water of Life*. Or they may run when the going gets rough, like Henry Fleming in *The Red Badge of Courage*. Sometimes, though, such a character doesn't even get his feet wet. Miniver is a good example of this last type. Basically, what is Miniver's problem? Why doesn't he budge? Why is he instead seemingly content to be without any kind of content, save dreams?

2. If Miniver Cheevy were a nextdoor neighbor, you would not describe him as a "failed hero." What would you call him? (Certainly, *lazy* is not entirely fitting.)

3. If, as was suggested in the introductory chapter, the hero must have some traits in common with all of us, what can be found in Miniver's make-up that would also be found in a true hero? Does he have any kind of quest in life, and does he actually pursue it?

4. The tone of this poem is grim, bitter; but there are moments of ironic humor here too. Specifically, what are they? How do they save Miniver from being merely an obnoxious loser?
5. Both Miniver Cheevy and Walter Mitty are failed heroes who spend much time indulging in fantasies. Otherwise, however, they are quite different. Compare them.
6. To what status does contemporary society relegate the failed hero? Prove it.

In Order To

1. Heracles (the Roman Hercules) is synonymous with physical strength. He is also famous for the twelve impossible labors he performed. Looking him up in any good collection of Greek myths will be worth your while; his story is fascinating. Finding out about Heracles will make your reading of *In Order To* more rewarding. It will also provide the necessary background for a paper comparing Patchen's speaker-hero with his famous model.
2. Unlike most selections in this book, *In Order To* represents a conscious borrowing from mythology, although Patchen takes obvious comic liberties with his ancient material. His is a humorous treatment of a serious theme—the plight of modern man confronted with the need for Heraclean strength just to survive in the "rat race." Is it possible to be competitive in the kind of dog-eat-dog society Patchen's poem suggests and still be a hero in the classical sense of the word? What is his hero's goal? What is the route of his quest? How does he change in the course of his journey? Could it be that by going through the hardening process that modern society forces on us, we ourselves are embarked on a quest of sorts?
3. Characterize the speaker. What kind of person would "burn up every man-made thing on the face of the earth"? (The last time something as totally devastating as that happened what were the results?) Who are the "they" who give him his orders? Can you think of instances in modern history where so-called heroes have excused dreadful acts by saying that they were only following orders?
4. After the speaker has blown everything "to hell and gone," leaving "nothing of any kind whatever," why does he refuse to put it back together? Was it simply too big a task, even for someone powerful enough to have destroyed it? His last comment is obviously an ironic understatement. Could it be that there were deeper reasons?
5. How many labors did "they" command the speaker to perform? Enumerate them. Compared with Heracles's labors, were they easier or more difficult?

Jack and King Marock

1. This is one of a great number of "Jack tales," folk stories concerning the trickster-hero Jack. The origin of the stories is not certain. Their central character is centuries old and has been traced to English and Irish sources. Jack became a favorite of the American Black, probably because he is not a favored, idealized hero like Gawain or the prince in *The Water of Life*, but a poor, devil-may-care fellow who must live by his wits and whatever good fortune comes his way. This is one feature that distinguishes the trickster-hero from his nobler and/or guileless counterpart.

   Can you think of other trickster-heroes like Jack, those who do not reach their goal in the time-honored hero's way, but instead use whatever and whoever happen to work best? (Odysseus was described by Homer as "wily," and Raven, the Indian hero, is a notorious trickster. Myth and literature are full of examples.)

2. What are the symbolic functions of the rod and the beer? Of the greyhound skins?

3. Just to be sure you understand what they are by now, isolate the following elements in this story:
   (a) the hero's wound
   (b) the dark descent
   (c) the guide
   (d) the winning of the "sword."

4. Here again is the lady of the quest acting out her classic role. She is the hero's protector, his source of wisdom, and his ultimate reward. She is young, beautiful, and innocent. (Whenever there are sisters, she is always the youngest.) How has this age-old, idealized image perhaps forced us today to perceive the female in a certain stereotyped way? What modern customs, values, and institutions keep this image alive?

5. How does the trickster-hero's success, largely though guile and good luck, fit into the greater system of American values? Account for how this might have something to do with the trickster's popularity among an oppressed minority.

III
OTHER MOTIFS

1
THE FALL
FROM INNOCENCE

•

Such, such were the joys
When we all, girls and boys,
In our youth time were seen
on the Echoing Green.

　　　　—William Blake, *The Echoing Green*

Not all myths deal solely with a heroic journey, although all major mythic patterns seemingly relate to it. The quest has been called the *monomyth* by some scholars—the one, universal mythic framework. But while it is possible to ponder the idea that all mythic expressions flow from one basic story, it is also difficult and misleading at this point.

For purposes of study, the story of Adam in The Bible serves more vividly as an example of the myth of the fall from innocence than it does as an example of the quest, although it is that too. *Sir Gawain and the Green Knight*, on the other hand, is so clearly a quest story that it is best studied that way, rather than as a "fall" story (which it is) or as an outgrowth of a fertility myth (which it also is).

Many myths focus mainly on the puzzling dualities that exist within and around us. They will be discussed in a section of this book devoted to duality myths, although it can be said that the hero's quest is at heart an attempt to reconcile these opposites—that this goal is what the quest is all about. Rather than pick apart a quest story to prove this thesis, it is probably better at this point to examine separately some clear-cut examples of duality themes in myth and literature.

All of the following sections—*The Fall from Innocence, Dualities*, and *Fertility: Cycles of Nature*—have a definite bearing on the quest story. At the beginning, however, it is easier to examine parts rather than wholes. Sooner or later, the parts should fall together. One should begin to sense the intricate relationships among mythic themes and to perceive their continuing relevance in human affairs.

> Now the serpent was more subtile than any beast of the field which the Lord God had made. And he said unto the woman, Yea, hath God said, Ye shall not eat of every tree of the garden? And the woman said unto the serpent, We may eat of the fruit of the trees of the garden: But of the fruit of the tree which is in the midst of the garden, God hath said, Ye shall not eat of it, neither shall ye touch it, lest ye die. And the serpent said unto the woman, Ye shall not surely die: For God doth know that in the day ye eat thereof, then your eyes shall be opened, and ye shall be as gods, knowing good and evil.
>
> And when the woman saw that the tree was good for food, and that it was pleasant to the eyes, and a tree to be desired to make one wise, she took of the fruit thereof, and did eat, and gave also unto her husband with her; and he did eat. And the eyes of them both were opened, and they knew that they were naked; and they sewed fig leaves together, and made themselves aprons.
>
> —*Genesis*, Chapter 3

Thus, in the best-known story in the Judeo-Christian world, did Adam, the first man, fall from a state of perfect innocence and enter the darker world of experience; and all who descended from him bear his original sin of disobedience and suffer the loss of paradise. Adam should be the most unpopular character in mythology, for look what he did to us!

Yet Adam is not a figure of hatred or contempt. His disobedience is childlike, despite its profound consequences. There is nothing monstrous in his act. The apple is a silly temptation, for although the serpent promised that by eating the apple they will come to know good and evil, Eve and Adam seem chiefly tempted by the look of the fruit. At any rate they cannot possibly be lured by the promise of the knowledge of good and evil, inasmuch as they know nothing about either. In fact, they know little about anything.

Consider that God has told Adam he will die if he tastes the fruit. Only one who is innocent of any understanding of death— a very young child, for example—would give in so readily, if at all. Consider also that while God warned Adam about the apple, He did not warn him about Satan. It would seem, if we take it in a literal sense, that the story is flawed by such an oversight. A slightly deeper reading reveals, of course, that Adam was meant to disobey —that if he hadn't, he and all who followed would be condemned to the blissful ignorance symbolized by Eden.

This seemingly simple story dealing with man's origin and his expulsion from paradise is in reality a wise and accurate psychological depiction of Everyman's journey from innocence to experience. Adam is not despicable because he chose to disobey. By endowing him with the ability to choose, God granted Adam not just suffering and eventual death, but his humanity. To wander forever sheeplike and innocent in a garden sounds ideal only at first. Eden can be beautiful, however, only after one has developed an awareness of beauty; and this is impossible until one has perceived its opposites. In such a garden, the story tells us, we learn nothing; we are without alternatives and therefore without knowledge. Thus there is no possibility for spiritual growth.

By tasting the apple—that is, by performing some act we know to violate familial or societal law—we, like Adam, come to realize the moral consequences of our choices in life. Just as important, we become conscious that the burden of choosing is up to us.

Unlike Adam we do not usually fall through a single disobedient act from a state of innocence to one of experience. Our fall is a long one, in essence a growing up. It takes time, hard knocks, and disillusionments. Along the way, we repeat Adam's original sin countless times. To disobey—to violate a moral code—is part of moving from childhood to adulthood. This doesn't mean, as some would have it, that we are inevitably drawn to evil ways, that we must suffer all our days because we are sinful and therefore damned. If we are free to choose, as Adam was, then it doesn't make sense that we will always choose evil. Nor does this idea square with the noble acts we are capable of.

What Adam's story tells us is that the potential for both good and evil exists within each of us, along with the intelligence to know the difference, and that we are individually responsible for determining which will prevail.

What about Satan, then, "more subtile than any beast of the field"? Is he a presence outworn, with no application in today's world? Not at all. While the potential for immoral acts dwells within each of us, we're also influenced by others. In fact, we tend to see evil acting on us from the outside more readily than we acknowledge it in ourselves. The serpent who tempted Eve is a symbol of the external call to disobedience, wickedness, the dissolution of our inner moral fiber.

When we were very young, we told our parents or our teacher, "Charlie made me do it." What we were really saying was, "I couldn't help it. The devil forced me to do it." Rather than blame the inner tuggings of temptation, we pin the blame on conditions beyond our control, whether it be Charlie, some other personification of wickedness, or society itself, where evil often seems to be running rampant.

This is not only a childish point of view. Some very interesting works of literature seem to say the same thing: that the world is a wicked place where goodness cannot possibly prevail; or that goodness itself is an illusion, as so much of the history of humanity seems to illustrate. Are we not cruel, warlike? Do we not steal, lie, murder? Do we not let the poor live like animals and the guilty go unpunished? Isn't the Satan who stalks us actually a projection of our inner appetite for evil? Isn't the whole idea of the fall simply this, that we grow from the innocence of childhood to the grim disillusionment of adulthood, where the sum total of experience seems to be that the person who attempts to live a virtuous life doesn't stand a chance?

Obviously, there is much available proof to support a belief in the hopelessness of trying to stay honest and decent. What such a belief doesn't take into account, however, is that if the good act survives under such conditions, then goodness must be at least as tough and enduring as the ageless Satan. The fatalistic point of view has another flaw too: It suggests that evil and goodness are total opposites, always poles apart. Either one is good, an impossibility, or one is evil, a likelihood. Along the way from innocence to experience, most of us develop enough wisdom to see that neither of these qualities is found in complete isolation. (If they were, life wouldn't be so confusing.) The great seventeenth century poet John Milton observed that "good and evil, we know, in the field of this world grow up together almost inseparably."

Such considerations have found various expression not only in mythology but in all kinds of writing, from ancient to modern; from philosophical treatises to nursery tales. Indeed, the questions raised by Adam's experience and our own have provided us with the largest thematic body of works in all of literature. The selections that follow consider some of these questions in very different ways.

The first is a paragraph from *The Adventures of Huckleberry Finn*. Huck has made for shore, pressured by his aching conscience to turn in the runaway slave Jim. When he is confronted by slave hunters, however, he cooks up an ingenious story to keep them away from the raft where Jim is hiding.

> They went off and I got aboard the raft, feeling bad and low, because I knowed very well I had done wrong, and I see it warn't no use for me to try to learn to do right; a

body that don't get *started* right when he's little ain't got
nothing to back him up and keep him to his work, and so
he gets beat. Then I thought a minute, and says to myself,
hold on; s'pose you'd 'a' done right and give Jim up would
you felt better than what you do now? No, says I, what's
the use you learning to do right when it's troublesome to do
right and ain't no trouble to do wrong, and the wages is
just the same? I was stuck. I couldn't answer that. So I
reckoned I wouldn't bother no more about it, but after this
always do whichever come handiest at the time.

NEUTRAL TONES

Thomas Hardy (1840–1928)

We stood by a pond that winter day,
And the sun was white as though chidden of God,
And a few leaves lay on the starving sod;
—They had fallen from an ash, and were gray.

Your eyes on me were as eyes that rove   5
Over tedious riddles solved years ago;
And some words played between us to and fro
    On which lost the more by our love.

The smile on your mouth was the deadest thing
Alive enough to have strength to die;   10
And a grin of bitterness swept thereby
    Like an ominous bird a-wing. . . .

Since then, keen lessons that love deceives,
And wrings with wrong, have shaped to me
Your face, and the God-curst sun, and a tree,   15
    And a pond edged with grayish leaves.

SPRING AND FALL

To a Young Child

Gerard Manley Hopkins (1844–1889)

Márgaret, are you gríeving
Over Goldengrove unleaving?
Leaves, líke the things of man, you
With your fresh thoughts care for, can you?

Ah! ás the heart grows older   5
It will come to such sights colder
By and by, nor spare a sigh
Though worlds of wanwood leafmeal° lie;
And yet you wíll weep and know why.
Now no matter, child, the name: 10
Sórrow's spríngs áre the same.

Nor mouth had, no nor mind, expressed
What heart heard of, ghost guessed:
It ís the blight man was born for,
It is Margaret you mourn for.   15

IN JUST-

E. E. Cummings (1894–1962)

in Just-
spring   when the world is mud-
luscious the little
lame balloonman

whistles   far   and wee   5

and eddieandbill come
running from marbles and
piracies and it's
spring

when the world is puddle-wonderful   10

the queer
old balloonman whistles
far   and   wee
and bettyandisbel come dancing

from hop-scotch and jump-rope and   15

it's
spring
and
     the

          goat-footed   20

°*wanwood leafmeal*: leaves rotting, turning to small pieces

balloonMan   whistles
far
and
wee

WHEN I WAS ONE-AND-TWENTY

A. E. Housman (1859–1936)

When I was one-and-twenty
  I heard a wise man say,
"Give crowns and pounds and guineas
  But not your heart away;
Give pearls away and rubies   5
  But keep your fancy free."
But I was one-and-twenty,
  No use to talk to me.

When I was one-and-twenty
  I heard him say again,   10
"The heart out of the bosom
  Was never given in vain;
'Tis paid with sighs a-plenty
  And sold for endless rue."
And I am two-and-twenty,   15
  And oh, 'tis true, 'tis true.

MARKHEIM

Robert Louis Stevenson (1850–1894)

"Yes," said the dealer, "our windfalls are of various kinds. Some customers are ignorant, and then I touch a dividend of my superior knowledge. Some are dishonest," and here he held up the candle, so that the light fell strongly on his visitor, "and in that case," he continued, "I profit by my virtue."

Markheim had but just entered from the daylight streets, and his eyes had not yet grown familiar with the mingled shine and darkness in the shop. At these pointed words, and before the near presence of the flame, he blinked painfully and looked aside.

The dealer chuckled. "You come to me on Christmas Day," he resumed, "when you know that I am alone in my house, put up my shutters, and make a point of refusing business. Well, you will have to pay for that; you will have to pay for my loss of time, when I should be balancing my books; you will have to pay, for a kind of manner that I remark in you today very strongly. I am the essence of discretion, and ask no awkward questions; but when a customer cannot look me in the eye, he has to pay for it." The dealer once more chuckled; and then, changing to his usual business voice, though still with a note of irony, "You can give, as usual, a clear account of how you came into the possession of the objects?" he continued. "Still your uncle's cabinet? A remarkable collector, sir!"

And the little pale, round-shouldered dealer stood almost on tiptoe, looking over the top of his gold spectacles, and nodding his head with every mark of disbelief. Markheim returned his gaze with one of infinite pity, and a touch of horror.

"This time," said he, "you are in error. I have not come to sell, but to buy. I have no curios to dispose of; my uncle's cabinet is bare to the wainscot; even were it still intact, I have done well on the Stock Exchange, and should more likely add to it than otherwise, and my errand today is simplicity itself. I seek a Christmas present for a lady," he continued, waxing more fluent as he struck into the speech he had prepared; "and certainly I owe you every excuse for thus disturbing you upon so small a matter. But the thing was neglected yesterday; I must produce my little compliment at dinner; and, as you very well know, a rich marriage is not a thing to be neglected."

There followed a pause, during which the dealer seemed to weigh this statement incredulously. The ticking of many clocks among the curious lumber of the shop, and the faint rushing of the cabs in a rear thoroughfare, filled up the interval of silence.

"Well, sir," said the dealer, "be it so. You are an old customer after all; and if, as you say, you have the chance of a good marriage, far be it from me to be an obstacle. —Here is a nice thing for a lady now," he went on, "this hand glass°—fifteenth century, warranted; comes from a good collection, too; but I reserve the name, in the interests of my customer, who was just like yourself, my dear sir, the nephew and sole heir of a remarkable collector."

The dealer, while he thus ran on in his dry and biting voice, had stooped to take the object from its place; and, as he had done so, a shock had passed through Markheim, a start both of hand and foot, a sudden leap of many tumultuous passions to the face. It passed as swiftly as it came, and left no trace beyond a certain trembling of the hand that now received the glass.

"A glass," he said hoarsely, and then paused, and repeated it more clearly. "A glass? For Christmas? Surely not?"

°*glass*: mirror

"And why not?" cried the dealer. "Why not a glass?"

Markheim was looking upon him with an indefinable expression. "You ask me why not?" he said. "Why, look here—look in it—look at yourself! Do you like to see it? No! nor I—nor any man."

The little man had jumped back when Markheim had so suddenly confronted him with the mirror; but now, perceiving there was nothing worse on hand, he chuckled. "Your future lady, sir, must be pretty hard-favored," said he.

"I ask you," said Markheim, "for a Christmas present, and you give me this—this damned reminder of years, and sins and follies—this hand conscience! Did you mean it? Had you a thought in your mind? Tell me. It will be better for you if you do. Come, tell me about yourself. I hazard a guess now, that you are in secret a very charitable man?"

The dealer looked closely at his companion. It was very odd, Markheim did not appear to be laughing; there was something in his face like an eager sparkle of hope, but nothing of mirth.

"What are you driving at?" the dealer asked.

"Not charitable?" returned the other, gloomily. "Not charitable; not pious; not scrupulous; unloving, unbeloved; a hand to get money, a safe to keep it. Is that all? Dear God, man, is that all?"

"I will tell you what it is," began the dealer, with some sharpness, and then broke off again into a chuckle. "But I see this is a love-match of yours, and you have been drinking the lady's health."

"Ah!" cried Markheim, with a strange curiosity. "Ah, have you been in love? Tell me about that."

"I," cried the dealer. "I in love! I never had the time, nor have I the time today for all this nonsense. Will you take the glass?"

"Where is the hurry?" returned Markheim. "It is very pleasant to stand here talking; and life is so short and insecure that I would not hurry away from any pleasure—no, not even from so mild a one as this. We should rather cling, cling to what little we can get, like a man at a cliff's edge. Every second is a cliff, if you think about it—a cliff a mile high—high enough, if we fall, to dash us out of every feature of humanity. Hence it is best to talk pleasantly. Let us talk of each other; why should we wear this mask? Let us be confidential. Who knows, we might become friends?"

"I have just one word to say to you," said the dealer. "Either make your purchase, or walk out of my shop."

"True, true," said Markheim. "Enough fooling. To business. Show me something else."

The dealer stooped once more, this time to replace the

glass upon the shelf, his thin blond hair falling over his eyes as he did so. Markheim moved a little nearer, with one hand in the pocket of his greatcoat; he drew himself up and filled his lungs; at the same time many different emotions were depicted together on his face—terror, horror, and resolve, fascination and a physical repulsion; and through a haggard lift of his upper lip, his teeth looked out.

"This, perhaps, may suit," observed the dealer; and then, as he began to rise, Markheim bounded from behind upon his victim. The long, skewer-like dagger flashed and fell. The dealer struggled like a hen, striking his temple on the shelf, and then tumbled on the floor in a heap.

Time had some score of small voices in that shop, some stately and slow as was becoming to their great age; others garrulous and hurried. All these told out the seconds in an intricate chorus of tickings. Then the passage of a lad's feet, heavily running on the pavement, broke in upon these smaller voices and startled Markheim into the consciousness of his surroundings. He looked about him awfully. The candle stood on the counter, its flame solemnly wagging in a draught; and by that inconsiderable movement, the whole room was filled with noiseless bustle and kept heaving like a sea; the tall shadows nodding, the gross blots of darkness swelling and dwindling as with respiration, the faces of the portraits and the china gods changing and wavering like images in water. The inner door stood ajar, and peered into that leaguer of shadows with a long slit of daylight like a pointing finger.

From these fear-stricken rovings, Markheim's eyes returned to the body of his victim, where it lay both humped and sprawling, incredibly small and strangely meaner than in life. In these poor, miserly clothes, in that ungainly attitude, the dealer lay like so much sawdust. Markheim had feared to sell it, and, lo! it was nothing. And yet, as he gazed, this bundle of old clothes and pool of blood began to find eloquent voices. There it must lie; there was none to work the cunning hinges or direct the miracle of locomotion —there it must lie till it was found. Found! ay, and then? Then would this dead flesh lift up a cry that would ring over England, and fill the world with the echoes of pursuit. Ay, dead or not, this was the enemy. "Time was that when the brains were out," he thought; and the first word struck into his mind. Time, now that the deed was accomplished—time, which had closed for the victim, had become instant, and momentous for the slayer.

The thought was yet in his mind, when, first one and then another, with every variety of pace and voice—one deep as the bell from a cathedral turret, another ringing on its treble notes the prelude of a waltz—the clocks began to strike the hour of three in the afternoon.

The sudden outbreak of so many tongues in that dumb chamber staggered him. He began to bestir himself, going to and fro with the candle, beleaguered by moving shadows, and startled to the soul by chance reflections. In many rich mirrors, some of home designs, some from Venice or Amsterdam, he saw his face repeated and repeated, as it were an army of spies; his own eyes met and detected him; and the sound of his own steps, lightly as they fell, vexed the surrounding quiet. And still as he continued to fill his pockets, his mind accused him, with a sickening iteration, of the thousand faults of his design. He should have chosen a more quiet hour; he should have prepared an alibi; he should not have used a knife; he should have been more cautious, and only bound and gagged the dealer, and not killed him; he should have been more bold, and killed the servant also; he should have done all things otherwise; poignant regrets, weary, incessant toiling of the mind to change what was unchangeable, to plan what was now useless, to be the architect of the irrevocable past. Meanwhile, and behind all this activity, brute terrors, like the scurrying of rats in a deserted attic, filled the more remote chambers of his brain with riot; the hand of the constable would fall heavy on his shoulder, and his nerves would jerk like a hooked fish; or he beheld, in galloping defile°, the dock, the prison, the gallows, and the black coffin.

Terror of the people in the street sat down before his mind like a besieging army. It was impossible, he thought, but that some rumor of the struggle must have reached their ears and set on edge their curiosity; and now, in all the neighboring houses, he divined them sitting motionless and with uplifted ear—solitary people, condemned to spend Christmas dwelling alone on memories of the past, and now startlingly recalled from that tender exercise; happy family parties, struck into silence round the table, the mother still with raised finger: every degree and age and humor, but all, by their own hearts, prying and hearkening and weaving the rope that was to hang him. Sometimes it seemed to him he could not move too softly; the clink of the tall Bohemian goblets rang out loudly like a bell; and alarmed by the bigness of the ticking, he was tempted to stop the clocks. And then, again, with a swift transition of his terrors, the very silence of the place appeared a source of peril, and a thing to strike and freeze the passerby; and he would step more

---

°*defile*: line of march

boldly, and bustle aloud among the contents of the shop, and imitate, with elaborate bravado, the movements of a busy man at ease in his own house.

But he was now so pulled about by different alarms that, while one portion of his mind was still alert and cunning, another trembled on the brink of lunacy. One hallucination in particular took a strong hold on his credulity. The neighbor hearkening with white face beside his window, the passerby arrested by a horrible surmise on the pavement—these could at worst suspect, they could not know; through the brick walls and shuttered windows only sounds could penetrate. But here, within the house, was he alone? He knew he was; he had watched the servant set forth sweethearting, in her poor best, "out for the day" written in every ribbon and smile. Yes, he was alone, of course; and yet, in the bulk of empty house above him, he could surely hear a stir of delicate footing—he was surely conscious, inexplicably conscious of some presence. Ay, surely; to every room and corner of the house his imagination followed it; and now it was a faceless thing, and yet had eyes to see with; and again it was a shadow of himself; and yet again beheld the image of the dead dealer, reinspired with cunning and hatred.

At times, with a strong effort, he would glance at the open door which still seemed to repel his eyes. The house was tall, the skylight small and dirty, the day blind with fog; and the light that filtered down to the ground story was exceedingly faint, and showed dimly on the threshold of the shop. And yet, in that strip of doubtful brightness, did there not hang wavering a shadow?

Suddenly, from the street outside, a very jovial gentleman began to beat with a staff on the shop door, accompanying his blows with shouts and railleries in which the dealer was continually called upon by name. Markheim, smitten into ice, glanced at the dead man. But no! he lay quite still; he was fled away far beyond earshot of these blows and shoutings; he was sunk beneath seas of silence; and his name, which would once have caught his notice above the howling of a storm, had become an empty sound. And presently the jovial gentleman desisted from his knocking and departed.

Here was a broad hint to hurry what remained to be done, to get forth from this accusing neighborhood, to plunge into a bath of London multitudes, and to reach, on the other side of day, that haven of safety and apparent innocence—his bed. One visitor had come: at any moment another might follow and be more obstinate. To have done the deed, and yet not to reap the profit would be too abhorrent a failure. The money, that was now Markheim's concern; and as a means to that, the keys.

He glanced over his shoulder at the open door, where the

shadow was still lingering and shivering; and with no conscious repugnance of the mind, yet with a tremor of the belly, he drew near the body of his victim. The human character had quite departed. Like a suit half stuffed with bran, the limbs lay scattered, the trunk doubled, on the floor; and yet the thing repelled him. Although so dingy and inconsiderable to the eye, he feared it might have more significance to the touch. He took the body by the shoulders, and turned it on its back. It was strangely light and supple, and the limbs, as if they had been broken, fell into the oddest postures. The face was robbed of all expression; but it was as pale as wax, and shockingly smeared with blood about one temple. That was, for Markheim, the one displeasing circumstance. It carried him back, upon the instant, to a certain fair day in a fishers' village: a grey day, a piping wind, a crowd upon the street, the blare of brasses, the booming of drums, the nasal voice of a ballad singer; and a boy going to and fro, buried over head in the crowd and divided between interest and fear, until coming out upon the chief place of concourse, he beheld a booth and a great screen with pictures, dismally designed, garishly colored: Brownrigg with her apprentice; the Mannings with their murdered guest; We are in the death-grip of Thurtell; and a score besides of famous crimes. The thing was as clear as an illusion; he was once again that little boy; he was looking once again, and with the same sense of physical revolt, at these vile pictures; he was still stunned by the thumping of the drums. A bar of that day's music returned upon his memory; and at that, for the first time, a qualm came over him, a breath of nausea, a sudden weakness of the joints, which he must instantly resist and conquer.

He judged it more prudent to confront than to flee from these considerations; looking the more hardily in the dead face, bending his mind to realize the nature and greatness of his crime. So little a while ago that face had moved with every change of sentiment, that pale mouth had spoken, that body had been all on fire with governable energies; and now, and by his act, that piece of life had been arrested, as the horologist, with interjected finger, arrests the beating of the clock. So he reasoned in vain; he could rise to no more remorseful consciousness; the same heart which had shuddered before the painted effigies of crime looked on its reality unmoved. At best, he left a gleam of pity for one who had been endowed in vain with all those faculties that can make the world a garden of enchantment, one who had never lived and who was now dead. But of penitence, no, not a tremor.

With that, shaking himself clear of these considerations, he found the keys and advanced towards the open door of the shop.

Outside, it had begun to rain smartly; and the sound of the shower upon the roof had banished silence. Like some dripping cavern, the chambers of the house were haunted by an incessant echoing, which filled the ear and mingled with the ticking of the clocks. And, as Markheim approached the door, he seemed to hear, in answer to his own cautious tread, the steps of another foot withdrawing up the stair. The shadow still palpitated loosely on the threshold. He threw a ton's weight of resolve upon his muscles, and drew back the door.

The faint, foggy daylight glimmered dimly on the bare floor and stairs; on the bright suit of armor posted, halbert in hand, upon the landing; and on the dark wood-carvings and framed pictures that hung against the yellow panels of the wainscot. So loud was the beating of the rain through all the house that, in Markheim's ears, it began to be distinguished into many different sounds. Footsteps and sighs, the tread of regiments marching in the distance, the chink of money in the counting, and the creaking of doors held stealthily ajar, appeared to mingle with the patter of the drops upon the cupola and the gushing of the water in the pipes. The sense that he was not alone grew upon him to the verge of madness. On every side he was haunted and begirt by presences. He heard them moving in the upper chambers; from the shop, he heard the dead man getting to his legs; and as he began with a great effort to mount the stairs, feet fled quietly before him and followed stealthily behind. If he were but deaf, he thought, how tranquilly he would possess his soul! And then again, and hearkening with ever fresh attention, he blessed himself for that unresting sense which held the outposts and stood a trusty sentinel upon his life. His head turned continually on his neck; his eyes, which seemed starting from their orbits, scouted on every side, and on every side were half rewarded as with the tail of something nameless vanishing. The four-and-twenty steps to the first floor were four-and-twenty agonies.

On that first story, the doors stood ajar, three of them like three ambushes, shaking his nerves like the throats of cannon. He could never again, he felt, be sufficiently immured and fortified from men's observing eyes; he longed to be home, girt in by walls, buried among bed-clothes, and invisible to all but God. And at that thought he wondered a little, recollecting tales of other murderers and the fear they were said to entertain of heavenly avengers. It was not so, at least, with him. He feared the laws of nature, lest, in their callous and immutable procedure, they should preserve some damning evidence of his crime. He feared tenfold more, with a slavish, superstitious terror, some scission in the continuity of man's experience, some wilful illegality of nature. He played a game of skill, depending on the rules, calculating consequence from cause;

and what if nature, as the defeated tyrant overthrew the chess-board, should break the mould of their succession? The like had befallen Napoleon (so writers said) when the winter changed the time of its appearance. The like might befall Markheim: the solid walls might become transparent and reveal his doings like those of bees in a glass hive; the stout planks might yield under his foot like quicksands and detain him in their clutch; ay, and there were so-berer accidents that might destroy him; if, for instance, the house should fall and imprison him beside the body of his victim; or the house next door should fly on fire, and the firemen invade him from all sides. These things he feared; and, in a sense, these things might be called the hands of God reached forth against sin. But about God himself he was at ease; his act was doubtless exceptional, but so were his excuses, which God knew; it was there, and not among men, that he felt sure of justice.

When he had got safe into the drawing-room, and shut the door behind him, he was aware of a respite from alarms. The room was quite dismantled, uncarpeted besides, and strewn with packing-cases and incongruous furniture; several great pier-glasses, in which he beheld himself at various angles, like an actor on a stage; many pictures, framed and unframed, standing, with their faces to the wall; a fine Sheraton sideboard, a cabinet of mar-quetry, and a great old bed, with tapestry hangings. The windows opened to the floor; but by great good-fortune the lower part of the shutters had been closed, and this concealed him from the neigh-bors. Here, then, Markheim drew in a packing-case before the cabi-net, and began to search among the keys. It was a long business, for there were many; and it was irksome, besides; for, after all, there might be nothing in the cabinet, and time was on the wing. But the closeness of the occupation sobered him. With the tail of his eye he saw the door—even glanced at it from time to time directly, like a besieged commander pleased to verify the good estate of his de-fenses. But in truth he was at peace. The rain falling in the street sounded natural and pleasant. Presently, on the other side, the notes of a piano were wakened to the music of a hymn, and the voices of many children took up the air and words. How stately, how com-fortable was the melody! How fresh the youthful voices! Markheim gave ear to it smilingly, as he sorted out the keys; and his mind was thronged with answerable ideas and images; church-going children and the pealing of the high organ; children afield, bathers by the brookside, ramblers on the brambly common, kite-fliers in the windy and cloud-navigated sky; and then, at another cadence of the hymn, back again to church, and the somnolence of summer Sun-days, and the high genteel voice of the parson (which he smiled a

little to recall) and the painted Jacobean tombs, and the dim letter-
ing of the Ten Commandments in the chancel.

And as he sat thus, at once busy and absent, he was startled to his feet. A flash of ice, a flash of fire, a bursting gush of
blood, went over him, and then he stood transfixed and thrilling. A
step mounted the stair slowly and steadily, and presently a hand
was laid upon the knob, and the lock clicked, and the door opened.

Fear held Markheim in a vise. What to expect he knew
not, whether the dead man walking, or the official ministers of
human justice, or some chance witness blindly stumbling in to con-
sign him to the gallows. But when a face was thrust into the aper-
ture, glanced round the room, looked at him, nodded and smiled as
if in friendly recognition, and then withdrew again, and the door
closed behind it, his fear broke loose from his control in a hoarse
cry. At the sound of this the visitant returned.

"Did you call me?" he asked, pleasantly and with that he
entered the room and closed the door behind him.

Markheim stood and gazed at him with all his eyes. Perhaps there was a film upon his sight, but the outlines of the new-
comer seemed to change and waver like those of the idols in the
wavering candlelight of the shop; and at times he thought he knew
him; and at times he thought he bore a likeness to himself; and
always, like a lump of living terror, there lay in his bosom the conviction that this thing was not of the earth and not of God.

And yet the creature had a strange air of the commonplace, as he stood looking on Markheim with a smile; and when he
added: "You are looking for the money, I believe?" it was in the
tones of everyday politeness.

Markheim made no answer.

"I should warn you," resumed the other, "that the maid
has left her sweetheart earlier than usual and will soon be here. If
Mr. Markheim be found in this house, I need not describe to him the
consequences."

"You know me?" cried the murderer.

The visitor smiled. "You have long been a favorite of
mine," he said; "and I have long observed and often sought to help
you."

"What are you?" cried Markheim: "the devil?"

"What I may be," returned the other, "cannot affect the
service I propose to render you."

"It can," cried Markheim; "it does! Be helped by you?
No, never; not by you! You do not know me yet; thank God, you do
not know me!"

"I know you," replied the visitant, with a sort of kind
severity or rather firmness. "I know you to the soul."

"Know me!" cried Markheim. "Who can do so? My life is but a travesty and slander on myself. I have lived to belie my nature. All men do; all men are better than this disguise that grows about and stifles them. You see each dragged away by life, like one whom bravos have seized and muffled in a cloak. If they had their own control—if you could see their faces, they would be altogether different, they would shine out for heroes and saints! I am worse than most; my self is more overlaid; my excuse is known to me and God. But, had I the time, I could disclose myself."

"To me?" inquired the visitant.

"To you before all," returned the murderer. "I supposed you were intelligent. I thought—since you exist—you would prove a reader of the heart. And yet you would propose to judge me by my acts! Think of it; my acts! I was born and I have lived in a land of giants; giants have dragged me by the wrists since I was born out of my mother—the giants of circumstance. And you would judge me by my acts! But can you not look within? Can you not understand that evil is hateful to me? Can you not see within me the clear writing of conscience, never blurred by any wilful sophistry, although too often disregarded? Can you not read me for a thing that surely must be common as humanity—the unwilling sinner?"

"All this is very feelingly expressed," was the reply, "but it regards me not. These points of consistency are beyond my province, and I care not in the least by what compulsion you may have been dragged away, so as you are but carried in the right direction. But time flies; the servant delays, looking in the faces of the crowd and at the pictures on the hoardings,° but still she keeps moving nearer; and remember, it is as if the gallows itself was striding towards you through the Christmas streets! Shall I help you; I, who know all? Shall I tell you where to find the money?"

"For what price?" asked Markheim.

"I offer you the service for a Christmas gift," returned the other.

Markheim could not refrain from smiling with a kind of bitter triumph. "No," he said, "I will taking nothing at your hands; if I were dying of thirst, and it was your hand that put the pitcher to my lips, I should find the courage to refuse. It may be credulous, but I will do nothing to commit my self to evil."

"I have no objection to a deathbed repentance," observed the visitant.

"Because you disbelieve their efficacy!" Markheim cried.

"I do not say so," returned the other; "but I look on these things from a different side, and when the life is done my interest

---

°*hoardings*: billboards

falls. The man has lived to serve me, to spread black looks under color of religion, or to sow tares in the wheatfield, as you do, in a course of weak compliance with desire. Now that he draws so near to his deliverance, he can add but one act of service—to repent, to die smiling, and thus to build up in confidence and hope the more timorous of my surviving followers. I am not so hard a master. Try me. Accept my help. Please yourself in life as you have done hitherto; please yourself more amply, spread your elbows at the board; and when the night begins to fall and the curtains to be drawn, I tell you, for your greater comfort, that you will find it even easy to compound your quarrel with your conscience, and to make a truckling peace with God. I came but now from such a deathbed, and the room was full of sincere mourners, listening to the man's last words: and when I looked into that face, which had been set as a flint against mercy, I found it smiling with hope."

"And do you, then, suppose me such a creature?" asked Markheim. "Do you think I have no more generous aspirations than to sin, and sin, and sin, and, at last, sneak into heaven? My heart rises at the thought. Is this, then, your experience of mankind? or is it because you find me with red hands that you presume such baseness? and is this crime of murder indeed so impious as to dry up the very springs of good?"

"Murder is to me no special category," replied the other. "All sins are murder, even as all life is war. I behold your face, like starving mariners on a raft, plucking crusts out of the hands of famine and feeding on each other's lives. I follow sins beyond the moment of their acting; I find in all that the last consequence is death; and to my eyes, the pretty maid who thwarts her mother with such taking graces on a question of a ball, drips no less visibly with human gore than such a murderer as yourself. Do I say that I follow sins? I follow virtues also; they differ not by the thickness of a nail, they are both scythes for the reaping angel of Death. Evil, for which I live, consists not in action but in character. The bad man is dear to me; not the bad act, whose fruits, if we could follow them far enough down the hurtling cataract of the ages, might yet be found more blessed than those of the rarest virtues. And it is not because you have killed a dealer, but because you are Markheim, that I offered to forward your escape."

"I will lay my heart open to you," answered Markheim. "This crime on which you find me is my last. On my way to it I have learned many lessons; itself is a lesson, a momentous lesson. Hitherto I have been driven with revolt to what I would not; I was a bond-slave to poverty, driven and scourged. There are robust virtues that can stand in these temptations; mine was not so: I had a thirst of pleasure. But today, and out of this deed, I pluck both warning and riches—both the power and a fresh resolve to be myself. I become in all things a free actor in the world; I begin to see myself all changed, these hands the agents of good, this heart at peace. Something comes over me out of the past; something of what I have dreamed on Sabbath evenings to the sound of the church organ, of what I forecast when I shed tears over noble books, or talked, an innocent child, with my mother. There lies my life; I have wandered a few years, but now I see once more my city of destination."

"You are to use this money on the Stock Exchange, I think?" remarked the visitor; "and there, if I mistake not, you have already lost some thousands?"

"Ah," said Markheim, "but this time I have a sure thing."

"This time, again, you will lose," replied the visitor quietly.

"Ah, but I keep back the half!" cried Markheim.

"That also you will lose," said the other.

The sweat started upon Markheim's brow. "Well, then, what matter?" he exclaimed. "Say it be lost, say I am plunged again in poverty, shall one part of me, and that the worst, continue until the end to override the better? Evil and good run strong in me, haling me both ways. I do not love the one thing, I love all. I can conceive great deeds, renunciations, martyrdoms; and though I be fallen to such a crime as murder, pity is no stranger to my thoughts. I pity the poor; who knows their trials better than myself? I pity and help them; I prize love, I love honest laughter; there is no good thing nor true thing on earth but I love it from my heart. And are my vices only to direct my life, and my virtues to lie without effect, like some passive lumber of the mind? Not so; good, also, is a spring of acts."

But the visitant raised his finger. "For the six-and-thirty years that you have been in this world," said he, "through many changes of fortune and varieties of humor, I have watched you steadily fall. Fifteen years ago you would have started at a theft. Three years back you would have blenched at the name of murder. Is there any crime, is there any cruelty of meanness, from which you still recoil?—five years from now I shall detect you in the fact! Downward, downward, lies your way; nor can anything but death avail to stop you."

"It is true," Markheim said huskily, "I have in some degree complied with evil. But it is so with all: the very saints, in the mere exercise of living, grow less dainty and take on the tone of their surroundings."

"I will propound to you one simple question," said the

other; "and as you answer, I shall read to you your moral horoscope. You have grown in many things more lax; possibly you do right to be so; and at any account, it is the same with all men. But granting that, are you in any one particular, however trifling, more difficult to please with your own conduct, or do you go in all things with a looser rein?"

"In any one?" repeated Markheim, with an anguish of consideration. "No," he added, with despair, "in none! I have gone down in all."

"Then," said the visitor, "content yourself with what you are, for you will never change; and the words of your part on this stage are irrevocably written down."

Markheim stood for a long while silent, and indeed it was the visitor who first broke the silence. "That being so," he said, "shall I show you the money?"

"And grace?" cried Markheim.

"Have you not tried it?" returned the other. "Two or three years ago, did I not see you on the platform of revival meetings, and was not your voice the loudest in the hymn?"

"It is true," said Markheim; "and I see clearly what remains for me by way of duty. I thank you for these lessons from my soul; my eyes are opened, and I behold myself at last for what I am."

At this moment, the sharp note of the doorbell rang through the house; and the visitant, as though this were some concerted signal for which he had been waiting, changed at once in his demeanor. "The maid!" he cried. "She has returned, as I forewarned you, and there is now before you one more difficult passage. Her master, you must say, is ill; you must let her in, with an assured but rather serious countenance—no smiles, no overacting, and I promise you success! Once the girl within, and the door closed, the same dexterity that has already rid you of the dealer will relieve you of this last danger in your path. Thenceforward you have the whole evening—the whole night, if needful—to ransack the treasures of the house and to make good your safety. This is help that comes to you with the mask of danger. Up!" he cried: "up, friend; your life hangs trembling in the scales: up, and act!"

Markheim steadily regarded his counsellor. "If I be condemned to evil acts," he said, "there is still one door of freedom open—I can cease from action. If my life be an ill thing, I can lay it down. Though I be, as you say truly, at the beck of every small temptation, I can yet, by one decisive gesture, place myself beyond the reach of all. My love of good is damned to barrenness; it may, and let it be! But I have still my hatred of evil; and from that, to your galling disappointment, you shall see that I can draw both energy and courage."

The features of the visitor began to undergo a wonderful and lovely change: they brightened and softened with a tender triumph; and, even as they brightened, faded and dislimned. But Markheim did not pause to watch or understand the transformation. He opened the door and went downstairs very slowly, thinking to himself. His past went soberly before him; he beheld it as it was, ugly and strenuous like a dream, random as chance-medley—a scene of defeat. Life, as he thus reviewed it, tempted him no longer; but on the further side he perceived a quiet haven for his bark. He paused in the passage, and looked into the shop, where the candle still burned by the dead body. It was strangely silent. Thoughts of the dealer swarmed into his mind, as he stood gazing. And then the bell once more broke out into impatient clamor.

He confronted the maid upon the threshold with something like a smile.

"You had better go for the police," said he: "I have killed your master."

QUESTIONS AND CONSIDERATIONS

• *Huckleberry Finn*

1. Huck's resolution to act according to "whichever come handiest at the time" is basically a disavowal of any moral code. How does it square with the act he has just performed? With his conviction that he has been defeated by the forces of wrong?
2. Huck is no more than 13 or 14 when this incident occurs. Already he figures he is doomed to a life of sinning. On the basis of this short passage, determine whether he has already left a state of relative innocence and speaks from experience; or that his thinking is a reflection of his extreme innocence.
3. Discuss Huck's belief that if one doesn't get the right start, "he gets beat"; that is, there there is little chance for him to lead a decent, moral life.

Neutral Tones

1. Love is the subject of much literature dealing with the fall. The reason is obvious: Part of growing up involves getting hurt, and

the pain of disillusionment that accompanies one's first serious in-volvement with another can be especially excruciating. Does the speaker of this poem look back to a time of innocence? To what does "Since then" (line 13) refer?

2. In what way does Hardy use the setting to help establish the tone of the poem? Be specific.

3. Is it possible to survive disillusionment without becoming bitter and cynical? What does the title suggest about the speaker's real feel-ings? Is there any significance in the fact that the speaker uses the second person "you," rather than "her" or "his"? What is meant by lines 5–8? If the speaker's feelings are as dead as he or she suggests, how can words lose "the more by our love"?

4. What does all this have to do with the fall from innocence anyhow? Is any such fall established in the poem?

Spring and Fall: To a Young Child

1. This is a difficult poem, particularly because Hopkins strains Eng-lish syntax to the point where many re-readings may be required just to unravel the sentence structure. But it is also a beautiful, worthwhile statement about the fall from innocence. Margaret has been a part of all of us.

   How old is Margaret when the speaker addresses her? Aside from the title itself, what makes it obvious that she is not an adult? Is her grieving in the first line childish? Why or why not? About what does she grieve? What is the tone of the first four lines—mocking? sympathetic? or what?

2. The speaker observes that colder sights will come, but then says it doesn't matter now what they will be. Why doesn't it matter? Colder sights than what? In this connection, what is meant by line 11, "Sórrow's springs áre the same"? Sorrow about what?

3. In line 13, "ghost" probably refers to one's soul; what the mind can-not grasp or the lips utter, the soul can sense. What might it be that "ghost guessed"? The thing that Margaret will weep about "and know why"?

4. The title is clearly a metaphor, as is the poem itself. What are "spring" and "fall" as the poet is using them? Merely youth and old age? Innocence and experience? Can you cite specific lines that relate to fall and to spring? Is fall synonymous with "the blight that man was born for"?

5. Notice Hopkins's shifts of tense. In line 6, he says "It *will* come . . . "; in line 9, "*will* weep. . . . " Why, then, does he not say in line 15, "It is Margaret you *will* mourn for"?

in Just-

1. Like Hopkins, Cummings too stretches language, although with different effect. This poem also deals with a season in one's life, at first glance in the carefree, puddle-wonderful way of spring itself. But on closer examination it suggests that "eddieandbill," "bettyandisbel," and everyone else have only a brief time in which to play at innocent games. Specifically how does Cummings suggest this? (Consider the consecutive ways he describes the balloonman.)
2. Account for why the last nine lines are typographically scattered down the page and why Cummings ends the poem with an abrupt break.
3. Who might the balloonman be? Why is he goat-footed? In myth what does the goat symbolize? What does this suggest about what will happen to eddieandbill and bettyandisbel?
4. Compare the impending fall experience of Cummings's characters with what Hopkins predicts for Margaret.

When I Was One-and-Twenty

1. There is nothing even faintly ominous about the tone of this poem. It is, despite the speaker's "endless rue," light, even funny. Yet it is the *tone* that makes it so, not the theme. Compare this poem with "Neutral Tones." Are they saying essentially the same thing?
2. What has happened to the speaker between the ages of twenty-one and twenty-two? Why wasn't the wise man heeded? Is youth perhaps a time when good advice is ignored?
3. Is the speaker overstating his rue? (Consider his age and the use of the word "endless.") Does this suggest that he still has much to learn about life? Is he as bitter as he makes himself sound?
4. What kind of person is the wise man? A man of true wisdom, or just someone a bit older and somewhat cynical? Would the poem be more, or less, humorous if the speaker were a man of forty?

Markheim

1. Markheim is not an innocent. His journey through life has been largely sordid; as a fortune hunter, thief, and murderer, he has fallen further from innocence than most people ever do. Still, his choice is the same as ours: whether to give in to evil or to resist it. It is never a simple choice. What, ultimately, is Markheim's choice? At what point in the story does he come to it?
2. Mirrors figure importantly in this story. What do they symbolize?

Is there a connection between them and Markheim's wish that he might be "invisible to all but God"?

3. Dostoevsky's great novel *Crime and Punishment* concerns a young man who commits murder with no other motive than to test his belief that he is above the law in killing a useless individual. Is there any evidence that Markheim feels his victim to be unimportant and obnoxious enough so that no great moral issue is involved in the crime?

4. What does Markheim mean when he refers to "the giants of circumstance"? How does he reconcile his act with his statement that "evil is hateful to me"? How can one "live to belie [his] nature"?

5. The man who interrupts Markheim's crime is obviously Satan, the personification of evil. Why has he sought out Markheim? What is the probable nature of the arrangement he seeks with him? (Consider that Satan's fall is the most dramatic and total in all of Judeo-Christian literature.)

6. In view of the brutal act Markheim has committed, why does he so firmly resist Satan's help? Are his arguments sound and convincing, or are they shallow and self-deceiving to the end?

7. Consider and discuss the implications of these lines:
   (a) "If I be condemned to evil acts, there is still one door of freedom open—I can cease from action."
   (b) "The features of the visitor began to undergo a wonderful and lovely change: they brightened and softened with a tender triumph. . . ."

8. In a paper, discuss whether this story points out that evil is an unconquerable adversary; or that it implies that the individual has the power to resist it and therefore is totally responsible for his acts.

2
DUALITIES

•

... a hot temper leaps o'er a cold decree.
—William Shakespeare, *The Merchant of Venice*

There was a little girl
Who had a little curl
Right in the middle of her forehead;
And when she was good,
She was very, very good,
And when she was bad, she was horrid.

—Anonymous

In grade school antonyms frequently formed part of the weekly spelling lesson, remember? As you waded through double-column lists of such words as wise–foolish, joy–sorrow, bravery–cowardice, and the like, you probably didn't realize that much of our language mirrors a puzzling irony: life is filled with conflicts, with dualities. It is, in fact, difficult to think of a single significant idea or act that does not have a counterpart. We have already touched upon the most dramatic and obvious duality—that of good and evil. But our moods, attitudes, reactions, indeed, our very characters, are based on many other dualities as well.

The good–evil idea was treated separately because it is so vividly an expression of the fall motif represented by Adam and Eve and also because to this day it is the center of the age-old philosophical question about free will—whether or not we really do have the innate power to choose between one and the other. Many of the dualistic aspects of life seemingly do not admit of choice, however. Take joy–misery, for example. There isn't much conscious deliberation involved. If we have reason to feel miserable, there often isn't much to be done about it. Love–hate falls into the same category. "Love your enemies" sounds good enough as an ideal but can seem almost impossible as a practice. Bravery–cowardice is another example. If all it took to be brave were the resolution not to be cowardly, heroes would be a dime a dozen.

Mythology has concerned itself with the paradox of duality for thousands of years. Long before the formal study of human behavior revealed that we are all more or less confused and sometimes anguished by our dual natures, myths recorded man's awareness of this aspect of his make-up. Perhaps because we are most often torn between the twin forces of emotion and reason, this motif is prevalent in myth. It goes by other names, too: the heart versus the head; the flesh versus the spirit; impulse versus reason; cerebrum (brain) against viscera (gut); even sanity versus insanity. Whatever the labels, no one has escaped the contrary pulls of these forces.

In Greek mythology, dualities were personified. Dionysus represented one, Apollo the other. Dionysus (Bacchus in later Greek and subsequently Roman mythology) was fathered by Zeus, as were many other mythological figures, including Apollo. (Zeus was an insatiable lover. His wife, the goddess Hera, spent most of her time breaking up his amorous affairs.) Dionysus was born twice, although there are conflicting versions as to how it happened. The generally accepted account is that Zeus seduced Semele, a mortal. Hera, understandably angry, tricked Semele into demanding that her lover appear before her in all his godly majesty, a sight too awesome for human eyes. Zeus reluctantly complied, visiting Semele as a thunderbolt. The spectacle (or the lightning) killed her.

Zeus snatched the unborn Dionysus from her womb and sewed the infant into his thigh, later removing him. This may be why Dionysus qualified as a full god, for by being born from Zeus the father and also in a sense from Zeus the mother, both sides of his parentage were divine.

Hera brought much misery to the young Dionysus and to those who reared him. It is said that Zeus changed him into a goat-child to disguise him from his vengeful wife; and that Hermes, the messenger god, carried him in that form to far-off Mount Nysa, where he was cared for by nymphs (minor female goddesses). Hera struck him with madness after he had been returned to human form, and he fled his nurses and wandered through many lands before arriving in Phrygia. There, he was cured of his madness by Cybele, who is identified with Rhea, mother of Zeus. Cybele was also said to have introduced Dionysus to the rites with which he became associated.

At any rate, it was in Phrygia that Dionysus began to wear the flowing oriental robes that came to mark him and his worshipers. He left Phrygia, picking up followers along the way. By the time he reached the eastern shores of the Mediterranean, he was fully acknowledged as a god. By this time, too, he had become associated with the cultivation of grapes and wine-making.

Dionysus was a traveling god and was always accompanied by maenads (frenzied female worshipers) and satyrs (manlike creatures but with various animal characteristics, such as small horns, pointed ears, and goatlike legs). The rites of Dionysus were usually climaxed by drunken, orgiastic revels, in which Dionysus appeared in the form of a goat. The maenads would sometimes tear apart kids or fawns and eat them raw as part of the rituals.

When Dionysus was honored in a particular place, he would bestow upon its citizens a knowledge of how to cultivate grapes, as well as the pleasures of wine. It isn't hard to imagine, however, that he and his wild-eyed crowd were often seen as a menace to the community they were visiting, and Dionysus sometimes met with strong local resistance. Dionysus's response to this was to destroy his opposition with madness, an affliction with which he was familiar.

One such victim was Lycurgus, king of the Edonians. After chasing out Dionysus and his band, he lost his mind long enough either to chop down all the grapevines in his kingdom, in one version, or to butcher his wife and son, in another. He regained his sanity, but his land became barren and his subjects killed him.

Dionysus eventually returned to Thebes, his birthplace. King Pentheus became incensed by the behavior of the Dionysian cult and their drastic influence on his subjects. He threw the maenads and (according to one version) Dionysus in jail. Dionysus, however, had little difficulty in influencing Pentheus's mind. The king not only released his prisoners but also accompanied Dionysus to a revel. He hid himself from the maenads, but at the height of their frenzy they discovered him and tore him limb from limb.° With Pentheus's death, Thebes became the site of the central shrine of Dionysian worship.

Dionysus is credited with many achievements, some of rather dubious merit. For one thing, he is said to have created the dolphin and to have placed in the sky the constellation Aries, along with a number of lesser-known constellations. It was also Dionysus, however, who granted Midas his golden touch, which proved to be that monarch's destruction; who drove the women of Attica to madness and suicide; and who crazed the women of Argos to the point of devouring their children. His crowning achievement, of course, was the introduction of wine, hence intoxication, to the world.

°One version of Dionysus's first birth has him torn apart by the Titans, acting on Hera's orders.

Dionysus was a fertility god. His association with the earth and the grape established him as an important deity not for the Greek ruling classes but for the common tillers of the soil. Dionysus's very nature is earthy. His Bacchanalian rites were marked by zest and passion, attended by music, dancing, and drinking. Such rites and celebrations, as we shall see, are typical of agrarian cultures and are usually seasonal, coinciding with planting or harvest time. Animal sacrifice in connection with fertility rites is an ancient practice. So too is the ritual killing of the so-called "year king," wherein a leader is put to death or commits ritual suicide at the end of a predetermined cycle. It is easy to find expression of these practices metaphorized in the myth of Dionysus.

Apollo was the son of Zeus and the Titaness Leto. Unlike Dionysus, his birth was not spectacular. Like Semele, however, Leto was the target for Hera's jealousy and suffered much misery because of it. Leto was forced to wander the earth throughout her pregnancy, looking for a place to give birth. Because of Hera's influence, no country dared offer her a resting place. Zeus finally intervened, as usual behind his wife's back, and Leto was given refuge on the island of Delos. There she gave birth to the twins Apollo and Artemis, the latter being the goddess of the moon, childbirth, and wild animals. (Artemis became Diana in Roman mythology.)

Apollo was fed on nectar and ambrosia, a concoction meant only for gods. Perhaps because of its potency, Apollo was only four days old when he called for a bow, arrows, and a lyre and ventured to Delphi. There he killed the snake monster Python, which had once threatened his mother during her travels and which now guarded the oracle° at Delphi. (The battle between Apollo and Python, in which Apollo's arrows were said to be like rays from the sun, became a ritualized part of celebrations honoring him.)

Apollo established his own cult at Delphi, which had originally been controlled by Ge, the great earth goddess. Another earth goddess, Themis, whose shrine it was when Apollo arrived, relinquished it to him without objection. Apollo selected Phenomoë to be the Pythia (prophetess) and gave her the task of speaking his prophecies. This she did while sitting on a three-legged stool placed over a fissure which emitted gaseous vapors. Her answers to sup-

---

°The term *oracle* has three related meanings. It is a shrine in which a specially gifted priest serves as a medium through which a god speaks prophetically; it also denotes the priest and the prophecy itself.

pliants were sometimes as hazy as her vapor-enshrouded image. When, for example, the young Oedipus traveled to Delphi to find out whether he was actually the son of the king and queen who had reared him, the oracle not only refused to listen to his question but chased him from the shrine after telling him that he would kill his father and marry his mother, an ambiguous bit of information that led to a great tragedy.

King Croesus suffered from Delphic double-talk, too. His kingdom of Lydia was under attack by Persians. Wishing to know whether he should mount a war against them, he consulted the oracle, who told him that if he did, he would destroy a powerful empire. Encouraged, Croesus went to war, was defeated, and witnessed the collapse of his own empire.

The oracle of Apollo, nevertheless, became very influential, not only in Delphi but throughout the Mediterranean world. The shrine itself flourished for more than 400 years, and followers of the Apollonian cult formed an influential segment of Greek society. As the god Apollo grew in significance, an interesting mythological evolution also occurred.

Figures in mythology do not spring full-blown from a single creative act. They, and what they are associated with, develop over centuries and are fed from many sources. They are mirrors in which societies see themselves, an idea discussed earlier in this book. The myths in which Apollo figures reflect the growth of Hellenic society toward its intellectual zenith.

Apollo was not originally native to Greece. His origins lie elsewhere, perhaps central Asia. Under another name, he was at one time worshiped as a god of mice. He was also identified with the sun god Helius and replaced that ancient god in certain myths. This early association with brightness endured but became figuratively connected with intellect rather than the cyclical life-giving property of the sun. Although Apollo became associated with rationality, many myths depict him as being typically godlike; that is, he was capable of brutality, foolishness, and betrayal. He killed a number of relatively innocent mortals who offended him; suffered poor King Midas to wear ass's ears; granted Cassandra the gift of prophecy but when she spurned him, fixed it so that she would never be listened to. He also had a hand in the death of Achilles and, accidentally, the fall of Troy.

Yet it was not Apollo's role in mythology to symbolize the weaknesses of gods (and mortals). An inscription on his temple read, "Nothing in excess," an appeal to temperate behavior. Another inscription, "Know thyself," established Apollo's advocacy of self-knowledge, the first step in the direction of wisdom. Further-more, there are few indications in any myth concerning Apollo that he enjoyed his lapses into frenzied behavior. Gradually, as his asso-ciation with the rational forces in humanity increased, he left behind much of his impetuosity.

Apollo's celebrated battle with Python symbolized his vic-tory over disorder. By taking over the oracle at Delphi from an earth goddess, he also established his primacy over a more primitive object of worship. Apollo became known as the god of prophecy, music, and healing°. A number of renowned seers claimed either to have descended from him or to have been taught by him. Orpheus was one of three sons of Apollo who became great minstrels; Ascle-pius, another son, is famous as a physician. Significantly, although he was also the god of archers, Apollo's lineage included no great warriors.

By the fifth century B.C., Apollo had become synonymous with the highest rational principles. Aeschylus, a great Greek play-wright of this period, depicts him presiding over courts of law, then as now symbols of the highest degree of disciplined rationality.

Apollo and Dionysus were never meant to represent the forces of right and wrong. Far from it. There is nothing wrong or unnatural about kicking up one's heels and indulging in what is purely gratifying. Abandoning one's intellect occasionally may actually make sense, which sounds like a contradiction but isn't. While we have been admonished from early childhood to beware such indulgences, the pull of the irrational simply cannot be resisted all the time.

To be sure, a headlong plunge into excess is destructive to the self and often to others. Dionysus paved the way for drunken-ness, an enduring social ill. His rites involved the kinds of joyful release that, carried to an extreme, can become expressive of the savage forces that sleep somewhere in all of us. But Dionysus is not synonymous with excess and debauchery alone, any more than a glass or two of wine is synonymous with alcoholism. Wine's pri-mary function in Dionysian rites was to liberate the individual from the restraints of rationalism that repress the natural and earthy side of us and to permit him to commune with the earth mother. What Dionysus stood for and the extremes his rites allowed are thus not necessarily the same.

°The dark side of Apollo's association with healing was that he was
    able to cause plagues. He could bring them to an end, too, which
    is healing of an ironic sort.

That Dionysus appealed chiefly to the common people is not surprising. Apart from his direct association with the soil, he stood for the kinds of relaxation and fun most working people earn the hard way and get too little of. The comic strip character Andy Capp is instinctively Dionysian, yet we chuckle at him affectionately. He is no monster. Neither is Archie Bunker, who blows off steam at the neighborhood tavern instead of going to the ballet or reading Shakespeare.

Apollo, as we have seen, was no more narrowly expressive of one force in life than Dionysus was of its opposite. The *essence* of each was different, to be sure; but the myths surrounding both gods portrayed a truth: that the things Dionysus and Apollo symbolized are not mutually exclusive and are dangerous when viewed in such a light. The coldly intellectual element in the latter has useful application in certain situations but as a way of life is as sterile as the Dionysian extreme is wanton. The wise man acknowledges both seeming opposites within himself, the myths suggest, and attempts to integrate them.

Many myths symbolize our dualistic aspects by casting them in the form of brothers or sisters (sometimes twins), companions, evenly matched adversaries, or strangers who are thrown together by chance. Cain and Abel are examples, as are Eteocles and Polyneices, both sons of Oedipus, who killed each other in the war of the Seven against Thebes.

In Greek drama, the chorus donned masks symbolizing comedy or tragedy, indicating that beneath the differing facial expressions the masks bore, both extremes lived in anyone. Before western movies became sophisticated, the good guy wore a white hat and the villain a black one, suggesting that otherwise the two would not be distinct enough to tell apart. Other interesting depictions of duality are found in such stories as *Dr. Jekyll and Mr. Hyde, Dracula, The Picture of Dorian Gray,* and *The Wolfman.*

A surface reading of any of these stories or countless similar examples from literature or the movies might indicate that they are all considerations of the good–evil theme we have already examined. Usually, however, it isn't as simple as that. The story of Cain and Abel has many meanings beyond suggesting that one brother was good and the other was evil. The first of the following selections, a chapter from John Steinbeck's novel *Tortilla Flat,* could be read simply as a condemnation of avarice. But it would take a humorless, narrow-minded prude to take it that way. Pilon is guilty of greed, deceit, and various minor depravities; but he is not evil; he is only human. And these two things are not the same.

FROM TORTILLA FLAT

John Steinbeck (1902–1969)

PREFACE

This is the story of Danny and of Danny's friends and of Danny's house. It is a story of how these three became one thing, so that in Tortilla Flat if you speak of Danny's house you do not mean a structure of wood flaked with old whitewash, overgrown with an ancient untrimmed rose of Castile. No, when you speak of Danny's house you are understood to mean a unit of which the parts are men, from which came sweetness and joy, philanthropy and, in the end, a mystic sorrow. For Danny's house was not unlike the Round Table, and Danny's friends were not unlike the knights of it. And this is the story of how that group came into being, of how it flourished and grew to be an organization beautiful and wise. This story deals with the adventuring of Danny's friends, with the good they did, with their thoughts and their endeavors. In the end, this story tells how the talisman was lost and how the group disintegrated.

In Monterey, that old city on the coast of California, these things are well known, and they are repeated and sometimes elaborated. It is well that this cycle be put down on paper so that in a future time scholars, hearing the legends, may not say as they say of Arthur and of Roland and of Robin Hood—"There was no Danny nor any group of Danny's friends, nor any house. Danny is a nature god and his friends primitive symbols of the wind, the sky, the sun." This history is designed now and ever to keep the sneers from the lips of sour scholars.

III

How the poison of possessions wrought with Pilon, and how evil temporarily triumphed in him.

The next day Pilon went to live in the other house. It was exactly like Danny's house, only smaller. It had its pink rose of Castile over the porch, its weed-grown yard, its ancient, barren fruit trees, its red geraniums—and Mrs. Soto's chicken yard was next door.

Danny became a great man, having a house to rent, and Pilon went up the social scale by renting a house.

It is impossible to say whether Danny expected any rent, or whether Pilon expected to pay any. If they did, both were disappointed. Danny never asked for it, and Pilon never offered it.

The two friends were often together. Let Pilon come by a jug of wine or a piece of meat and Danny was sure to drop in to visit. And, if Danny were lucky or astute in the same way, Pilon spent a riotous night with him. Poor Pilon would have paid the money if he ever had any, but he never did have—not long enough to locate Danny. Pilon was an honest man. It worried him sometimes to think of Danny's goodness and his own poverty.

One night he had a dollar, acquired in a manner so astounding that he tried to forget it immediately for fear the memory might make him mad. A man in front of the San Carlos hotel had put the dollar in his hand, saying, "Run down and get four bottles of ginger ale. The hotel is out." Such things were almost miracles, Pilon thought. One should take them on faith, not worry and question them. He took the dollar up the road to give to Danny, but on the way he bought a gallon of wine, and with the wine he lured two plump girls into his house.

Danny, walking by, heard the noise and joyfully went in. Pilon fell into his arms and placed everything at Danny's disposal. And later, after Danny had helped to dispose of one of the girls and half of the wine, there was a really fine fight. Danny lost a tooth, and Pilon had his shirt torn off. The girls stood shrieking by and kicked whichever man happened to be down. At last Danny got up off the floor and butted one of the girls in the stomach, and she went out the door croaking like a frog. The other girl stole two cooking pots and followed her.

For a little while Danny and Pilon wept over the perfidy of women.

"Thou knowest not what bitches women are," Danny said wisely.

"I do know," said Pilon.

"Thou knowest not."

I do know."

"Liar."

There was another fight, but not a very good one.

After that Pilon felt better about the unpaid rent. Had he not been host to his landlord?

A number of months passed. Pilon began again to worry about the rent. And as time went by the worry grew intolerable. At last in desperation he worked a whole day cleaning squids for Chin Kee and made two dollars. In the evening he tied his red handkerchief around his neck, put on his father's revered hat, and started up the hill to pay Danny the two dollars on account.

But on the way he bought two gallons of wine. "It is better so," he thought. "If I give him hard money, it does not express how warmly I feel toward my friend. But a present, now. And I will tell him the two gallons cost five dollars." This was silly, and Pilon knew it, but he indulged himself. No one in Monterey better knew the price of wine than Danny.

Pilon was proceeding happily. His mind was made up; his nose pointed straight toward Danny's house. His feet moved, not quickly, but steadily in the proper direction. Under each arm he carried a paper bag, and a gallon of wine was in each bag.

It was purple dusk, that sweet time when the day's sleeping is over, and the evening of pleasure and conversation has not begun. The pine trees were very black against the sky, and all objects on the ground were obscured with dark; but the sky was as mournfully bright as memory. The gulls flew lazily home to the sea rocks after a day's visit to the fish canneries of Monterey.

Pilon was a lover of beauty and a mystic. He raised his face into the sky and his soul arose out of him into the sun's afterglow. That not too perfect Pilon, who plotted and fought, who drank and cursed, trudged slowly on; but a wistful and shining Pilon went up to the sea gulls where they bathed on sensitive wings in the evening. That Pilon was beautiful, and his thoughts were unstained with selfishness and lust. And his thoughts are good to know.

"Our Father is in the evening," he thought. "These birds are flying across the forehead of the Father. Dear birds, dear sea gulls, how I love you all. Your slow wings stroke my heart as the hand of a gentle master strokes the full stomach of a sleeping dog, as the hand of Christ stroked the heads of little children. Dear birds," he thought, "fly to our Lady of Sweet Sorrows with my open heart." And then he said the loveliest words he knew, *"Ave Maria, gratia plena—"*°

The feet of the bad Pilon had stopped moving. In truth the bad Pilon for the moment had ceased to exist. (Hear this, recording angel!) There was, nor is, nor ever has been a purer soul than Pilon's at that moment. Galvez' bad bulldog came to Pilon's deserted legs standing alone in the dark. And Galvez' bulldog sniffed and went away without biting the legs.

A soul washed and saved is a soul doubly in danger, for everything in the world conspires against such a soul. "Even the straws under my knees," says Saint Augustine, "shout to distract me from prayer."

Pilon's soul was not even proof against his own memories; for as he watched the birds, he remembered that Mrs. Pastano

---

°*Ave Maria, gratia plena*: The prayer beginning "Hail Mary, full
   of **grace**"

used sea gulls sometimes in her tamales, and that memory made him hungry, and hunger tumbled his soul out of the sky. Pilon moved on, once more a cunning mixture of good and evil. Galvez' bad bulldog turned snarling and stalked back, sorry now that he had let go such a perfect chance at Pilon's legs.

Pilon hunched his arms to ease the weight of the bottles.

It is a fact verified and recorded in many histories that the soul capable of the greatest good is also capable of the greatest evil. Who is there more impious than a backsliding priest? Who more carnal than a recent virgin? This, however, may be a matter of appearance.

Pilon, just back from Heaven, was, although he did not know it, singularly receptive of every bitter wind, toward every evil influence that crowded the night about him. True, his feet still moved toward Danny's house, but there was neither intention nor conviction in them. They awaited the littlest signal to turn about. Already Pilon was thinking how stupendously drunk he could get on two gallons of wine, and more, how long he could stay drunk.

It was almost dark now. The dirt road was no longer visible, nor the ditches on either side. No moral conclusion is drawn from the fact that at this moment, when Pilon's impulses were balanced as precariously as a feather, between generosity and selfishness, at this very moment Pablo Sanchez happened to be sitting in the ditch at the side of the road, wishing he had a cigarette and a glass of wine.

Ah, the prayers of the millions, how they must fight and destroy each other on their way to the throne of God.

Pablo first heard footsteps, then saw a blurred figure, and then recognized Pilon. "Ai, *amigo*," he called enthusiastically. "What great burden is it thou carriest?"

Pilon stopped dead and faced the ditch. "I thought you were in jail," he said severely. "I heard about a goose."

"So I was, Pilon," Pablo said jocularly. "But I was not well received. The judge said the sentence did me no good, and the police said I ate more than the allowance for three men. And so," he finished proudly, "I am on parole."

Pilon was saved from selfishness. True, he did not take the wine to Danny's house, but instantly he invited Pablo to share it at the rented house. If two generous paths branch from the highroad of life and only one can be followed, who is to judge which is best?

Pilon and Pablo entered the little house joyfully. Pilon lighted a candle and produced two fruit jars for glasses.

"Health!" said Pablo.

"*Salud!*"° said Pilon.

And in a few moments, "*Salud!*" said Pablo.

"Mud in your eye!" said Pilon.

They rested a little while. "*Su servidor*,"° said Pilon.

"Down the rat-hole," said Pablo.

Two gallons is a great deal of wine, even for two paisa-nos. Spiritually the jugs may be graduated thus: Just below the shoulder of the first bottle, serious and concentrated conversation. Two inches farther down, sweetly sad memory. Three inches more, thoughts of old and satisfactory loves. An inch, thoughts of bitter loves. Bottom of the first jug, general and undirected sadness. Shoulder of the second jug, black, unholy despondency. Two fingers down a song of death or longing. A thumb, every other song each one knows. The graduations stop there, for the trail splits and there is no certainty. From this point on anything can happen.

But let us go back to the first mark, which says serious and concentrated conversation, for it was at that place that Pilon made his coup. "Pablo," he said, "dost thou never get tired of sleep-ing in ditches, wet and homeless, friendless and alone?"

"No," said Pablo.

Pilon mellowed his voice persuasively. "So *I* thought, my friend, when I was a dirty gutter-dog. I too was content, for I did not know how sweet a little house is, and a roof, and a garden. Ah, Pablo, this is indeed living."

"It's pretty nice," Pablo agreed.

Pilon pounced. "See, Pablo, how would you like to rent part of my house? There would never be the cold ground for you any more. Never the hard sand under the wharf with crabs getting in your shoes. How would you like to live here with me?"

"Sure," said Pablo.

"Look, you will pay only fifteen dollars a month! And you may use all the house except my bed, and all the garden. Think of it, Pablo! And if someone should write you a letter, he will have some place to send it to."

"Sure," said Pablo. "That's swell."

Pilon sighed with relief. He had not realized how the debt to Danny rode on his shoulders. The fact that he was fairly sure Pablo would never pay any rent did not mitigate his triumph. If Danny should ever ask for money, Pilon could say, "I will pay when Pablo pays."

They moved on to the next graduation, and Pilon remem-

°*Salud!*: Your health!

°*Su servidor*: Your servant

bered how happy he had been when he was a little boy. "No care then, Pablo. I knew not sin. I was very happy."

"We have never been happy since," Pablo agreed sadly.

IROQUOIS CREATION MYTH

Anonymous

One day, when the girl° had grown to womanhood, a man appeared. No one knows for sure who this man was. He had something to do with the gods above. Perhaps he was the West Wind. As the girl looked at him, she was filled with terror, and amazement, and warmth, and she fainted dead away. As she lay on the ground, the man reached into his quiver, and he took out two arrows, one sharp and one blunt, and he laid them across the body of the girl, and quietly went away.

When the girl awoke from her faint, she and her mother continued to walk around the earth. After a while, they knew that the girl was to bear a child. They did not know it, but the girl was to bear twins.

Within the girl's body, the twins began to argue and quarrel with one another. There could be no peace between them. As the time approached for them to be born, the twins fought about their birth. The right-handed twin wanted to be born in the normal way, as all children are born. But the left-handed twin said no. He said he saw light in another direction, and said he would be born that way. The right-handed twin beseeched him not to, saying that he would kill their mother. But the left-handed twin was stubborn. He went in the direction where he saw light. But he could not be born through his mother's mouth or her nose. He was born through her left armpit, and killed her. And meanwhile, the right-handed twin was born in the normal way, as all children are born.

The twins met in the world outside, and the right-handed twin accused his brother of murdering their mother. But the grandmother told them to stop their quarreling. They buried their mother. And from her grave grew the plants which the people still use. From her head grew the corn, the beans, and the squash—"our supporters, the three sisters." And from her heart grew the sacred tobacco, which the people still use in the ceremonies and by whose upward-floating smoke they send thanks. The women call her "our mother," and they dance and sing in the rituals so that the corn, the beans, and the squash may grow to feed the people.

°The girl is the daughter of the archetypal Earth Mother (or goddess), in Greek myth Demeter, whose daughter was Persephone.

But the conflict of the twins did not end at the grave of their mother. And, strangely enough, the grandmother favored the left-handed twin.

The right-handed twin was angry, and he grew more angry as he thought how his brother had killed their mother. The right-handed twin was the one who did everything just as he should. He said what he meant, and he meant what he said. He always told the truth, and he always tried to accomplish what seemed to be right and reasonable. The left-handed twin never said what he meant or meant what he said. He always lied, and he always did things backward. You could never tell what he was trying to do because he always made it look as if he were doing the opposite. He was the devious one.

These two brothers, as they grew up, represented two ways of the world which are in all people. The Indians did not call these the right and the wrong. They called them the straight mind and the crooked mind, the upright man and the devious man, the right and the left.

The twins had creative powers. They took clay and modeled it into animals, and they gave these animals life. And in this they contended with one another. The right-handed twin made the deer, and the left-handed twin made the mountain lion which kills the deer. But the right-handed twin knew there would always be more deer than mountain lions. And he made another animal. He made the ground squirrel. The left-handed twin saw that the mountain lion could not get to the ground squirrel, who digs a hole, so he made the weasel. And although the weasel can go into the ground squirrel's hole and kill him, there are lots of ground squirrels and not so many weasels. Next the right-handed twin decided he would make an animal that the weasel could not kill, so he made the porcupine. But the left-handed twin made the bear, who flips the porcupine over on his back and tears out his belly.

And the right-handed twin made berries and fruits of other kinds for his creatures to live on. The left-handed twin made briars and poison ivy, and the poisonous plants like the baneberry and the dogberry, and the suicide root with which people kill themselves when they go out of their minds. And the left-handed twin made medicines, for good and for evil, for doctoring and for witchcraft.

And finally, the right-handed twin made man. The people do not know just how much the left-handed twin had to do with making man. Man was made of clay, like pottery, and baked in the fire. [At a later time the idea was added that some men were baked too little: these were white men. Some men were baked too much: these were Negroes. But some were baked just right: these were Indians. Those who were baked too little or too much were thrown away, but the Indians were settled upon the land.]

The world the twins made was a balanced and orderly world, and this was good. The plant-eating animals created by the right-handed twin would eat up all the vegetation if their number was not kept down by the meat-eating animals which the left-handed twin created. But if these carnivorous animals ate too many other animals, then they would starve, for they would run out of meat. So the right- and the left-handed twins built balance into the world.

As the twins became men full grown, they still contested with one another. No one had won, and no one had lost. And they knew that the conflict was becoming sharper and sharper and one of them would have to vanquish the other.

And so they came to the duel. They started with gambling. They took a wooden bowl, and in it they put wild plum pits. One side of the pits was burned black, and by tossing the pits in the bowl, and betting on how these would fall, they gambled against one another, as the people still do in the New Year's rites. All through the morning they gambled at this game, and all through the afternoon, and the sun went down. And when the sun went down, the game was done, and neither one had won.

So they went on to battle one another at the lacrosse game. And they contested all day, and the sun went down, and the game was done. And neither had won.

And now they battled with clubs, and they fought all day, and the sun went down, and the fight was done. But neither had won.

And they went from one duel to another to see which one would succumb. Each one knew in his deepest mind that there was something, somewhere, that would vanquish the other. But what was it? Where to find it?

Each knew somewhere in his mind what it was that was his own weak point. They talked about this as they contested in these duels, day after day, and somehow the deep mind of each entered into the other. And the deep mind of the right-handed twin lied to his brother, and the deep mind of the left-handed twin told the truth.

On the last day of the duel, as they stood, they at last knew how the right-handed twin was to kill his brother. Each selected his weapon. The left-handed twin chose a mere stick that would do him no good. But the right-handed twin picked out the deer antler, and with one touch he destroyed his brother. And the left-handed twin died, but he died and he didn't die. The right-handed twin picked up the body and cast it off the edge of the earth. And some place below the world, the left-handed twin still lives and reigns.

When the sun rises from the east and travels in a huge arc along the sky dome, which rests like a great upside-down cup on the saucer of the earth, the people are in the daylight realm of the right-handed twin. But when the sun slips down in the west at nightfall and the dome lifts to let it escape at the western rim, the people are again in the domain of the left-handed twin—the fearful realm of night.

Having killed his brother, the right-handed twin returned home to his grandmother. And she met him in anger. She threw the food out of the cabin onto the ground, and said that he was a murderer, for he had killed his brother. He grew angry and told her she had always helped his brother, who had killed their mother. In his anger, he grabbed her by the throat and cut her head off. Her body he threw into the ocean, and her head, into the sky. There "Our Grandmother, the Moon," still keeps watch at night over the realm of her favorite grandson.

The right-handed twin has many names. One of them is Sapling. It means smooth, young, green and fresh and innocent, straightforward, straight-growing, soft and pliable, teachable and trainable. These are the old ways of describing him. But since he has gone away, he has other names. He is called "He Holds Up the Skies," "Master of Life," and "Great Creator."

The left-handed twin also has many names. One of them is Flint. He is called the devious one, the one covered with boils, Old Warty. He is stubborn. He is thought of as being dark in color.

These two beings rule the world and keep an eye on the affairs of men. The right-handed twin, the Master of Life, lives in the Sky-World. He is content with the world he helped to create and with his favorite creatures, the humans. The scent of sacred tobacco rising from the earth comes gloriously to his nostrils.

In the world below lives the left-handed twin. He knows the world of men, and he finds contentment in it. He hears the sounds of warfare and torture, and he finds them good.

In the daytime, the people have rituals which honor the right-handed twin. Through the daytime rituals they thank the Master of Life. In the nighttime, the people dance and sing for the left-handed twin.

HOLY SONNET 14

John Donne (1572–1631)

Batter my heart, three-personed God; for you
As yet but knock, breathe, shine, and seek to mend.
That I may rise and stand, o'erthrow me and bend
Your force to break, blow, burn, and make me new.
I, like an usurped town, to another due,   5
Labor to admit you, but, oh, to no end;
Reason, your viceroy in me, me should defend,
But is captived and proves weak or untrue.

Yet dearly I love you and would be lovèd fain,
But am betrothed unto your enemy: 10
Divorce me, untie or break that knot again,
Take me to you, imprison me, for I,
Except you enthrall me, never shall be free,
Nor ever chaste, except you ravish me.

THE USE OF FORCE

William Carlos Williams (1883–1963)

They were new patients to me, all I had was the name, Olson. Please come down as soon as you can, my daughter is very sick.

When I arrived I was met by the mother, a big startled looking woman, very clean and apologetic who merely said, Is this the doctor? and let me in. In the back, she added. You must excuse us, doctor, we have her in the kitchen where it is warm. It is very damp here sometimes.

The child was fully dressed and sitting on her father's lap near the kitchen table. He tried to get up, but I motioned for him not to bother, took off my overcoat and started to look things over. I could see that they were all very nervous, eyeing me up and down distrustfully. As often, in such cases, they weren't telling me more than they had to, it was up to me to tell them; that's why they were spending three dollars on me.

The child was fairly eating me up with her cold, steady eyes, and no expression to her face whatever. She did not move and seemed, inwardly, quiet; an unusually attractive little thing, and as strong as a heifer in appearance. But her face was flushed, she was breathing rapidly, and I realized that she had a high fever. She had magnificent blonde hair, in profusion. One of those picture children often reproduced in advertising leaflets and the photogravure sections of the Sunday papers.

She's had a fever for three days, began the father and we don't know what it comes from. My wife has given her things, you know, like people do, but it don't do no good. And there's been a lot of sickness around. So we tho't you'd better look her over and tell us what is the matter.

As doctors often do I took a trial shot at it as a point of departure. Has she had a sore throat?

Both parents answered me together, No . . . No, she says her throat don't hurt her.

Does your throat hurt you? added the mother to the child. But the little girl's expression didn't change nor did she move her eyes from my face.

Have you looked?

I tried to, said the mother, but I couldn't see.

As it happens we had been having a number of cases of diphtheria in the school to which this child went during that month and we were all, quite apparently, thinking of that, though no one had as yet spoken of the thing.

Well, I said, suppose we take a look at the throat first. I smiled in my best professional manner and asking for the child's first name I said, come on, Mathilda, open your mouth and let's take a look at your throat.

Nothing doing.

Aw, come on, I coaxed, just open your mouth wide and let me take a look. Look, I said opening both hands wide, I haven't anything in my hands. Just open up and let me see.

Such a nice man, put in the mother. Look how kind he is to you. Come on, do what he tells you to. He won't hurt you.

At that I ground my teeth in disgust. If only they wouldn't use the word "hurt" I might be able to get somewhere. But I did not allow myself to be hurried or disturbed but speaking quietly and slowly I approached the child again.

As I moved my chair a little nearer suddenly with one cat-like movement both her hands clawed instinctively for my eyes and she almost reached them too. In fact she knocked my glasses flying and they fell, though unbroken, several feet away from me on the kitchen floor.

Both the mother and father almost turned themselves inside out in embarrassment and apology. You bad girl, said the mother, taking her and shaking her by one arm. Look what you've done. The nice man . . .

For heaven's sake, I broke in. Don't call me a nice man to her. I'm here to look at her throat on the chance that she might have diphtheria and possibly die of it. But that's nothing to her. Look here, I said to the child, we're going to look at your throat. You're old enough to understand what I'm saying. Will you open it now by yourself or shall we have to open it for you?

Not a move. Even her expression hadn't changed. Her breaths however were coming faster and faster. Then the battle began. I had to do it. I had to have a throat culture for her own protection. But first I told the parents that it was entirely up to them. I explained the danger but said that I would not insist on a throat examination so long as they would take the responsibility.

If you don't do what the doctor says you'll have to go to the hospital, the mother admonished her severely.

Oh yeah? I had to smile to myself. After all, I had already fallen in love with the savage brat; the parents were contemptible to me. In the ensuing struggle they grew more and more abject, crushed, exhausted while she surely rose to magnificent heights of insane fury of effort bred of her terror of me.

The father tried his best, and he was a big man but the fact that she was his daughter, his shame at her behavior and his dread of hurting her made him release her just at the critical times when I had almost achieved success, till I wanted to kill him. But his dread also that she might have diphtheria made him tell me to go on, go on though he himself was almost fainting, while the mother moved back and forth behind us raising and lowering her hands in an agony of apprehension.

Put her in front of you on your lap, I ordered, and hold both her wrists.

But as soon as he did the child let out a scream. Don't, you're hurting me. Let go of my hands. Let them go I tell you. Then she shrieked terrifyingly, hysterically. Stop it! Stop it! You're killing me!

Do you think she can stand it, doctor! said the mother.

You get out, said the husband to his wife. Do you want her to die of diphtheria?

Come on now, hold her, I said.

Then I grasped the child's head with my left hand and tried to get the wooden tongue depressor between her teeth. She fought, with clenched teeth, desperately! But now I also had grown furious—at a child. I tried to hold myself down but I couldn't. I know how to expose a throat for inspection. And I did my best. When finally I got the wooden spatula behind the last teeth and just the point of it into the mouth cavity, she opened up for an instant but before I could see anything she came down again and gripping the wooden blade between her molars she reduced it to splinters before I could get it out again.

Aren't you ashamed, the mother yelled at her. Aren't you ashamed to act like that in front of the doctor?

Get me a smooth-handled spoon of some sort, I told the mother. We're going through with this. The child's mouth was already bleeding. Her tongue was cut and she was screaming in wild hysterical shrieks. Perhaps I should have desisted and come back in an hour or more. No doubt it would have been better. But I have seen at least two children lying dead in bed of neglect in such cases, and feeling that I must get a diagnosis now or never I went at it again. But the worst of it was that I too had got beyond reason. I could have torn the child apart in my own fury and enjoyed it. It was a pleasure to attack her. My face was burning with it.

The damned little brat must be protected against her own idiocy, one says to one's self at such times. Others must be protected against her. It is a social necessity. And all these things are true. But a blind fury, a feeling of adult shame, bred of a longing for muscular release are the operatives. One goes on to the end.

In a final unreasoning assault I overpowered the child's neck and jaws. I forced the heavy silver spoon back of her teeth and down her throat till she gagged. And there it was—both tonsils covered with membrane. She had fought valiantly to keep me from knowing her secret. She had been hiding that sore throat for three days at least and lying to her parents in order to escape just such an outcome as this.

Now truly she was furious. She had been on the defensive before but now she attacked. Tried to get off her father's lap and fly at me while tears of defeat blinded her eyes.

QUESTIONS AND CONSIDERATIONS

Tortilla Flat

1. Pilon is a drunk, a womanizer, a con man, and a thief. What saves him from being as despicable as these traits would suggest about their owner? How can it be said that "Pilon was an honest man"? Or is this statement meant ironically? The preface states that "Danny's friends were not unlike the knights of [the Round Table]." Do you detect any knightly qualities in Pilon or in Danny himself? Consider Pilon's attempts to make it all the way to Danny's house to pay the rent, and the temptations which befall him when he tries.

2. Basically what conflicting forces are at work in Pilon to make such a simple and honest gesture as paying the rent a mighty struggle? (Obviously, they are not just goodness versus evil.)

3. It could be observed that Steinbeck's characterizations are tongue-in-cheek; that he is satirizing serious matters. Is Pilon merely a caricature, romanticized and white-washed past all possibility of being human? If not, what saves him from this? What about him is recognizable, even familiar?

4. Pilon's dual nature is most specifically captured in these lines: "That not too perfect Pilon, who plotted and fought, who drank and cursed, trudged slowly on; but a wistful and shining Pilon went up to the sea gulls where they bathed on sensitive wings in the evening. That Pilon was beautiful, and his thoughts were unstained with selfishness and lust." Look for other lines that deal with the two sides of Pilon. Do they resemble the Dionysian–Apollonian sides of human nature? Are they depicted as being separate, entirely distinct?

Iroquois Creation Myth

1. This selection offers a vivid insight into why and what myths are. It is a remarkably thorough and penetrating study of human nature. The adversary forces of life are here metaphorized as the twin creators, a common mythological motif. They begin quarreling while still in the womb, demonstrating that it is not our acquired education in life that makes us perverse, dualistic, but our very natures. Why is it that the two brothers are not called right and wrong, but rather "the straight mind and the crooked mind"? Is there any wisdom in acknowledging that "the two ways of the world" are indeed "in all people," rather than viewing unfavorable behavior as being unnatural and having no connection with favorable behavior? How does our society view the two ways? Explain how the mythical motif of the twins is an attempt to explain and reconcile what might otherwise be maddening opposites.

2. How could the world the twins made be "balanced and orderly"? What great truth lies in this seeming paradox?

3. Why is it necessary that one brother vanquish the other? The gaming and dueling form the most fascinating part of this tale. What condition is necessary for the right-handed brother to win? What does this reveal about human nature? Does the right-handed brother really win? Explain the following lines:
   (a) " . . . the deep mind of each entered into the other."
   (b) "And the left-handed twin died, but he died and he didn't die."

4. What kinds of dualities are depicted in this tale? How many of them are important aspects of the human condition today? (Are there any which are not?)

Holy Sonnet 14

1. This sonnet first appeared nearly 350 years ago. Its author, John Donne, was not only a renowned poet but the most distinguished preacher of his time. Here, he examines a profound paradox which will always be with us: the devout individual, no matter how he strives to deserve God's perfect love, knows that he must always fail. In the contest of flesh versus spirit, temptation versus faith, the latter can never wholly triumph.

    Perhaps because of the paradoxical nature of his theme, Donne uses paradox as a poetic device. One example is, "Except you enthrall me [I] never shall be free." Find others. What does each have to do with the weaknesses and contrary forces that the speaker finds within himself? Together, how do they establish the impossibility of reaching the Judeo-Christian ideal: to rid one's self of sin and to lead an unblemished, God-centered life?

2. In the first eight lines what does the speaker compare himself to? Specifically, how does he develop the metaphor?

3. What does Donne mean by "reason"? Why is it weak, untrue?

4. This is not a conventionally pious poem. It is a gutty, passionate expression of the paradox mentioned above. Consider and discuss the many ways that society attempts to tell us that the good, devout life is an easy pursuit and that such virtues as honesty, selflessness, humility, piety, industry, chastity, etc., are not at all paradoxical.

The Use of Force

1. This is not a simple tale about a day in the life of a doctor. The narrator in this taut little story is outwardly a calm, level-headed professional with a humane concern about people's suffering. Yet in a matter of minutes a small child uncovers another side of him— an element of character that rages somewhere inside everyone. How, generally, can this element be described?

2. What suggestions about the narrator's dual nature emerge relatively early in the story?

3. Who, Mathilda or the doctor, acts more savagely, more unreasonably? Support your point of view closely.

4. The doctor finally forces the child's jaws apart, but is it this necessary act to which the title refers? Or is it another kind of force?

5. How exactly does the author depict the alteration in the doctor's

character? Refer to specific lines. Would this depiction have been possible without the first-person narration?

6. The child's parents act typically, with concern, alarm, and an anxious desire to help. Why is it then that the narrator says about one or both of them: ". . . I ground my teeth in disgust"; ". . . the parents were contemptible to me"; ". . . I wanted to kill him"?

7. Account for Mathilda's fiercely stubborn resistance to the doctor. Was it based on more than an urgent fear about hiding her illness?

8. That side of the doctor's nature revealed in this story seeks outward expression in many ways. What approved outlets does society afford it, and in what kinds of circumstances is its expression condemned?

3

FERTILITY:
CYCLES OF NATURE

•

...I had seen birth and death,
But had thought they were different....
—T. S. Eliot, *Journey of the Magi*

The religions of Apollo and Dionysus eventually died out, seemingly because each became an increasingly narrow end in itself. The Apollonian cult grew brittle, so self-consciously rational that it lost its religious appeal; whereas the cult of Dionysus had earlier waned, probably because it became so thoroughly physical in its practices that the religious aspects became blurred or secondary.

In Dionysus, however, lay the early foreshadowings of the coming of Christ. At the center of Dionysian worship was the theme of fertility—the soil–song of planting, growth, fullness, and harvest, which is reflected not only in the vineyards and the fields but in all of life. It was Orpheus, son of Apollo and divine singer, who came to symbolize this ancient religious theme, but whose cult drew away from the physical emphasis represented by Dionysus and incorporated into their pagan creed a mystical, spiritual element.

Orpheus, you recall, failed in his attempt to bring Eurydice back from Hades. After wandering disconsolately for a while, he was torn to pieces by a pack of Thracian women, perhaps because he had neglected to pay proper homage to Dionysus, or because he had ignored their advances. His resurrection is uncertain. One story is that his head floated to sea and eventually lodged in a rock, where it became an oracle. At any rate, a shrine was erected in his name and the Orphic cult which developed around it celebrated a mystical death and resurrection rite. The resemblances between Orpheus and Christ are perhaps less obvious now than they were then, when society was more directly and openly involved with its mythology. In the dead, dismembered, and resurrected Orpheus resided the promise of a rebirth. Even though Orphism reached back to Dionysus in emphasizing the former's cyclical, earth-centered aspects, it also looked ahead toward Christ in its celebration of the divine elevation of this theme, wherein the god-king transcends the birth-death cycle and reaches the final state of Heaven.

Orpheus was a demigod; that is, one of his parents was a god, the other a mortal. He, like Christ, was involved with nature in a loving way, which held great appeal for pastoral and agrarian peoples. His music and singing lulled savage beasts and even charmed trees, rivers, and rocks. A pre-Christian Roman mosaic depicting Orpheus charming a field full of animals bears a striking resemblance to a sixth-century A.D. mosaic depicting Christ as the good shepherd.

As quoted in *Man and His Symbols*, edited by C. G. Jung, a Swiss author, Linda Fierz-David, observed about a fresco at Pompeii that depicts an Orphic rite: "Everything becomes light and all creatures are appeased when the mediator, in the act of worshipping, represents the light of nature. Orpheus is the embodiment of devotion and piety; he symbolizes the religious attitude that solves all conflicts, since thereby the whole soul is turned toward that which lies on the other side of all conflict. . . . And as he does this, he is truly Orpheus; that is, a good shepherd, his primitive embodiment. . . ."

Many pagan rites, some of them Orphic, were incorporated into early Christian practices and beliefs. A few of them survive to this day in one form or the other. Joseph Henderson in *Man and His Symbols* comments on several of them:

> At Christmas we may express our inner feeling for the mythological birth of a semidivine child, even though we may not believe in the doctrine of the virgin birth of Christ or have any kind of conscious religious faith. Unknowingly, we have fallen in with the symbolism of rebirth. This is a relic of an immensely older solstice festival, which carries the hope that the fading winter landscape of the northern hemisphere will be renewed. For all our sophistication we find satisfaction in this symbolic festival, just as we join with our children at Easter in the pleasant ritual of Easter eggs and Easter rabbits.

> But do we understand what we do, or see the connection between the story of Christ's birth, death, and resurrection and the folk symbolism of Easter? Usually we do not even care to consider such things intellectually.

> Yet they complement each other. Christ's crucifixion on Good Friday seems at first sight to belong to the same pat-

tern of fertility symbolism that one finds in the rituals of such other saviors as Osiris, Tammuz, Orpheus, and Balder. They too were of divine or semidivine birth; they flourished, were killed, and were reborn. They belonged, in fact, to cyclic religions in which the death and rebirth of the god-king was an eternally recurring myth.

Expressions of fertility (or renewal) motifs surround us. Usually they are joyous, even Dionysian, although they may be Christian in context or without any apparent religious basis. Mardi Gras is one obvious example of the former in its wild commemoration of Shrove Tuesday. May Day is an age-old celebration of the return of spring and with it the renewal of the earth's fertility. The German Oktoberfest is marked by beer drinking but is not so much a tribute to beer as a celebration of the harvest. Thanksgiving is a blander version of the same thing. The festivities accompanying New Year include both drinking and feasting, obviously Dionysian in nature and intent. The idea of years and seasons themselves, so much a part of our lives as to have become mere practical demarcations of time, have mythological origins directly connected with fertility cycles.

Literature has given eloquent if sometimes unconscious expression to the renewal motifs found in all mythology. Following are several examples, widely different in style, origin, and subject. Each, however, is reflective of some kind of cyclical rebirth or regeneration. The first is a metaphorical call to American Plains Indians to resist the white man. It describes a vision experienced by a medicine man while in a religious trance. From it grew the Ghost Dance religion, which was quickly stamped out by United States military forces.

The Ghost Dance

Wovoka (1856?—1932), the Paiute Messiah

All Indians must dance, everywhere, keep on dancing. Pretty soon in next spring Great Spirit come. He bring back all game of every kind. The game be thick everywhere. All dead Indians come back and live again. They all be strong just like young men, be young again. Old blind Indian see again and get young and have fine time. When Great Spirit comes this way, then all the Indians go to mountains, high up away from whites. Whites can't hurt Indians then. Then while Indians way up high, big flood comes like water and all white people die, get drowned. After that, water go way and then nobody but Indians everywhere and game all kinds thick. Then medicine man tell Indians to send word to all Indians to keep up dancing and the good time will come. Indians who don't dance, who don't believe in this word, will grow little, just about a foot high, and stay that way. Some of them will be turned into wood and be burned in fire.

La Guerre°

E. E. Cummings (1894–1962)

I

the bigness of cannon
is skilful,

but i have seen
death's clever enormous voice
which hides in a fragility   5
of poppies. . . .

i say that sometimes
on these long talkative animals
are laid fists of huger silence.

I have seen all the silence   10
filled with vivid noiseless boys

at Roupy
i have seen
between barrages,

the night utter ripe unspeaking girls.   15

II

O sweet spontaneous
earth how often have
the
doting

         fingers of   20
prurient philosophers pinched

°*La Guerre*: War

and
poked

thee
, has the naughty thumb   25
of science prodded
thy

    beauty   . how
often have religions taken
thee upon their scraggy knees   30
squeezing and

buffeting thee that thou mightest conceive
gods
     (but
true   35

to the incomparable
couch of death thy
rhythmic
lover

     thou answerest   40

them only with

      spring)

PHILOMELA

Matthew Arnold (1822–1888)

Hark! ah, the nightingale—
The tawny-throated!
Hark, from that moonlit cedar what a burst!
What triumph! hark!—what pain!

O wanderer from a Grecian shore,   5
Still, after many years, in distant lands,
Still nourishing in thy bewildered brain
That wild, unquenched, deep-sunken, old-world
    pain—
Say, will it never heal?
And can this fragrant lawn   10

With its cool trees, and night,
And the sweet, tranquil Thames,
And moonshine, and the dew,
To thy racked heart and brain
Afford no balm?   15

Dost thou tonight behold,
Here, through the moonlight on this English grass,
The unfriendly palace in the Thracian° wild?
Dost thou again peruse
With hot cheeks and seared eyes   20
The too clear web, and thy dumb sister's shame?
Dost thou once more assay
Thy flight, and feel come over thee,
Poor fugitive, the feathery change
Once more, and once more seem to make resound   25
With love and hate, triumph and agony,
Lone Daulis°, and high Cephissian° vale?

Listen, Eugenia°—
How thick the bursts come crowding through the
        leaves!
Again—thou hearest?   30
Eternal passion!
Eternal pain!

ODE TO A NIGHTINGALE
John Keats (1795–1821)

I

My heart aches, and a drowsy numbness pains
    My sense, as though of hemlock° I had drunk,
Or emptied some dull opiate to the drains
    One minute past, and Lethe-wards° had sunk:

°*Thracian*: the region of Thrace is now a part of both Turkey and
    Greece.
°*Daulis*: a town in Thrace
°*Cephissian*: a valley of the river Cephissus in Thrace
°*Eugenia*: the speaker's companion
°*hemlock*: a poison; the kind Socrates drank
°*Lethe-wards*: Lethe was the river of forgetfulness in Hades; hence,
    into oblivion

'Tis not through envy of thy happy lot,   5
    But being too happy in thine happiness,—
        That thou, light-wingèd Dryad° of the
            trees,
        In some melodious plot
Of beechen green, and shadows numberless,
        Singest of summer in full-throated ease.   10

II

O, for a draught of vintage!° that hath been
    Cooled a long age in the deep-delvèd earth,
Tasting of Flora° and the country green,
        Dance, and Provençal° song, and sunburnt
            mirth!
O, for a beaker full of the warm South,   15
    Full of the true, the blushful Hippocrene,°
        With beaded bubbles winking at the brim,
           And purple-stainèd mouth;
    That I might drink, and leave the world
           unseen,
        And with thee fade away into the forest
           dim: 20

III

Fade far away, dissolve, and quite forget
    What thou among the leaves hast never known,
The weariness, the fever, and the fret
        Here, where men sit and hear each other
           groan;
Where palsy shakes a few, sad, last gray hairs,   25
        Where youth grows pale, and specter-thin, and
           dies;
        Where but to think is to be full of sorrow
        And leaden-eyed despairs,
    Where Beauty cannot keep her lustrous eyes,
        Or new Love pine at them beyond
           tomorrow.   30

°*Dryad*: wood nymph
°*vintage*: wine
°*Flora*: spring; Flora was the goddess of flowers
°*Provençal*: The troubadours first came from Provence, in southern
    France
°*Hippocrene*: the Muses' fountain, source of poetic inspiration

IV

Away! away! for I will fly to thee,
   Not charioted by Bacchus° and his pards,°
But on the viewless° wings of Poesy,
   Though the dull brain perplexes and retards:
Already with thee! tender is the night,   35
And haply the Queen-Moon is on her throne,
   Clustered around by all her starry Fays;
      But here there is no light,
Save what from heaven is with the breezes blown
   Through verdurous glooms and winding
      mossy ways.   40

V

I cannot see what flowers are at my feet,
   Nor what soft incense hangs upon the boughs,
But, in embalmèd° darkness, guess each sweet
   Wherewith the seasonable month endows
The grass, the thicket, and the fruit-tree wild;   45
   White hawthorn, and the pastoral eglantine;
      Fast fading violets covered up in leaves;
      And mid-May's eldest child,
The coming musk-rose, full of dewy wine,
      The murmurous haunt of flies on summer
      eves.   50

VI

Darkling I listen; and, for many a time
   I have been half in love with easeful Death,
Called him soft names in many a musèd rhyme,
   To take into the air my quiet breath;
Now more than ever seems it rich to die,   55
   To cease upon the midnight with no pain,
      While thou art pouring forth thy soul
         abroad
      In such an ecstasy!
Still wouldst thou sing, and I have ears in
      vain—
      To thy high requiem become a sod.   60

°*Bacchus*: god of wine. *Pards*: leopards, who drew Bacchus's chariot
°*viewless*: invisible
°*embalmèd*: fragrant

VII

Thou wast not born for death, immortal Bird!
    No hungry generations tread thee down;
The voice I hear this passing night was heard
    In ancient days by emperor and clown:
Perhaps the self-same song that found a path   65
    Through the sad heart of Ruth,° when, sick for
        home,
        She stood in tears amid the alien corn,°
    The same that oft-times hath
Charmed magic casements, opening on the
        foam
    Of perilous seas, in faery lands forlorn.   70

VIII

Forlorn! the very word is like a bell
    To toll me back from thee to my sole self!
Adieu! the fancy° cannot cheat so well
    As she is famed to do, deceiving elf.
Adieu! adieu! thy plaintive anthem fades   75
    Past the near meadows, over the still stream,
        Up the hillside; and now 'tis buried deep
    In the next valley glades:
Was it a vision, or a waking dream?
    Fled is that music:—Do I wake or sleep?   80

THE THREE STRANGERS

Thomas Hardy (1840–1928)

Among the few features of agricultural England which
retain an appearance but little modified by the lapse of centuries
may be reckoned the high, grassy and furzy downs, coombs, or ewe-
leases, as they are indifferently called, that fill a large area of certain counties in the south and southwest. If any mark of human
occupation is met with hereon, it usually takes the form of the solitary cottage of some shepherd.

°*Ruth*: the girl of Moab whose loyalty in accompanying her Hebrew mother-
    in-law into a wholly alien land and culture is recounted in the Old
    Testament Book of Ruth
°*corn*: grain
°*fancy*: imagination

Fifty years ago such a lonely cottage stood on such a down, and may possibly be standing there now. In spite of its loneliness, however, the spot, by actual measurement, was not more than five miles from a county-town. Yet that affected it little. Five miles of irregular upland, during the long inimical seasons, with their sleets, snows, rains, and mists, afford withdrawing space enough to isolate a Timon or a Nebuchadnezzar; much less, in fair weather, to please that less repellent tribe, the poets, philosophers, artists, and others who "conceive and meditate of pleasant things."

Some old earthen camp or barrow, some clump of trees, at least some starved fragment of ancient hedge is usually taken advantage of in the erection of these forlorn dwellings. But, in the present case, such a kind of shelter had been disregarded. Higher Crowstairs, as the house was called, stood quite detached and undefended. The only reason for its precise situation seemed to be the crossing of two footpaths at right angles hard by, which may have crossed there and thus for a good five hundred years. Hence the house was exposed to the elements on all sides. But, though the wind up here blew unmistakably when it did blow, and the rain hit hard whenever it fell, the various weathers of the winter season were not quite so formidable on the coomb as they were imagined to be by dwellers on low ground. The raw rimes were not so pernicious as in the hollows, and the frosts were scarcely so severe. When the shepherd and his family who tenanted the house were pitied for their sufferings from the exposure, they said that upon the whole they were less inconvenienced by "wuzzes and flames" (hoarses and phlegms) than when they had lived by the stream of a snug neighboring valley.

The night of March 28, 182– was precisely one of the nights that were wont to call forth these expressions of commiseration. The level rainstorm smote walls, slopes, and hedges like the clothyard shafts of Senlac and Crecy. Such sheep and outdoor animals as had no shelter stood with their buttocks to the winds; while the tails of little birds trying to roost on some scraggy thorn were blown inside-out like umbrellas. The gable-end of the cottage was stained with wet, and the eavesdroppings flapped against the wall. Yet never was commiseration for the shepherd more misplaced. For that cheerful rustic was entertaining a large party in glorification of the christening of his second girl.

The guests had arrived before the rain began to fall, and they were all now assembled in the chief or living room of the dwelling. A glance into the apartment at eight o'clock on this eventful evening would have resulted in the opinion that it was as cozy and comfortable a nook as could be wished for in boisterous

weather. The calling of its inhabitant was proclaimed by a number
of highly polished sheep-crooks without stems that were hung orna-
mentally over the fireplace, the curl of each shining crook varying
from the antiquated type engraved in the patriarchal pictures of old
family Bibles to the most approved fashion of the last local sheep-
fair. The room was lighted by half-a-dozen candles, having wicks
only a trifle smaller than the grease which enveloped them, in candlesticks that were never used but at high-days, holy-days, and
family feasts. The lights were scattered about the room, two of
them standing on the chimney-piece. This position of candles was in
itself significant. Candles on the chimney-piece always meant a
party.

On the hearth, in front of a back-brand to give substance,
blazed a fire of thorns, that crackled "like the laughter of the fool."

Nineteen persons were gathered here. Of these, five
women, wearing gowns of various bright hues, sat in chairs along
the wall; girls shy and not shy filled the window-bench; four men,
including Charley Jake the hedge-carpenter, Elijah New the parish-clerk, and John Pitcher, a neighboring dairyman, the shepherd's
father-in-law, lolled in the settle; a young man and maid, who were
blushing over tentative *pourparlers*° on a life-companionship, sat
beneath the corner-cupboard; and an elderly engaged man of fifty
or upward moved restlessly about from spots where his betrothed
was not to the spot where she was. Enjoyment was pretty general,
and so much the more prevailed in being unhampered by conventional restrictions. Absolute confidence in each other's good opinion
begat perfect ease, while the finishing stroke of manner, amounting
to a truly princely serenity, was lent to the majority by the absence
of any expression or trait denoting that they wished to get on in the
world, enlarge their minds, or do any eclipsing thing whatever—
which nowadays so generally nips the bloom and *bonhomie* of all
except the two extremes of the social scale.

Shepherd Fennel had married well, his wife being a dairyman's daughter from a vale at a distance, who brought fifty guineas in her pocket—and kept them there, till they should be required
for ministering to the needs of a coming family. This frugal woman
had been somewhat exercised as to the character that should be
given to the gathering. A sit-still party had its advantages; but an
undisturbed position of ease in chairs and settles was apt to lead on
the men to such an unconscionable deal of toping that they would
sometimes fairly drink the house dry. A dancing party was the
alternative; but this, while avoiding the foregoing objection on the

---

°*pourparlers*: preliminary talks

score of good drink, had a counterbalancing disadvantage in the matter of good victuals, the ravenous appetites engendered by the exercise causing immense havoc in the buttery. Shepherdess Fennel fell back upon the intermediate plan of mingling short dances with short periods of talk and singing, so as to hinder any ungovernable rage in either. But this scheme was entirely confined to her own gentle mind: the shepherd himself was in the mood to exhibit the most reckless phases of hospitality.

The fiddler was a boy of those parts, about twelve years of age, who had a wonderful dexterity in jigs and reels, though his fingers were so small and short as to necessitate a constant shifting for the high notes, from which he scrambled back to the first position with sounds not of unmixed purity of tone. At seven the shrill tweedle-dee of this youngster had begun, accompanied by a booming ground-bass from Elijah New, the parish-clerk, who had thoughtfully brought with him his favorite musical instrument, the serpent. Dancing was instantaneous, Mrs. Fennel privately enjoining the players on no account to let the dance exceed the length of a quarter of an hour.

But Elijah and the boy, in the excitement of their position, quite forgot the injunction. Moreover, Oliver Giles, a man of seventeen, one of the dancers, who was enamored of his partner, a fair girl of thirty-three rolling years, had recklessly handed a new crown-piece to the musicians, as a bribe to keep going as long as they had muscle and wind. Mrs. Fennel, seeing the steam begin to generate on the countenances of her guests, crossed over and touched the fiddler's elbow and put her hand on the serpent's mouth. But they took no notice, and fearing she might lose her character of genial hostess if she were to interfere too markedly, she retired and sat down helpless. And so the dance whizzed on with cumulative fury, the performers moving in their planet-like courses, direct and retrograde, from apogee to perigee, till the hand of the well-kicked clock at the bottom of the room had traveled over the circumference of an hour.

While these cheerful events were in course of enactment within Fennel's pastoral dwelling, an incident having considerable bearing on the party had occurred in the gloomy night without. Mrs. Fennel's concern about the growing fierceness of the dance corresponded in point of time with the ascent of a human figure to the solitary hill of Higher Crowstairs from the direction of the distant town. This personage strode on through the rain without a pause, following the little-worn path which, further on in its course, skirted the shepherd's cottage.

It was nearly the time of full moon, and on this account,

though the sky was lined with a uniform sheet of dripping cloud, ordinary objects out of doors were readily visible. The sad wan light revealed the lonely pedestrian to be a man of supple frame; his gait suggested that he had somewhat passed the period of perfect and instinctive agility, though not so far as to be otherwise than rapid of motion when occasion required. At a rough guess, he might have been about forty years of age. He appeared tall, but a recruiting sergeant, or other person accustomed to the judging of men's heights by the eye, would have discerned that this was chiefly owing to his gauntness, and that he was not more than five-feet-eight or nine.

Notwithstanding the regularity of his tread, there was caution in it, as in that of one who mentally feels his way; and despite the fact that it was not a black coat nor a dark garment of any sort that he wore, there was something about him which suggested that he naturally belonged to the black-coated tribes of men. His clothes were of fustian, and his boots hobnailed, yet in his progress he showed not the mud-accustomed bearing of hobnailed and fustianed peasantry.

By the time that he had arrived abreast of the shepherd's premises the rain came down, or rather came along, with yet more determined violence. The outskirts of the little settlement partially broke the force of wind and rain, and this induced him to stand still. The most salient of the shepherd's domestic erections was an empty sty at the forward corner of his hedgeless garden, for in these latitudes the principle of masking the homelier features of your establishment by a conventional frontage was unknown. The traveler's eye was attracted to this small building by the pallid shine of the wet slates that covered it. He turned aside, and, finding it empty, stood under the pent-roof for shelter.

While he stood, the boom of the serpent within the adjacent house, and the lesser strains of the fiddler, reached the spot as an accompaniment to the surging hiss of the flying rain on the sod, its louder beating on the cabbage-leaves of the garden, on the eight or ten beehives just discernible by the path, and its dripping from the eaves into a row of buckets and pans that had been placed under the walls of the cottage. For at Higher Crowstairs, as at all such elevated domiciles, the grand difficulty of housekeeping was an insufficiency of water; and a casual rainfall was utilized by turning out, as catchers, every utensil that the house contained. Some queer stories might be told of the contrivances for economy in suds and dishwaters that are absolutely necessitated in upland habitations during the droughts of summer. But at this season there were no such exigencies; a mere acceptance of what the skies bestowed was sufficient for an abundant store.

At last the notes of the serpent ceased and the house was silent. This cessation of activity aroused the solitary pedestrian from the reverie into which he had lapsed, and, emerging from the shed, with an apparently new intention, he walked up the path to the house-door. Arrived here, his first act was to kneel down on a large stone beside the row of vessels, and to drink a copious draught from one of them. Having quenched his thirst he rose and lifted his hand to knock, but paused with his eye upon the panel. Since the dark surface of the wood revealed absolutely nothing, it was evident that he must be mentally looking through the door, as if he wished to measure thereby all the possibilities that a house of this sort might include, and how they might bear upon the question of his entry.

In his indecision he turned and surveyed the scene around. Not a soul was anywhere visible. The garden-path stretched downward from his feet, gleaming like the track of a snail; the roof of the little well (mostly dry), the well-cover, the top rail of the garden-gate, were varnished with same dull liquid gaze; while, far away in the vale, a faint whiteness of more than usual extent showed that the rivers were high in the meads. Beyond all this winked a few bleared lamplights through the beating drops—lights that denoted the situation of the county-town from which he had appeared to come. The absence of all notes of life in that direction seemed to clinch his intentions, and he knocked at the door.

Within, a desultory chat had taken the place of movement and musical sound. The hedge-carpenter was suggesting a song to the company, which nobody just then was inclined to undertake, so that the knock afforded a not unwelcome diversion.

"Walk in!" said the shepherd promptly.

The latch clicked upward, and out of the night our pedestrian appeared upon the doormat. The shepherd arose, snuffed two of the nearest candles, and turned to look at him.

Their light disclosed that the stranger was dark in complexion and not unprepossessing as to feature. His hat, which for a moment he did not remove, hung low over his eyes, without concealing that they were large, open, and determined, moving with a flash rather than a glance round the room. He seemed pleased with his survey, and, baring his shaggy head, said, in a rich deep voice, "The rain is so heavy, friends, that I ask leave to come in and rest awhile."

"To be sure, stranger," said the shepherd. "And faith, you've been lucky in choosing your time, for we are having a bit of a fling for a glad cause—though, to be sure, a man could hardly wish that glad cause to happen more than once a year."

"Nor less," spoke up a woman. "For 'tis best to get your

family over and done with, as soon as you can, so as to be all the earlier out of the fag o't."

"And what may be this glad cause?" asked the stranger.

"A birth and christening," said the shepherd.

The stranger hoped his host might not be made unhappy, either by too many or too few of such episodes, and being invited by a gesture to a pull at the mug, he readily acquiesced. His manner, which, before entering, had been so dubious, was now altogether that of a careless and candid man.

"Late to be traipsing athwart this coomb—hey?" said the engaged man of fifty.

"Late it is, master, as you say—I'll take a seat in the chimney-corner, if you have nothing to urge against it, ma'am; for I am a little moist on the side that was next the rain."

Mrs. Shepherd Fennel assented, and made room for the self-invited comer, who, having got completely inside the chimney-corner, stretched out his legs and his arms with the expansiveness of a person quite at home.

"Yes, I am rather cracked in the vamp," he said freely, seeing that the eyes of the shepherd's wife fell upon his boots, "and I am not well fitted either. I have had some rough times lately, and have been forced to pick up what I can get in the way of wearing, but I must find a suit better fit for working-days when I reach home."

"One of hereabouts?" she inquired.

"Not quite that—further up the country."

"I thought so. And so be I; and by your tongue you come from my neighborhood."

"But you would hardly have heard of me," he said quickly. "My time would be long before yours, ma'am, you see."

This testimony to the youthfulness of his hostess had the effect of stopping her cross-examination.

"There is only one thing more wanted to make me happy," continued the new-comer. "And that is a little baccy, which I am sorry to say I am out of."

"I'll fill your pipe," said the shepherd.

"I must ask you to lend me a pipe likewise."

"A smoke, and no pipe about 'ee?"

"I have dropped it somewhere on the road."

The shepherd filled and handed him a new clay pipe, saying, as he did so, "Hand me your baccy-box—I'll fill that too, now I am about it."

The man went through the movement of searching his pockets.

"Lost that too?" said his entertainer, with some surprise.

"I am afraid so," said the man with some confusion. "Give it to me in a screw of paper." Lighting his pipe at the candle with a suction that drew the whole flame into the bowl, he re-settled himself in the corner and bent his looks upon the faint steam from his damp legs, as if he wished to say no more.

Meanwhile the general body of guests had been taking little notice of this visitor by reason of an absorbing discussion in which they were engaged with the band about a tune for the next dance. The matter being settled, they were about to stand up when an interruption came in the shape of another knock at the door.

At sound of the same the man in the chimney-corner took up the poker and began stirring the brands as if doing it thoroughly were the one aim of his existence; and a second time the shepherd said, "Walk in!" In a moment another man stood upon the straw-woven doormat. He too was a stranger.

This individual was one of a type radically different from the first. There was more of the commonplace in his manner, and a certain jovial cosmopolitanism sat upon his features. He was several years older than the first arrival, his hair being slightly frosted, his eyebrows bristly, and his whiskers cut back from his cheeks. His face was rather full and flabby, and yet it was not altogether a face without power. A few grog-blossoms marked the neighborhood of his nose. He flung back his long drab greatcoat, revealing that beneath it he wore a suit of cinder-gray shade throughout, large heavy seals, of some metal or other that would take a polish, dangling from his fob as his only personal ornament. Shaking the waterdrops from his low-crowned glazed hat, he said, "I must ask for a few minutes' shelter, comrades, or I shall be wetted to my skin before I get to Casterbridge."

"Make yourself at home, master," said the shepherd, perhaps a trifle less heartily than on the first occasion. Not that Fennel had the least tinge of niggardliness in his composition; but the room was far from large, spare chairs were not numerous, and damp companions were not altogether desirable at close quarters for the women and girls in their bright-colored gowns.

However, the second comer, after taking off his greatcoat, and hanging his hat on a nail in one of the ceiling-beams as if he had been specially invited to put it there, advanced and sat down at the table. This had been pushed so closely into the chimney-corner, to give all available room to the dancers, that its inner edge grazed the elbow of the man who had ensconced himself by the fire; and thus the two strangers were brought into close companionship. They nodded to each other by way of breaking the ice of unacquaintance, and the first stranger handed his neighbor the family mug—a huge vessel of brown ware, having its upper edge worn away like a threshold by the rub of whole generations of thirsty lips that had gone the way of all flesh, and bearing the following inscription burnt upon its rotound side in yellow letters:

THERE IS NO FUN

UNTILL I CUM

The other man, nothing loth, raised the mug to his lips, and drank on, and on, and on—till a curious blueness overspread the countenance of the shepherd's wife, who had regarded with no little surprise the first stranger's free offer to the second of what did not belong to him to dispense.

"I knew it!" said the toper to the shepherd with much satisfaction. "When I walked up your garden before coming in, and saw the hives all of a row, I said to myself, 'Where there's bees there's honey, and where there's honey there's mead.' But mead of such a truly comfortable sort as this I really didn't expect to meet in my older days." He took yet another pull at the mug, till it assumed an ominous elevation.

"Glad you enjoy it!" said the shepherd warmly.

"It is goodish mead," assented Mrs. Fennel, with an absence of enthusiasm which seemed to say that it was possible to buy praise for one's cellar at too heavy a price. "It is trouble enough to make—and really I hardly think we shall make any more. For honey sells well, and we ourselves can make shift with a drop o' small mead and metheglin for common use from the comb-washings."

"O, but you'll never have the heart!" reproachfully cried the stranger in cinder-gray, after taking up the mug a third time and setting it down empty. "I love mead, when 'tis old like this, as I love to go to church o' Sundays, or to relieve the needy any day of the week."

"Ha, ha, ha!" said the man in the chimney-corner, who, in spite of the taciturnity induced by the pipe of tobacco, could not or would not refrain from this slight testimony to his comrade's humor.

Now the old mead of those days, brewed of the purest first year or maiden honey, four pounds to the gallon—with its due complement of white of eggs, cinnamon, ginger, cloves, mace, rosemary, yeast, and processes of working, bottling and cellaring— tasted remarkably strong; but it did not taste so strong as it actually was. Hence, presently, the stranger in cinder-gray at the table, moved by its creeping influence, unbuttoned his waistcoat, threw himself back in his chair, spread his legs, and made his presence felt in various ways.

"Well, well, as I say," he resumed, "I am going to Casterbridge, and to Casterbridge I must go. I should have been almost there by this time; but the rain drove me into your dwelling, and I'm not sorry for it."

"You don't live in Casterbridge?" said the shepherd.

"Not as yet; though I shortly mean to move there."

"Going to set up in trade, perhaps?"

"No, no," said the shepherd's wife. "It is easy to see that the gentleman is rich, and don't want to work at anything."

The cinder-gray stranger paused, as if to consider whether he would accept that definition of himself. He presently rejected it by answering, "Rich is not quite the word for me, dame. I do work, and I must work. And even if I only get to Casterbridge by midnight I must begin work there at eight tomorrow morning. Yes, het or wet, blow or snow, famine or sword, my day's work tomorrow must be done."

"Poor man! Then, in spite o' seeming, you be worse off than we?" replied the shepherd's wife.

"'Tis the nature of my trade, men and maidens. 'Tis the nature of my trade more than my poverty. . . . But really and truly I must up and off, or I shan't get a lodging in the town." However, the speaker did not move, and directly added, "There's time for one more draught of friendship before I go; and I'd perform it at once if the mug were not dry."

"Here's a mug o' small," said Mrs. Fennel. "Small, we call it, though to be sure 'tis only the first wash o' the combs."

"No," said the stranger disdainfully. "I won't spoil your first kindness by partaking o' your second."

"Certainly not," broke in Fennel. "We don't increase and multiply every day, and I'll fill the mug again." He went away to the dark place under the stairs where the barrel stood. The shepherdess followed him.

"Why should you do this?" she said reproachfully, as soon as they were alone. "He's emptied it once, though it held enough for ten people; and now he's not contented wi' the small, but must needs call for more o' the strong! And a stranger unbeknown to any of us. For my part, I don't like the look o' the man at all."

"But he's in the house, my honey, and 'tis a wet night, and a christening. Daze it, what's a cup of mead more or less? There'll be plenty more next bee-burning."

"Very well—this time, then," she answered, looking wistfully at the barrel. "But what is the man's calling, and where is he one of, that he should come in and join us like this?"

"I don't know. I'll ask him again."

The catastrophe of having the mug drained dry at one pull by the stranger in cinder-gray was effectually guarded against this time by Mrs. Fennel. She poured out his allowance in a small cup, keeping the large one at a discreet distance from him. When he had tossed off his portion the shepherd renewed his inquiry about the stranger's occupation.

The latter did not immediately reply, and the man in the chimney-corner, with sudden demonstrativeness, said, "Anybody may know my trade—I'm a wheelwright."

"A very good trade for these parts," said the shepherd.

"And anybody may know mine—if they've the sense to find it out," said the stranger in cinder-gray.

"You may generally tell what a man is by his claws," observed the hedge-carpenter, looking at his own hands. "My fingers be as full of thorns as an old pincushion is of pins."

The hands of the man in the chimney-corner instinctively sought the shade, and he gazed into the fire as he resumed his pipe. The man at the table took up the hedge-carpenter's remark, and added smartly, "True; but the oddity of my trade is that, instead of setting a mark upon me, it sets a mark upon my customers."

No observation being offered by anybody in elucidation of this enigma, the shepherd's wife once more called for a song. The same obstacles presented themselves as at the former time—one had no voice, another had forgotten the first verse. The stranger at the table, whose soul had now risen to a good working temperature, relieved the difficulty by exclaiming that, to start the company, he would sing himself. Thrusting one thumb into the arm-hole of his waistcoat, he waved the other hand in the air, and, with an extemporizing gaze at the shining sheep-crooks above the mantelpiece, began:

O my trade it is the rarest one,
  Simple shepherds all—
For my customers I tie, and take them up on high,
  And waft 'em to a far countree!

The room was silent when he had finished the verse—with one exception, that of the man in the chimney-corner, who, at the singer's word, "Chorus!" joined him in a deep bass voice of musical relish:

And waft 'em to a far countree!

Oliver Giles, John Pitcher the dairyman, the parish-clerk, the engaged man of fifty, the row of young women against the wall, seemed lost in thought not of the gayest kind. The shepherd looked meditatively on the ground, the shepherdess gazed keenly at the singer, and with some suspicion; she was doubting whether this stranger were merely singing an old song from recollection, or was composing one there and then for the occasion. All were as per-plexed at the obscure revelation as the guests at Belshazzar's Feast, except the man in the chimney-corner, who quietly said, "Second verse, stranger," and smoked on.

The singer thoroughly moistened himself from his lips inwards, and went on with the next stanza as requested:

My tools are but common ones,
                        Simple shepherds all—

My tools are no sight to see:
A little hempen string, and a post whereon to
    swing
            Are implements enough for me!

Shepherd Fennel glanced round. There was no longer any doubt that the stranger was answering his question rhythmically. The guests one and all started back with suppressed exclamations. The young woman engaged to the man of fifty fainted half-way, and would have proceeded, but finding him wanting in alacrity for catching her she sat down trembling.

"O, he's the——" whispered the people in the background, mentioning the name of an ominous public officer. "He's come to do it! 'Tis to be at Casterbridge jail tomorrow—the man for sheep-stealing—the poor clock-maker we heard of, who used to live away at Shottsford and had no work to do—Timothy Summers, whose family were a-starving, and so he went out of Shottsford by the high-road, and took a sheep in open daylight, defying the farmer and the farmer's wife and the farmer's lad, and every man jack among 'em. He" (and they nodded towards the stranger of the deadly trade) "is come from up the country to do it because there's not enough to do in his own county-town, and he's got the place here now our own county man's dead; he's going to live in the same cot-tage under the prison wall."

The stranger in cinder-gray took no notice of this whispered string of observations, but again wetted his lips. Seeing that his friend in the chimney-corner was the only one who reciprocated his joviality in any way, he held out his cup towards that apprecia-tive comrade, who also held out his own. They clinked together, the eyes of the rest of the room hanging upon the singer's actions. He parted his lips for the third verse; but at that moment another knock was audible upon the door. This time the knock was faint and hesitating.

The company seemed scared; the shepherd looked with consternation towards the entrance, and it was with some effort that he resisted his alarmed wife's deprecatory glance, and uttered for the third time the welcoming words, "Walk in!"

The door was gently opened, and another man stood upon the mat. He, like those who had preceded him, was a stranger. This time it was a short, small personage, of fair complexion, and dressed in a decent suit of dark clothes.

"Can you tell me the way to—?" he began: when, gazing round the room to observe the nature of the company amongst whom he had fallen, his eyes lighted on the stranger in cinder-gray. It was just at the instant when the latter, who had thrown his mind into his song with such a will that he scarcely heeded the interrup-tion, silenced all whispers and inquiries by bursting into his third verse.

> Tomorrow is my working day,
> 　　　　Simple shepherds all—
> 　Tomorrow is a working day for me:
> For the farmer's sheep is slain, and the lad who
> 　　did it ta'en,
> 　　　And on his soul may God ha' merc-y!

The stranger in the chimney-corner, waving cups with the singer so heartily that his mead splashed over on the hearth, repeated in his bass voice as before.

> 　　And on his soul may God ha' merc-y!

All this time the third stranger had been standing in the doorway. Finding now that he did not come forward or go on speaking, the guests particularly regarded him. They noticed to their surprise that he stood before them the picture of abject terror—his knees trembling, his hand shaking so violently that the door-latch by which he supported himself rattled audibly: his white lips were parted, and his eyes fixed on the merry officer of justice in the middle of the room. A moment more and he had turned, closed the door, and fled.

"What a man can it be?" said the shepherd.

The rest, between the awfulness of their late discovery and the odd conduct of this third visitor, looked as if they knew not what to think, and said nothing. Instinctively they withdrew further and further from the grim gentleman in their midst, whom some of them seemed to take for the Prince of Darkness himself, till they formed a remote circle, an empty space of floor being left between them and him:

>   ... *circulus, cujus centrum diabolus.*°

The room was so silent—though there were more than twenty people in it—that nothing could be heard but the patter of the rain against the window-shutters, accompanied by the occasional hiss of a stray drop that fell down the chimney into the fire, and the steady puffing of the man in the corner, who had now resumed his pipe of long clay.

The stillness was unexpectedly broken. The distant sound of a gun reverberated through the air—apparently from the direction of the county-town.

"Be jiggered!" cried the stranger who had sung the song, jumping up.

"What does that mean?" asked several.

"A prisoner escaped from the jail—that's what it means."

All listened. The sound was repeated, and none of them spoke but the man in the chimney-corner, who said quietly, "I've often been told that in this county they fire a gun at such times; but I never heard it till now."

"I wonder if it is *my* man?" murmured the personage in cinder-gray.

"Surely it is!" said the shepherd involuntarily. "And surely we've zeed him! That little man who looked in at the door by now, and quivered like a leaf when he zeed ye and heard your song!"

"His teeth chattered, and the breath went out of his body," said the dairyman.

"And his heart seemed to sink within him like a stone," said Oliver Giles.

"And he bolted as if he'd been shot at," said the hedge-carpenter.

°*circulus, cujus centrum diabolus*: Latin for "a circle, the center of which is the devil"

"True—his teeth chattered, and his heart seemed to sink; and he bolted as if he'd been shot at," slowly summed up the man in the chimney-corner.

"I didn't notice it," remarked the hangman.

"We were all a-wondering what made him run off in such a fright," faltered one of the women against the wall, "and now 'tis explained!"

The firing of the alarm-gun went on at intervals, low and sullenly, and their suspicions became a certainty. The sinister gentleman in cinder-gray roused himself. "Is there a constable here?" he asked, in thick tones. "If so, let him step forward."

The engaged man of fifty stepped quavering out from the wall, his betrothed beginning to sob on the back of the chair.

"You are a sworn constable?"

"I be, sir."

"Then pursue the criminal at once, with assistance, and bring him back here. He can't have gone far."

"I will, sir, I will—when I've got my staff. I'll go home and get it, and come sharp here, and start in a body."

"Staff!—never mind your staff; the man'll be gone!"

"But I can't do nothing without my staff—can I, William, and John, and Charles Jake? No; for there's the king's royal crown a painted on en in yaller and gold, and the lion and the unicorn, so as when I raise on up and hit my prisoner, 'tis made a lawful blow thereby. I wouldn't 'tempt to take up a man without my staff—no, not I. If I hadn't the law to gie me courage, why, instead o' my taking up him he might take up me!"

"Now, I'm a king's man myself, and can give you authority enough for this," said the formidable officer in gray. "Now then, all of ye, be ready. Have ye any lanterns?"

"Yes—have ye any lanterns?—I demand it!" said the constable.

"And the rest of you able-bodied—"

"Able-bodied men—yes—the rest of ye!" said the constable.

"Have you some good stout staves and pitchforks—"

"Staves and pitchforks—in the name o' the law! And take 'em in yer hands and go in quest, and do as we in authority tell ye!"

Thus aroused, the men prepared to give chase. The evidence was, indeed, though circumstantial, so convincing, that but little argument was needed to show the shepherd's guests that after what they had seen it would look very much like connivance if they did not instantly pursue the unhappy third stranger who could not as yet have gone more than a few hundred yards over such uneven country.

A shepherd is always well provided with lanterns; and, lighting these hastily, and with hurdle-staves in their hands, they poured out of the door, taking a direction along the crest of the hill, away from the town, the rain having fortunately a little abated.

Disturbed by the noise, or possibly by unpleasant dreams of her baptism, the child who had been christened began to cry heart-brokenly in the room overhead. These notes of grief came down through the chinks of the floor to the ears of the women below, who jumped up one by one, and seemed glad of the excuse to ascend and comfort the baby, for the incidents of the last half-hour greatly oppressed them. Thus in the space of two or three minutes the room on the ground-floor was deserted quite.

But it was not for long. Hardly had the sound of footsteps died away when a man returned round the corner of the house from the direction the pursuers had taken. Peeping in at the door, and seeing nobody there, he entered leisurely. It was the stranger of the chimney-corner, who had gone out with the rest. The motive of his return was shown by his helping himself to a cut piece of skimmer-cake that lay on a ledge beside where he had sat, and which he had apparently forgotten to take with him. He also poured out half a cup more mead from the quantity that remained, ravenously eating and drinking these as he stood. He had not finished when another figure came in just as quietly—his friend in cinder-gray.

"O—you here?" said the latter, smiling. "I thought you had gone to help in the capture." And this speaker also revealed the object of his return by looking solicitously round for the fascinating mug of old mead.

"And I thought you had gone," said the other, continuing his skimmer-cake with some effort.

"Well, on second thoughts, I felt there were enough without me," said the first confidentially, "and such a night as it is, too. Besides, 'tis the business o' the Government to take care of its criminals—not mine."

"True; so it is. And I felt as you did, that there were enough without me."

"I don't want to break my limbs running over the humps and hollows of this wild country."

"Nor I neither, between you and me."

"These shepherd-people are used to it—simple-minded souls, you know, stirred up to anything in a moment. They'll have him ready for me before morning, and no trouble to me at all."

"They'll have him, and we shall have saved ourselves all labor in the matter."

"True, true. Well, my way is to Casterbridge; and 'tis as

much as my legs will do to take me that far. Going the same way?"

"No, I am sorry to say! I have to get home over there" (he nodded indefinitely to the right), "and I feel as you do, that it is quite enough for my legs to do before bedtime."

The other had by this time finished the mead in the mug, after which, shaking hands heartily at the door, and wishing each other well, they went their several ways.

In the meantime the company of pursuers had reached the end of the hog's-back elevation which dominated this part of the down. They had decided on no particular plan of action; and, finding that the man of the baleful trade was no longer in their company, they seemed quite unable to form any such plan now. They descended in all directions down the hill, and straightway several of the party fell into the snare set by Nature for all misguided midnight ramblers over this part of the cretaceous formation. The "lanchets," or flint slopes, which belted the escarpment at intervals of a dozen yards, took the less cautious ones unawares, and losing their footing on the rubbly steep they slid sharply downwards, the lanterns rolling from their hands to the bottom, and there lying on their sides till the horn was scorched through.

When they had again gathered themselves together, the shepherd, as the man who knew the country best, took the lead, and guided them round these treacherous inclines. The lanterns, which seemed rather to dazzle their eyes and warn the fugitive than to assist them in the exploration, were extinguished, due silence was observed; and in this more rational order they plunged into the vale. It was a grassy, briery, moist defile, affording some shelter to any person who had sought it; but the party perambulated it in vain, and ascended on the other side. Here they wandered apart, and after an interval closed together again to report progress. At the second time of closing in they found themselves near a lonely ash, the single tree on this part of the coomb, probably sown there by a passing bird some fifty years before. And here, standing a little to one side of the trunk, as motionless as the trunk itself, appeared the man they were in quest of, his outline being well defined against the sky beyond. The band noiselessly drew up and faced him.

"Your money or your life!" said the constable sternly to the still figure.

"No, no," whispered John Pitcher. " 'Tisn't our side ought to say that. That's the doctrine of vagabonds like him, and we be on the side of the law."

"Well, well," replied the constable impatiently; "I must say something, mustn't I? and if you had all the weight o' this undertaking upon your mind, perhaps you'd say the wrong thing too—Prisoner at the bar, surrender, in the name of the Father—the Crown, I mane!"

The man under the tree seemed now to notice them for the first time, and, giving them no opportunity whatever for exhibiting their courage, he strolled slowly towards them. He was, indeed, the little man, the third stranger; but his trepidation had in a great measure gone.

"Well, travelers," he said, "did I hear ye speak to me?"

"You did: you've got to come and be our prisoner at once!" said the constable. "We arrest 'ee on the charge of not biding in Casterbridge jail in a decent proper manner to be hung tomorrow morning. Neighbors, do your duty, and seize the culpet!"

On hearing the charge, the man seemed enlightened, and, saying not another word, resigned himself with preternatural civility to the search-party, who, with their staves in their hands, surrounded him on all sides, and marched him back towards the shepherd's cottage.

It was eleven o'clock by the time they arrived. The light shining from the open door, a sound of men's voices within, proclaimed to them as they approached the house that some new events had arisen in their absence. On entering they discovered the shepherd's living room to be invaded by two officers from the Casterbridge jail, and a well-known magistrate who lived at the nearest county-seat, intelligence of the escape having become generally circulated.

"Gentlemen," said the constable, "I have brought back your man—not without risk and danger; but every one must do his duty! He is inside this circle of able-bodied persons, who have lent me useful aid, considering their ignorance of Crown work. Men, bring forward your prisoner!" And the third stranger was led to the light.

"Who is this?" said one of the officials.

"The man," said the constable.

"Certainly not," said the turnkey; and the first corroborated his statement.

"But how can it be otherwise?" asked the constable. "Or why was he so terrified at sight o' the singing instrument of the law who sat there?" Here he related the strange behavior of the third stranger on entering the house during the hangman's song.

"Can't understand it," said the officer coolly. "All I know is that it is not the condemned man. He's quite a different character from this one; a gauntish fellow, with dark hair and eyes, rather good-looking, and with a musical bass voice that if you heard it once you'd never mistake as long as you lived."

"Why, souls—'twas the man in the chimney-corner!"

"Hey—what?" said the magistrate, coming forward after inquiring particulars from the shepherd in the background. "Haven't you got the man after all?"

"Well, sir," said the constable, "he's the man we were in search of, that's true; and yet he's not the man we were in search of. For the man we were in search of was not the man we wanted, sir, if you understand my every-day way; for 'twas the man in the chimney-corner."

"A pretty kettle of fish altogether!" said the magistrate. "You had better start for the other man at once."

The prisoner now spoke for the first time. The mention of the man in the chimney-corner seemed to have moved him as nothing else could do. "Sir," he said, stepping forward to the magistrate, "take no more trouble about me. The time is come when I may as well speak. I have done nothing; my crime is that the condemned man is my brother. Early this afternoon I left home at Shottsford to tramp it all the way to Casterbridge jail to bid him farewell. I was benighted, and called here to rest and ask the way. When I opened the door I saw before me the very man, my brother, that I thought to see in the condemned cell at Casterbridge. He was in the chimney-corner; and jammed close to him, so that he could not have got out if he had tried, was the executioner who'd come to take his life, singing a song about it and not knowing that it was his victim who was close by, joining in to save appearances. My brother looked a glance of agony at me, and I knew he meant, 'Don't reveal what you see; my life depends on it.' I was so terror-struck that I could hardly stand, and, not knowing what I did, I turned and hurried away."

The narrator's manner and tone had the stamp of truth, and his story made a great impression on all around. "And do you know where your brother is at the present time?" asked the magistrate.

"I do not. I have never seen him since I closed this door."

"I can testify to that, for we've been between ye ever since," said the constable.

"Where does he think to fly to?—what is his occupation?"

"He's a watch-and-clock-maker, sir."

" 'A said 'a was a wheelwright—a wicked rogue," said the constable.

"The wheels of clocks and watches he meant, no doubt," said Shepherd Fennel. "I thought his hands were palish for's trade."

"Well, it appears to me that nothing can be gained by retaining this poor man in custody," said the magistrate; "your business lies with the other, unquestionably."

And so the little man was released off-hand; but he looked nothing the less sad on that account, it being beyond the power of magistrate or constable to raze out the written troubles in his brain, for they concerned another whom he regarded with more solicitude than himself. When this was done, and the man had gone his way, the night was found to be so far advanced that it was deemed useless to renew the search before the next morning.

Next day, accordingly, the quest for the clever sheep-stealer became general and keen, to all appearance at least. But the intended punishment was cruelly disproportioned to the transgression, and the sympathy of a great many country-folk in that district was strongly on the side of the fugitive. Moreover, his marvelous coolness and daring in hob-and-nobbing with the hangman, under the unprecedented circumstances of the shepherd's party, won their admiration. So that it may be questioned if all those who ostensibly made themselves so busy in exploring woods and fields and lanes were quite so thorough when it came to the private examination of their own lofts and outhouses. Stories were afloat of a mysterious figure being occasionally seen in some overgrown trackway or other, remote from turnpike roads; but when a search was instituted in any of these suspected quarters nobody was found. Thus the days and weeks passed without tidings.

In brief, the bass-voiced man of the chimney-corner was never recaptured. Some said that he went across the sea, others that he did not, but buried himself in the depths of a populous city. At any rate, the gentleman in cinder-gray never did his morning's work at Casterbridge, nor met anywhere at all, for business purposes, the genial comrade with whom he had passed an hour of relaxation in the lonely house on the coomb.

The grass has long been green on the graves of Shepherd Fennel and his frugal wife; the guests who made up the christening party have mainly followed their entertainers to the tomb; the baby in whose honor they all had met is a matron in the sere and yellow leaf. But the arrival of the three strangers at the shepherd's that night, and the details connected therewith, is a story as well known as ever in the country about Higher Crowstairs.

QUESTIONS AND CONSIDERATIONS

The Ghost Dance

1. For the American Indian in the latter half of the nineteenth century, nearly all hope for a return to the old ways was gone. The white man was too powerful, his encroachments too irresistible. It would take a miracle to stop him. The Ghost Dance religion was in response to the need for such a miracle. The myth from which it grew is not entirely an ancient one, although its elements suggest age-old roots. Regardless of the myth's age, it is a valid example of the myth-making process. In fewer than 200 words it offers what all myths do —a statement of positive metaphorical truths to which its audience can relate. It would be wrong to read this merely as an expedient story cooked up to rally Indians to a cause. There is too much that relates to even larger purposes and to ancient themes. What does the flood symbolize? Is it meant to stand only for the destruction of an enemy? What does it symbolize in The Bible? Account for the universality of the flood motif. (For a fuller account of the Ghost Dance religion, and the white man's harsh response to it, read Dee Brown's *Bury My Heart at Wounded Knee.*)
2. Why will the Great Spirit not arrive before spring? What specific things will happen in conjunction with the arrival of spring (and the Great Spirit)?
3. Why might the white man sense a threat in what was essentially a response to a Bible-like fertility myth?

La Guerre

1. Despite its title, this is not a poem about war. Cummings uses "the bigness of cannon" as an ironic symbol for the ineffectual devices we have thrown in the way of an unconquerable force—the regenerative power of nature.
    Discuss the idea that there are two poems here. What makes them distinct? What is different about the tone, subject, form of address? What essential cycle of nature does each deal with?
2. Considered together, the two stanzas illustrate the paradox of nature itself. What is this paradox? How does it relate to the mythic theme of regeneration?
3. The earth's fertility is always metaphorized in myth as a female. Prove that Cummings uses the same metaphor.
4. Account for the poet's use of seemingly contradictory metaphors. How can bigness be skillful; how can a voice hide or be seen; how can the night utter?
5. Who or what is the earth's rhythmic lover? Why rhythmic? How

is the rhythm itself depicted as being greater by far than the human forces that seek to alter it?
6. How are philosophy, science, and religion metaphorized? Be specific. Note Cummings's choice of verbs—"pinched," "poked," "prodded," "squeezing," "buffeting."

Philomela and Ode to a Nightingale

1. In the generally accepted version of the Greek myth of Philomela, she is the younger sister of Procne, wife of Tereus, king of Thrace. When Tereus became enamored of Philomela, he sent Procne away on some pretext, told Philomela that her sister was dead, seduced her, and cut out her tongue to silence her. Philomela, however, wove her story into a robe, which she sent to Procne. In a fit of rage over the betrayal, Procne killed their child and served its remains to her husband. When he discovered the horrible vengeance his wife had carried out, he attempted to kill both sisters. As they fled him, Philomela was changed into a nightingale, Procne into a swallow. Arnold switches the sisters' roles, making Philomela the wife of the faithless Tereus. Otherwise, the story is the same. Compare the transcendent symbol of the nightingale, whose eternal song suggests to Arnold the "old-world pain," with the "immortal bird" of John Keats's "Ode to a Nightingale."
2. How does each poem emphasize the theme of nature's endlessly renewing ways? What does Keats mean by "What thou among the leaves hast never known"? Compare this with Arnold's lines, "Eternal passion! Eternal pain!" Is Keats suggesting that the bird symbolizes eternal, mindless bliss, and Arnold an opposite view? Why then does Keats refer to the bird's song as a "plaintive anthem"?
3. Compare the pastoral (idealized, nature-centered) settings of the two works. Which is the more real, the less a projection of the poet's imagination?
4. Might it be significant that in both poems the nightingale whose song stirs the poet is hidden from sight—that it is the *sound* into which each reads a message from the ancient past? Why or why not?
5. What lines from each poem bear on the theme of "La Guerre"?

The Three Strangers

1. Everyone enjoys a well-told story, particularly if it involves the elements of suspense and surprise. Perhaps your enjoyment of Hardy's *The Three Strangers* will become even richer when you find in it examples of how mythic themes repeat their vital truths in literature of any age or form. Consider how this story can be taken as a reiteration of the birth-death-rebirth cycle. For example, the

action takes place on March 28, seven days after the beginning of spring. The host and his invited guests are pastoral people. Inside the cottage, the hearth is hung with sheep-crooks engraved with Biblical figures. Ceremonial candlesticks marking "high-days, holy-days and family feasts" have been brought out for the occasion. The revelers partake of mead, a drink from honey. There is, in fact, an obvious Dionysian tone to the gathering. Look for other signs, some not so obvious, that symbolize fertility.

2. What does the cottage's being located by a crossroads suggest? What two forces have met on this rainy spring night? How can it be said that they cross? Do they cross in "La Guerre"? In the Ghost Dance myth?

3. Why is it significant (or isn't it?) that the three strangers are all dressed in dark colors?

4. How do the following lines bear out the fertility theme in this story?

   (a) "Yes, het or wet, blow or snow, famine or sword, my day's work tomorrow must be done."

   (b) "Daze it, what's a cup of mead more or less? There'll be plenty more next bee-burning."

   (c) "THERE IS NO FUN UNTILL I CUM."

   (d) "Disturbed by the noise, or possibly by unpleasant dreams of her baptism, the child who had been christened began to cry heart-brokenly in the room overhead."

   (e) "When they had again gathered themselves together, the shepherd, as the man who knew the country best, took the lead, and guided them round these treacherous inclines."

   (f) " . . . the baby in whose honor they all had met is a matron in the sere and yellow leaf."

5. If the executioner didn't have to perform his duty until eight in the morning, why did he attach importance to getting to Casterbridge by midnight? Why do we not learn his name?

6. Look up one or two myths that embody fertility themes. Persephone figures in two interesting stories, those of Demeter and Persephone and of Adonis and Persephone. A number of mythic figures were turned into plants, trees, and flowers. Find out about Daphne, Narcissus, and Hyacinth, for example. Try to relate any of their stories to modern counterparts in literature, movies, or television drama.

IV

SELECTED READINGS

The readings gathered in this section are meant to mirror the major mythic themes which you have examined thus far. This shouldn't suggest that reading them will be a chore; they all have the power to fascinate, in addition to being appropriate.

They may be used as extensions of the readings offered earlier in the book; as supplemental thematic materials; as sources for additional research; or simply as representative literature, to be read, enjoyed, and perhaps discussed.

There are no "Questions and Considerations" in this section, an omission which should delight you. By now you have gained important insights into myth and its profound connections with literature. They should carry over into whatever you read from now on without the props and guidelines such questionings have provided to this point.

1
THE HERO'S QUEST

•

OISIN IN TIR NA NÓG°

or

THE LAST OF THE FENA°
Anonymous

According to an ancient legend, Oisin, the hero-poet,
was the son of Finn, a king of a race of gods known
as the Dedannans. He is said to have survived to the
time of St. Patrick, two hundred years after the
other Fena. On a certain occasion, when the saint
asked him how he had lived to such a great age, the
old hero related the following story.

A short time after the fatal battle of Gavra,° where so
many of our heroes fell, we were hunting on a dewy morning near
the brink of Loch Lein, where the trees and hedges around us were
all fragrant with blossoms, and the little birds sang melodious
music on the branches. We soon roused the deer from the thickets,
and as they bounded over the plain, our hounds followed after them
in full cry.

We were not long so engaged, when we saw a rider
coming swiftly towards us from the west; and we soon perceived
that it was a maiden on a white steed. We all ceased from the chase
on seeing the lady, who reined in as she approached. And Finn and
the Fena were greatly surprised, for they had never before seen so

°*Tír na nóg*: the land of Eternal Youth
°*Fena*: standing army
°*Gavra*: now Jarristown, in North County, Dublin

161

lovely a maiden. A slender golden diadem encircled her head; and she wore a brown robe of silk, spangled with stars of red gold, which was fastened in front by a golden brooch, and fell from her shoulders till it swept the ground. Her yellow hair flowed far down over her robe in bright, golden ringlets. Her blue eyes were as clear as the drops of dew on the grass; and while her small, white hand held the bridle and curbed her steed with a golden bit, she sat more gracefully than the swan on Loch Lein. The white steed was covered with a smooth, flowing mantle. He was shod with four shoes of pure yellow gold, and in all Erin a better or more beautiful steed could not be found.

As she came slowly to the presence of Finn, he addressed her courteously:

"Who art thou, O lovely youthful princess? Tell us thy name and the name of thy country, and relate to us the cause of thy coming."

She answered in a sweet and gentle voice. "Noble king of the Fena, I have had a long journey this day, for my country lies far off in the Western Sea. I am the daughter of the king of Tír na nÓg, and my name is Niamh of the Golden Hair."

"And what is it that has caused thee to come so far across the sea? Has thy husband forsaken thee; or what other evil has befallen thee?"

"My husband has not forsaken me, for I have never been married or betrothed to any man. But I love thy noble son, Oisin; and this is what has brought me to Erin. It is not without reason that I have given him my love, and that I have undertaken this long journey: for I have often heard of his bravery, his gentleness, and the nobleness of his person. Many princes and high chiefs have sought me in marriage; but I was quite indifferent to all men, and never consented to wed, till my heart was moved with love for thy gentle son, Oisin."

When I heard these words, and when I looked on the lovely maiden with her glossy, golden hair, I was all over in love with her. I came near, and, taking her small hand in mine, I told her she was a mild star of brightness and beauty, and that I preferred her to all the princesses in the world for my wife.

"Then," said she, "I place you under geasa,° which true heroes never break through, to come with me on my white steed to Tír na nÓg, the land of never-ending youth. It is the most delightful

---

°*geasa*: chivalrous obligation

and the most renowned country under the sun. There is abundance of gold and silver and jewels, of honey and wine; and the trees bear fruit and blossoms and green leaves together all the year round. You will get a hundred swords and a hundred robes of silk and satin, a hundred swift steeds, and a hundred slender, keen-scenting hounds. You will get herds of cows without number, and flocks of sheep with fleeces of gold; a coat of mail that cannot be pierced, and a sword that never missed a stroke and from which no one ever escaped alive. There are feasting and harmless pastimes each day. A hundred warriors fully armed shall always await you at call, and harpers shall delight you with their sweet music. You will wear the diadem of the king of Tír na nÓg, which he never yet gave to any one under the sun, and which will guard you day and night, in tumult and battle and danger of every kind. Lapse of time shall bring neither decay nor death, and you shall be forever young, and gifted with unfading beauty and strength. All these delights you shall enjoy, and many others that I do not mention; and I myself will be your wife if you come with me to Tír na nÓg."

I replied that she was my choice above all the maidens in the world, and that I would willingly go with her to the Land of Youth.

When my father, Finn, and the Fena heard me say this, and knew that I was going from them, they raised three shouts of grief and lamentation. And Finn came up to me and took my hand in his, saying sadly: "Woe is me, my son, that you are going away from me, for I do not expect that you will ever return to me!"

The manly beauty of his countenance became quite dimmed with sorrow; and though I promised to return after a little time, and fully believed that I should see him again, I could not check my tears, as I gently kissed my father's cheek.

I then bade farewell to my dear companions, and mounted the white steed, while the lady kept her seat before me. She gave the signal, and the steed galloped swiftly and smoothly towards the west, till he reached the strand; and when his gold-shod hoofs touched the waves, he shook himself and neighed three times. He made no delay, but plunged forward at once, moving over the face of the sea with the speed of a cloud-shadow on a March day. The wind overtook the waves and we overtook the wind, so that we straightway lost sight of land; and we saw nothing but billows tumbling before us and billows tumbling behind us.

Other shores came into view, and we saw many wonderful things on our journey—islands and cities, lime-white mansions, bright grianáns° and lofty palaces. A hornless fawn once crossed our course, bounding nimbly along from the crest of one wave to the crest of another; and close after, in full chase, a white hound with red ears. We saw also a lovely young maiden on a brown steed, with a golden apple in her hand; and as she passed swiftly by, a young warrior on a white steed plunged after her, wearing a long, flowing mantle of yellow silk, and holding a gold-hilted sword in his hand.

I knew naught of these things, and, marvelling much, I asked the princess what they meant.

"Heed not what you see here, Oisin," she said, "for all these wonders are as nothing compared with what you shall see in Tír na nóg."

At last we saw at a great distance, rising over the waves on the very verge of the sea, a palace more splendid than all the others; and, as we drew near, its front glittered like the morning sun. I asked the lady what royal house this was, and who was the prince that ruled over it.

"This country is the Land of Virtues," she replied. "Its king is the giant, Fomor of the Blows, and its queen the daughter of the king of the Land of Life. This Fomor brought the lady away by force from her own country, and keeps her in his palace; but she has put him under geasa that he cannot break through, never to ask her to marry him till she can find a champion to fight him in single combat. But she still remains in bondage; for no hero has yet come hither who has the courage to meet the giant."

"A blessing on you, golden-haired Niamh," I replied; "I have never heard music sweeter than your voice; and although I feel pity for this princess, yet your story is pleasant to me to hear; for of a certainty I will go to the palace, and try whether I cannot kill this Fomor, and free the lady."

So we came to land; and as we drew nigh to the palace, the lovely young queen met us and bade us welcome. She led us in and placed us on chairs of gold; after which choice food was placed before us, and drinking-horns filled with mead, and golden goblets of sweet wine.

When we had eaten and drunk, the mild young princess told us her story, while tears streamed from her soft, blue eyes; and she ended by saying: "I shall never return to my own country and to my father's house, so long as this great and cruel giant is alive!"

When I heard her sad words, and saw her tears falling, I

°*Grianán*: a summer-house; a house in a bright, sunny spot

was moved with pity; and telling her to cease from her grief, I gave her my hand as a pledge that I would meet the giant, and either slay him or fall myself in her defense.

While we were yet speaking, we saw the giant coming towards the palace, large of body, and ugly and hateful in appearance, carrying a load of deerskins on his back, and holding a great iron club in his hand. He threw down his load when he saw us, turned a surly look on the princess, and, without greeting us or showing the least mark of courtesy, he forthwith challenged me to battle in a loud, rough voice.

It was not my wont to be dismayed by a call to battle, or to be terrified at the sight of an enemy; and I went forth at once without the least fear in my heart. But though I had fought many battles in Erin against wild boars and enchanters and foreign invaders, never before did I find it so hard to preserve my life. We fought for three days and three nights without food or drink or sleep; for the giant did not give me a moment for rest, and neither did I give him. At length, when I looked at the two princesses weeping in great fear, and when I called to mind my father's deeds in battle, the fury of my valor arose; and with a sudden onset I felled the giant to the earth; and instantly, before he could recover himself, I cut off his head.

When the maidens saw the monster lying on the ground dead, they uttered three crys of joy; and they came to me, and led me into the palace. For I was indeed bruised all over, and covered with gory wounds; and a sudden dizziness of brain and feebleness of body seized me. But the daughter of the king of the Land of Life applied precious balsam and healing herbs to my wounds; and in a short time I was healed, and my cheerfulness of mind returned.

Then I buried the giant in a deep and wide grave; and I raised a great cairn over him, and placed on it a stone with his name graved in Ogham.

We rested that night, and at the dawn of next morning Niamh said to me that it was time for us to resume our journey to Tír na nóg. So we took leave of the daughter of the king of the Land of Life; and though her heart was joyful after her release, she wept at our departure, and we were not less sorry at parting from her. When we had mounted the white steed, he galloped towards the strand; and as soon as his hoofs touched the wave, he shook himself and neighed three times. We plunged forward over the clear, green sea with the speed of a March wind on a hillside; and soon we saw nothing but billows tumbling before us and billows tumbling behind us. We saw again the fawn chased by the white hound with red ears; and the maiden with the golden apple passed swiftly by, followed by the young warrior in yellow silk on his white steed. And again we passèd many strange islands and cities and white palaces.

The sky now darkened, so that the sun was hidden from our view. A storm arose, and the sea was lighted up with constant flashes. But though the wind blew from every point of the heavens, and the waves rose up and roared around us, the white steed kept his course straight on, moving as calmly and swiftly as before, through the foam and blinding spray, without being delayed or disturbed in the least, and without turning either to the right or to the left.

At length the storm abated, and after a time the sun again shone brightly; and when I looked up, I saw a country near at hand, all green and full of flowers, with beautiful smooth plains, blue hills, and bright lakes and waterfalls. Not far from the shore stood a palace of surpassing beauty and splendor. It was covered all over with gold and with gems of every color—blue, green, crimson, and yellow; and on each side were grianáns shining with precious stones, built by artists the most skilful that could be found. I asked Niamh the name of that delightful country, and she replied:

"This is my native country. Tír na nóg; and there is nothing I have promised you that you will not find in it."

As soon as we reached the shore, we dismounted; and now we saw advancing from the palace a troop of noble-looking warriors, all clad in bright garments, who came forward to meet and welcome us. Following these we saw a stately glittering host, with the king at their head wearing a robe of bright yellow satin covered with gems, and a crown that sparkled with gold and diamonds. The queen came after, attended by a hundred lovely young maidens; and as they advanced towards us, it seemed to me that this king and queen exceeded all the kings and queens of the world in beauty and gracefulness and majesty.

After they had kissed their daughter, the king took my hand, and said aloud in the hearing of the host:

"This is Oisin, the son of Finn, for whom my daughter, Niamh, travelled over the sea to Erin. This is Oisin, who is to be the husband of Niamh of the Golden Hair. We give you a hundred thousand welcomes, brave Oisin. You will be for ever young in this land. All kinds of delights and innocent pleasures are awaiting you, and my daughter, the gentle, golden-haired Niamh, shall be your wife; for I am the king of Tír na nóg."

I gave thanks to the king, and I bowed low to the queen; after which we went into the palace, where we found a banquet prepared. The feasting and rejoicing lasted for ten days, and on the last day, I was wedded to the gentle Niamh of the Golden Hair.

I lived in the Land of Youth more than three hundred years; but it appeared to me that only three years had passed since the day I parted from my friends. At the end of that time, I began to have a longing desire to see my father, Finn, and all my old companions, and I asked leave of Niamh and of the king to visit Erin. The king gave permission, and Niamh said:

"I will give consent, though I feel sorrow in my heart, for I fear much you will never return to me."

I replied that I would surely return, and that she need not feel any doubt or dread, for that the white steed knew the way, and would bring me back in safety. Then she addressed me in these words, which seemed very strange to me.

"I will not refuse this request, though your journey afflicts me with great grief and fear. Erin is not now as it was when you left it. The great king Finn and his Fena are all gone; and you will find, instead of them, a holy father and hosts of priests and saints. Now, think well on what I say to you, and keep my words in your mind. If once you alight from the white steed, you will never come back to me. Again I warn you, if you place your feet on the green sod in Erin, you will never return to this lovely land. A third time, O Oisin, my beloved husband, a third time I say to you, if you alight from the white steed, you will never see me again."

I promised that I would faithfully attend to her words, and that I would not alight from the white steed. Then, as I looked into her gentle face and marked her grief, my heart was weighed down with sadness, and my tears flowed plentifully; but even so, my mind was bent on coming back to Erin.

When I had mounted the white steed, he galloped straight towards the shore. We moved as swiftly as before over the clear sea. The wind overtook the waves and we overtook the wind, so that we straightway left the Land of Youth behind; and we passed by many islands and cities, till at length we landed on the green shores of Erin.

As I travelled on through the country, I looked closely around me; but I scarcely knew the old places, for everything seemed strangely altered. I saw no sign of Finn and his host, and I began to dread that Niamh's saying was coming true. At length, I espied at a distance a company of little men and women,° all mounted on horses as small as themselves; and when I came near, they greeted me kindly and courteously. They looked at me with wonder and curiosity, and they marvelled much at my great size, and at the beauty and majesty of my person.

I asked them about Finn and the Fena; whether they were still living, or if any sudden disaster had swept them away. And one replied:

"We have heard of the hero Finn, who ruled the Fena of Erin in times of old, and who never had an equal for bravery and wisdom. The poets of the Gael have written many books concerning his deeds and the deeds of the Fena, which we cannot now relate; but they are all gone long since, for they lived many ages ago. We have heard also, and we have seen it written in very old books, that Finn had a son named Oisin. Now this Oisin went with a young fairy maiden to Tír na nÓg, and his father and his friends sorrowed greatly after him, and sought him long; but he was never seen again."

When I heard all this, I was filled with amazement, and my heart grew heavy with great sorrow. I silently turned my steed away from the wondering people, and set forward straightway for Allen of the mighty deeds, on the broad, green plains of Leinster. It was a miserable journey to me; and though my mind, being full of sadness at all I saw and heard, forecasted further sorrows, I was grieved more than ever when I reached Allen. For there, indeed, I found the hill deserted and lonely, and my father's palace all in ruins and overgrown with grass and weeds.

I turned slowly away, and afterwards fared through the land in every direction in search of my friends. But I met only crowds of little people, all strangers, who gazed on me with wonder; and none knew me. I visited every place throughout the country where I knew the Fena had lived; but I found their houses all like Allen, solitary and in ruins.

At length I came to Glenasmole,° where many a time I had hunted in days of old with the Fena, and there I saw a crowd of people in the glen. As soon as they saw me, one of them came forward and said:

"Come to us, thou mighty hero, and help us out of our strait; for thou art a man of vast strength."

I went to them, and found a number of men trying in vain

°The gigantic race of the Fena had all passed away, and their descendants looked very small in Oisin's eyes.

°*Glenasmole*: a valley about seven miles south of Dublin, through which the river Dodder flows to raise a large, flat stone. It was half-lifted from the ground; but those who were under it were not strong enough either to raise it further or to free themselves from its weight. And they were in great distress, and on the point of being crushed to death.

I thought it a shameful thing that so many men should be unable to lift this stone, which Oscar, if he were alive, would take in his right hand and fling over the heads of the feeble crowd. After I had looked a little while, I stooped forward and seized the flag with one hand; and, putting forth my strength, I flung it seven perches from its place, and relieved the little men. But with the great strain the golden saddle-girth broke, and, bounding forward to keep myself from falling, I suddenly came to the ground on my two feet.

The moment the white steed felt himself free, he shook himself and neighed. Then, starting off with the speed of a cloud-shadow on a March day, he left me standing helpless and sorrowful. Instantly a woeful change came over me: the sight of my eyes began to fade, the ruddy beauty of my face fled, I lost all my strength, and I fell to the earth, a poor, withered old man, blind and wrinkled and feeble.

The white steed was never seen again. I never recovered my sight, my youth, or my strength; and I have lived in this manner, sorrowing without ceasing for my gentle, golden-haired wife, Niamh, and thinking ever of my father, Finn, and of the lost companions of my youth.

ULYSSES

Alfred, Lord Tennyson (1809–1892)

It little profits that an idle king,°
By this still hearth, among these barren crags,
Matched with an agèd wife, I mete and dole
Unequal laws unto a savage race,
That hoard, and sleep, and feed, and know not me.   5
I cannot rest from travel. I will drink
Life to the lees. All times I have enjoyed
Greatly, have suffered greatly, both with those
That loved me, and alone; on shore, and when
Through scudding drifts the rainy Hyades°   10
Vext the dim sea. I am become a name;

°*idle king*: Ulysses, after the Trojan War and his years of adventure before reaching his home island, Ithaca
°*Hyades*: star group, supposedly bringer of rain

For always roaming with a hungry heart
Much have I seen and known,—cities of men
And manners, climates, councils, governments,
Myself not least, but honored of them all,—   15
And drunk delight of battle with my peers,
Far on the ringing plains of windy Troy.
I am a part of all that I have met;
Yet all experience is an arch where-through
Gleams that untraveled world, whose margin fades   20
Forever and forever when I move.
How dull it is to pause, to make an end,
To rust unburnished, not to shine in use!
As though to breathe were life! Life piled on life
Were all too little, and of one to me   25
Little remains; but every hour is saved
From that eternal silence, something more,
A bringer of new things; and vile it were
For some three suns to store and hoard myself,
And this gray spirit yearning in desire   30
To follow knowledge like a sinking star,
Beyond the utmost bound of human thought.

This is my son, mine own Telemachus,
To whom I leave the scepter and the isle—
Well-loved of me, discerning to fulfill   35
This labor, by slow prudence to make mild
A rugged people, and through soft degrees
Subdue them to the useful and the good.
Most blameless is he, centered in the sphere
Of common duties, decent not to fail   40
In offices of tenderness, and pay
Meet adoration to my household gods,
When I am gone. He works his work, I mine.

There lies the port; the vessel puffs her sail;
There gloom the dark, broad seas. My mariners,   45
Souls that have toiled, and wrought, and thought
          with me,—
That ever with a frolic welcome took
The thunder and the sunshine, and opposed
Free hearts, free foreheads,—you and I are old;
Old age hath yet his honor and his toil.   50
Death closes all; but something ere the end,
Some work of noble note, may yet be done,

Not unbecoming men that strove with gods.
The lights begin to twinkle from the rocks;
The long day wanes: the slow moon climbs; the
    deep°   55
Moans round with many voices. Come, my friends.
'Tis not too late to seek a newer world.
Push off, and sitting well in order° smite
The sounding furrows; for my purpose holds
To sail beyond the sunset, and the baths°   60
Of all the western stars, until I die.
It may be that the gulfs will wash us down;
It may be we shall touch the Happy Isles,°
And see the great Achilles,° whom we knew.
Though much is taken, much abides; and though   65
We are not now that strength which in old days
Moved earth and heaven, that which we are,
    we are,—
One equal temper of heroic hearts
Made weak by time and fate, but strong in will
To strive, to seek, to find, and not to yield.   70

THE QUEST

George Garrett (1929–   )

The road was menaced by a dwarf,
sharp-tongued with a mind like a trap
for tigers. Later a dragon loomed,
snorted fire and made his wings flap

like starchy washing in brisk wind.   5
Farther still, the obsolete castle and
the improbable giant overlooked
nothing living in the land.

One is a long time coming to the point
where the enchanted may be free,   10
all charms be neutralized and everything
be what it, shining, seems to be.

°*deep*: sea
°*sitting . . . order*: Ulysses's ship is a galley; the oarsmen sit in rows
°*baths*: the seas into which the stars seem to sink
°*Happy Isles*: Greek heroes' heaven
°*Achilles*: greatest of the Greek warriors at Troy

BLOOD CLOT BOY

Anonymous

Kut-o-yis, or "Blood Clot Boy," when he had been taken from the pot and had grown to manhood in a day, slew the murderous son-in-law of his foster parents, then proceeded against the ogres of the countryside. He exterminated a tribe of cruel bears, with the exception of one female who was about to become a mother. She pleaded so pitifully for her life, that he spared her. If he had not done this, there would have been no bears in the world. Then he slaughtered a tribe of snakes, but again with the exception of one who was about to become a mother. Next he deliberately walked along a road which he had been told was dangerous. As he was going along, a great windstorm struck him and at last carried him into the mouth of a great fish. This was a suckerfish and the wind was its sucking. When he got into the stomach of the fish, he saw a great many people. Many of them were dead, but some were still alive. He said to the people, 'Ah, there must be a heart somewhere here. We will have a dance.' So he painted his face white, his eyes and mouth with black circles, and tied a white rock knife on his head, so that the point stuck up. Some rattles made of hoofs were also brought. Then the people started in to dance. For a while Blood Clot sat making wing-motions with his hands, and singing songs. Then he stood up and danced, jumping up and down until the knife on his head struck the heart. Then he cut the heart down. Next he cut through between the ribs of the fish, and let all the people out.

Again Blood Clot said he must go on his travels. Before starting, the people warned him, saying that after a while he would see a woman who was always challenging people to wrestle with her, but that he must not speak to her. He gave no heed to what they said, and, after he had gone a little way, he saw a woman who called him to come over. 'No,' said Blood Clot. 'I am in a hurry.' However, at the fourth time the woman asked him to come over, he said, 'Yes, but you must wait a little while, for I am tired. I wish to rest. When I have rested, I will come over and wrestle with you.' Now, while he was resting, he saw many large knives sticking up from the ground almost hidden by straw. Then he knew that the woman killed the people she wrestled with by throwing them down on the knives. When he was rested, he went on. The woman asked him to stand up in the place where he had seen the knives; but he said, 'No, I am not quite ready. Let us play a little, before we begin.' So he began to play with the woman, but quickly caught hold of her, threw her upon the knives, and cut her in two.

Blood Clot took up his travels again, and after a while

came to a camp where there were some old women. The old women told him that a little farther on he would come to a woman with a swing, but on no account must he ride with her. After a time he came to a place where he saw a swing on the bank of a swift stream. There was a woman swinging on it. He watched her a while, and saw that she killed people by swinging them out and dropping them into the water. When he found this out, he came up to the woman. 'You have a swing here; let me see you swing,' he said. 'No,' said the woman, 'I want to see you swing.' 'Well,' said Blood Clot, 'but you must swing first.' 'Well,' said the woman, 'now I shall swing. Watch me. Then I shall see you do it.' So the woman swung out over the stream. As she did this, he saw how it worked. Then he said to the woman, 'You swing again while I am getting ready'; but as the woman swung out this time, he cut the vine and let her drop into the water. This happened on Cut Bank Creek.

LEGEND

Judith Wright (1915–   )

The blacksmith's boy went out with a rifle
and a black dog running behind.
Cobwebs snatched at his feet,
rivers hindered him,
thorn branches caught at his eyes to make him
    blind   5
and the sky turned into an unlucky opal,
but he didn't mind,
I can break branches, I can swim rivers, I can
    stare out any spider I meet,
said he to his dog and his rifle.

The blacksmith's boy went over the paddocks   10
with his old black hat on his head.
Mountains jumped in his way,
rocks rolled down on him,
and the old crow cried, You'll soon be dead.
And the rain came down like mattocks.   15
But he only said
I can climb mountains, I can dodge rocks, I can
    shoot an old crow any day,
and he went on over the paddocks.

When he came to the end of the day the sun began
    falling.

Up came the night ready to swallow him,   20
like the barrel of a gun,
like an old black hat,
like a black dog hungry to follow him.
Then the pigeon, the magpie and the dove began
      wailing
and the grass lay down to billow him.   25
His rifle broke, his hat flew away and his dog was
      gone
and the sun was falling.

But in front of the night the rainbow stood on a
      mountain,
just as his heart foretold.
He ran like a hare,   30
he climbed like a fox;
he caught in his hands, the color and the cold—
like a bar of ice, like the column of a fountain,
like a ring of gold.
The pigeon, the magpie and the dove flew up to
      stare,   35
and the grass stood up again on the mountain.

The blacksmith's boy hung the rainbow on his
      shoulder
instead of his broken gun.
Lizards ran out to see,
snakes made way for him,
and the rainbow shone as brightly as the sun.   40
All the world said, Nobody is braver, nobody is
      bolder,
nobody else has done
anything to equal it. He went home as bold as he
      could be
with the swinging rainbow on his shoulder.   45

A MYSTERY OF HEROISM

Stephen Crane (1871–1900)

The dark uniforms of the men were so coated with dust from the incessant wrestling of the two armies that the regiment almost seemed a part of the clay bank which shielded them from the shells. On the top of the hill a battery was arguing in tremendous roars with some other guns, and to the eye of the infantry the artil-

lerymen, the guns, the caissons, the horses, were distinctly outlined
upon the blue sky. When a piece was fired, a red streak as round as
a log flashed low in the heavens, like a monstrous bolt of lightning.
The men of the battery wore white duck trousers, which somehow
emphasized their legs; and when they ran and crowded in little
groups at the bidding of the shouting officers, it was more impres-
sive than usual to the infantry.

Fred Collins, of A Company, was saying, "Thunder! I
wisht I had a drink. Ain't there any water round here?" Then somebody yelled, "There goes th' bugler!"

As the eyes of half the regiment swept in one machine-
like movement, there was an instant's picture of a horse in a great,
convulsive leap of a death wound and a rider leaning back with a
crooked arm and spread fingers before his face. On the ground was
the crimson terror of an exploding shell, with fibers of flame that
seemed like lances. A glittering bugle swung clear of the rider's
back as fell headlong the horse and the man. In the air was an odor
as from a conflagration.

Sometimes they of the infantry looked down at a fair
little meadow which spread at their feet. Its long, green grass was
rippling gently in a breeze. Beyond it was the gray form of a house
half torn to pieces by shells and by the busy axes of soldiers who
had pursued firewood. The line of an old fence was now dimly
marked by long weeds and by an occasional post. A shell had blown
the well house to fragments. Little lines of gray smoke ribboning
upward from some embers indicated the place where had stood the
barn.

From beyond a curtain of green woods there came the
sound of some stupendous scuffle, as if two animals of the size of
islands were fighting. At a distance there were occasional appearances of swift-moving men, horses, batteries, flags, and with the
crashing of infantry volleys were heard, often, wild and frenzied
cheers. In the midst of it all Smith and Ferguson, two privates of A
Company, were engaged in a heated discussion which involved the
greatest questions of the national existence.

The battery on the hill presently engaged in a frightful
duel. The white legs of the gunners scampered this way and that
way, and the officers redoubled their shouts. The guns, with their
demeanors of stolidity and courage, were typical of something
infinitely self-possessed in this clamor of death that swirled around
the hill.

One of a "swing" team was suddenly smitten quivering to
the ground, and his maddened brethren dragged his torn body in
their struggle to escape from this turmoil and danger. A young sol-
dier astride one of the leaders swore and fumed in his saddle and

furiously jerked at the bridle. An officer screamed out an order so violently that his voice broke and ended the sentence in a falsetto shriek.

The leading company of the infantry regiment was somewhat exposed, and the colonel ordered it moved more fully under the shelter of the hill. There was the clank of steel against steel.

A lieutenant of the battery rode down and passed them, holding his right arm carefully in his left hand. And it was as if this arm was not at all a part of him, but belonged to another man. His sober and reflective charger went slowly. The officer's face was grimy and perspiring, and his uniform was tousled as if he had been in direct grapple with an enemy. He smiled grimly when the men stared at him. He turned his horse toward the meadow.

Collins, of A Company, said, "I wisht I had a drink. I bet there's water in that there ol' well yonder!"

"Yes; but how you goin' to git it?"

For the little meadow which intervened was now suffering a terrible onslaught of shells. Its green and beautiful calm had vanished utterly. Brown earth was being flung in monstrous handfuls. And there was a massacre of the young blades of grass. They were being torn, burned, obliterated. Some curious fortune of the battle had made this gentle little meadow the object of the red hate of the shells, and each one as it exploded seemed like an imprecation in the face of a maiden.

The wounded officer who was riding across this expanse said to himself: "Why, they couldn't shoot any harder if the whole army was massed here!"

A shell struck the gray ruins of the house, and as, after the roar, the shattered wall fell in fragments, there was a noise which resembled the flapping of shutters during a wild gale of winter. Indeed, the infantry paused in the shelter of the bank appeared as men standing upon a shore contemplating a madness of the sea. The angel of calamity had under its glance the battery upon the hill. Fewer white-legged men labored about the guns. A shell had smitten one of the pieces, and after the flare, the smoke, the dust, the wrath of this blow were gone, it was possible to see white legs stretched horizontally upon the ground. And at that interval, to the rear, where it is the business of battery horses to stand with their noses to the fight, awaiting the command to drag the guns out of the destruction, or into it, or wheresoever these incomprehensible humans demanded with whip and spur—in this line of passive and dumb spectators, whose fluttering hearts yet would not let them forget the iron laws of man's control of them—in this rank of brute-soldiers there had been relentless and hideous carnage. From the ruck of bleeding and prostrate horses, the men of the infantry could see one animal raising its stricken body with its forelegs and turning its nose with mystic and profound eloquence toward the sky.

Some comrades joked Collins about his thirst. "Well, if yeh want a drink so bad, why don't yeh go git it?"

"Well, I will in a minnet, if yeh don't shut up!"

A lieutenant of artillery floundered his horse straight down the hill with as little concern as if there were level ground. As he galloped past the colonel of the infantry, he threw up his hand in swift salute. "We've got to get out of that," he roared angrily. He was a black-bearded officer, and his eyes, which resembled beads, sparkled like those of an insane man. His jumping horse sped along the column of infantry.

The fat major, standing carelessly with his sword held horizontally behind him and with his legs far apart, looked after the receding horseman and laughed. "He wants to get back with orders pretty quick, or there'll be no batt'ry left," he observed.

The wise young captain of the second company hazarded to the lieutenant colonel that the enemy's infantry would probably soon attack the hill, and the lieutenant colonel snubbed him.

A private in one of the rear companies looked out over the meadow, and then turned to a companion and said, "Look there, Jim!' It was the wounded officer from the battery, who some time before had started to ride across the meadow, supporting his right arm carefully with his left hand. This man had encountered a shell, apparently, at a time when no one perceived him, and he could now be seen lying face downward with a stirruped foot stretched across the body of his dead horse. A leg of the charger extended slantingly upward, precisely as stiff as a stake. Around this motionless pair the shells still howled.

There was a quarrel in A Company. Collins was shaking his fist in the faces of some laughing comrades. "Dern yeh! I ain't afraid t'go. If yeh say much, I will go!"

"Of course, yeh will! You'll run through that there medder, won't yeh?"

Collins said, in a terrible voice, "You see now!"

At this ominous threat, his comrades broke into renewed jeers.

Collins gave them a dark scowl, and went to find his captain. The latter was conversing with the colonel of the regiment.

"Captain," said Collins, saluting and standing at attention—in those days all trousers bagged at the knees—"Captain, I want t' get permission to go git some water from that there well over yonder!"

The colonel and the captain swung about simultaneously

and stared across the meadow. The captain laughed. "You must be pretty thirsty, Collins?"

"Yes, sir, I am."

"Well—ah," said the captain. After a moment, he asked, "Can't you wait?"

"No, sir."

The colonel was watching Collins's face. "Look here, my lad," he said, in a pious sort of voice, "look here, my lad"—Collins was not a lad—"don't you think that's taking pretty big risks for a little drink of water?"

"I dunno," said Collins uncomfortably. Some of the resentment toward his companions, which perhaps had forced him into this affair, was beginning to fade. "I dunno w'ether 'tis."

The colonel and the captain contemplated him for a time.

"Well," said the captain finally.

"Well," said the colonel, "if you want to go, why, go."

Collins saluted. "Much obliged t' yeh."

As he moved away, the colonel called after him. "Take some of the other boys' canteens with you, an' hurry back, now."

"Yes, sir, I will."

The colonel and the captain looked at each other then, for it had suddenly occurred that they could not for the life of them tell whether Collins wanted to go or whether he did not.

They turned to regard Collins, and as they perceived him surrounded by gesticulating comrades, the colonel said, "Well, by thunder! I guess he's going."

Collins appeared as a man dreaming. In the midst of the questions, the advice, the warnings, all the excited talk of his company mates, he maintained a curious silence.

They were very busy in preparing him for his ordeal. When they inspected him carefully, it was somewhat like the examination that grooms give a horse before a race; and they were amazed, staggered, by the whole affair. Their astonishment found vent in strange repetitions.

"Are yeh sure a-goin'?" they demanded again and again.

"Certainly I am," cried Collins at last, furiously.

He strode sullenly away from them. He was swinging five or six canteens by their cords. It seemed that his cap would not remain firmly on his head, and often he reached and pulled it down over his brow.

There was a general movement in the compact column. The long animal-like thing moved slightly. Its four hundred eyes were turned upon the figure of Collins.

"Well, sir, if that ain't th' derndest thing! I never thought Fred Collins had the blood in him for that kind of business."

"What's he goin' to do, anyhow?"

"He's goin to that well there after water."

"We ain't dyin' of thirst, are we? That's foolishness."

"Well, somebody put him up to it, an' he's doin' it."

"Say, he must be a desperate cuss."

When Collins faced the meadow and walked away from the regiment, he was vaguely conscious that a chasm, the deep valley of all prides, was suddenly between him and his comrades. It was provisional, but the provision was that he return as a victor. He had blindly been led by quaint emotions, and laid himself under an obligation to walk squarely up to the face of death.

But he was not sure that he wished to make a retraction, even if he could do so without shame. As a matter of truth, he was sure of very little. He was mainly surprised.

It seemed to him supernaturally strange that he had allowed his mind to maneuver his body into such a situation. He understood that it might be called dramatically great.

However, he had no full appreciation of anything, excepting that he was actually conscious of being dazed. He could feel his dulled mind groping after the form and color of this incident. He wondered why he did not feel some keen agony of fear cutting his sense like a knife. He wondered at this, because human expression had said loudly for centuries that men should feel afraid of certain things, and that all men who did not feel this fear were phenomena —heroes.

He was, then, a hero. He suffered that disappointment which we would all have if we discovered that we were ourselves capable of those deeds which we most admire in history and legend. This, then, was a hero. After all, heroes were not much.

No, it could not be true. He was not a hero. Heroes had no shames in their lives, and as for him, he remembered borrowing fifteen dollars from a friend and promising to pay it back the next day, and then avoiding that friend for ten months. When, at home, his mother had aroused him for the early labor of his life on the farm, it had often been his fashion to be irritable, childish, diabolical; and his mother had died since he had come to the war.

He saw that in this matter of the well, the canteens, the shells, he was an intruder in the land of fine deeds.

He was now about thirty paces from his comrades. The regiment had just turned its many faces toward him.

From the forest of terrific noises there suddenly emerged a little uneven line of men. They fired fiercely and rapidly at distant foliage on which appeared little puffs of white smoke. The spatter of skirmish firing was added to the thunder of the guns on the hill. The little line of men ran forward. A color sergeant fell flat with his flag as if he had slipped on ice. There was hoarse cheering from this distant field.

Collins suddenly felt that two demon fingers were pressed into his ears. He could see nothing but flying arrows, flaming red. He lurched from the shock of this explosion, but he made a mad rush for the house, which he viewed as a man submerged to the neck in a boiling surf might view the shore. In the air little pieces of shell howled, and the earthquake explosions drove him insane with the menace of their roar. As he ran, the canteens knocked together with a rhythmical tinkling.

As he neared the house, each detail of the scene became vivid to him. He was aware of some bricks of the vanished chimney lying on the sod. There was a door which hung by one hinge.

Rifle bullets called forth by the insistent skirmishers came from the far-off bank of foliage. They mingled with the shells and the pieces of shells until the air was torn in all directions by hootings, yells, howls. The sky was full of fiends who directed all their wild rage at his head.

When he came to the well, he flung himself face downward and peered into its darkness. There were furtive silver glintings some feet from the surface. He grabbed one of the canteens, and unfastening its cap, swung it down by the cord. The water flowed slowly in with an indolent gurgle.

And now, as he lay with his face turned away, he was suddenly smitten with the terror. It came upon his heart like the grasp of claws. All that power faded from his muscles. For an instant he was no more than a dead man.

The canteen filled with a maddening slowness, in the manner of all bottles. Presently he recovered his strength and addressed a screaming oath to it. He leaned over until it seemed as if he intended to try to push water into it with his hands. His eyes as he gazed down into the well shone like two pieces of metal, and in their expression was a great appeal and a great curse. The stupid water derided him.

There was the blaring thunder of a shell. Crimson light shone through the swift-boiling smoke and made a pink reflection on part of the wall of the well. Collins jerked out his arm and canteen with the same motion that a man would use in withdrawing his head from a furnace.

He scrambled erect and glared and hesitated. On the ground near him lay the old well bucket, with a length of rusty chain. He lowered it swiftly into the well. The bucket struck the water and then, turning lazily over, sank. When, with hand reaching tremblingly over hand, he hauled it out, it knocked often against the walls of the well and spilled some of its contents.

In running with a filled bucket, a man can adopt but one kind of gait. So, through this terrible field over which screamed practical angels of death, Collins ran in the manner of a farmer chased out of a dairy by a bull.

His face went staring white with anticipation—anticipation of a blow that would whirl him around and down. He would fall as he had seen other men fall, the life knocked out of them so suddenly that their knees were no more quick to touch the ground than their heads. He saw the long blue line of the regiment, but his comrades were standing looking at him from the edge of an impossible star. He was aware of some deep wheel ruts and hoofprints in the sod beneath his feet.

The artillery officer who had fallen in this meadow had been making groans in the teeth of the tempest of sound. These futile cries, wrenched from him by his agony, were heard only by shells, bullets. When wild-eyed Collins came running, this officer raised himself. His face contorted and blanched from pain, he was about to utter some great beseeching cry. But suddenly his face straightened, and he called. "Say, young man, give me a drink of water, will you?"

Collins had no room amid his emotions for surprise. He was mad from the threats of destruction.

"I can't!" he screamed, and in his reply was a full description of his quaking apprehension. His cap was gone and his hair was riotous. His clothes made it appear that he had been dragged over the ground by the heels. He ran on.

The officer's head sank down, and one elbow crooked. His foot in its brass-bound stirrup still stretched over the body of his horse, and the other leg was under the steed.

But Collins turned. He came dashing back. His face had now turned gray, and in his eyes was all terror. "Here it is! Here it is!"

The officer was as a man gone in drink. His arm bent like a twig. His head drooped as if his neck were of willow. He was sinking to the ground, to lie face downward.

Collins grabbed him by the shoulder. "Here it is. Here's your drink. Turn over. Turn over, man, for God's sake!"

With Collins hauling at his shoulder, the officer twisted his body and fell with his face turned toward that region where lived the unspeakable noises of the swirling missiles. There was the faintest shadow of a smile on his lips as he looked at Collins. He gave a sigh, a little primitive breath like that from a child.

Collins tried to hold the bucket steadily, but his shaking hands caused the water to splash all over the face of the dying man. Then he jerked it away and ran on.

The regiment gave him a welcoming roar. The grimed faces were wrinkled in laughter.

His captain waved the bucket away. "Give it to the men!"

The two genial, skylarking young lieutenants were the first to gain possession of it. They played over it in their fashion.

When one tried to drink, the other teasingly knocked his elbow. "Don't, Billie! You'll make me spill it," said the one. The other laughed.

Suddenly there was an oath, the thud of wood on the ground, and a swift murmur of astonishment among the ranks. The two lieutenants glared at each other. The bucket lay on the ground, empty.

KEMP OWYNE

Anonymous

Her mother died when she was young,
    Which gave her cause to make great moan:
Her father married the warst woman
    That ever lived in Christendom.

She served her with foot and hand,   5
    In every thing that she could dee,
Till once, in an unlucky time,
    She threw her in ower Craigy's sea.

Says, "Lie you there, dove Isabel,
    And all my sorrows lie with thee;   10
Till Kemp Owyne come ower the sea,
    And borrow you with kisses three,
Let all the warld do what they will,
    Oh borrowed shall you never be!"

Her breath grew strang, her hair grew lang,   15
    And twisted thrice about the tree,
And all the people, far and near,
    Thought what a savage beast was she.

These news did come to Kemp Owyne,
    Where he lived, far beyond the sea;   20
He hasted him to Craigy's sea,
    And on the savage beast looked he.

Her breath was strang, her hair was lang,

And twisted was about the tree,
And with a swing she came about: 25
    "Come to Craigy's sea and kiss with me.

"Here is a royal belt," she cried,
    "That I have found in the green sea;
And while your body it is on,
    Drawn shall your blood never be;   30
But if you touch me, tail or fin,
    I vow my belt your death will be."

He stepped in, gave her a kiss,
    The royal belt he brought him wi;
Her breath was strang, her hair was lang,   35
    And twisted twice about the tree,
And with a swing she came about:
    "Come to Craigy's sea and kiss with me.

"Here is a royal ring," she said,
    "That I have found in the green sea;   40
And while your finger it is on,
    Drawn shall your blood never be;
But if you touch me, tail or fin,
    I swear my ring your death shall be."

He stepped in, gave her a kiss,   45
    The royal ring he brought him wi;
Her breath was strang, her hair was lang,
    And twisted ance about the tree,
And with a swing she came about:
    "Come to Craigy's sea and kiss with me.   50

"Here is a royal brand," she said,
    "That I have found in the green sea;
And while your body it is on,
    Drawn shall your blood never be;
But if you touch me, tail or fin,   55
    I swear my brand your death shall be."

He stepped in, gave her a kiss,
    The royal brand he brought him wi;
Her breath was sweet, her hair grew short,
    And twisted nane about the tree,   60
And smilingly she came about,
    As fair a woman as fair could be.

EXPLORATION OVER THE RIM
William Dickey (1928–   )

Beyond that sandbar is the river's turning.
There a new country opens up to sight,
Safe from the fond researches of our learning.
Here it is day; there it is always night.

Around this corner is a certain danger.   5
The streets are streets of hell from here on in.
The Anthropophagi° and beings stranger
Roast in the fire and meditate on sin.

After this kiss will I know who I'm kissing?
Will I have reached the point of no return?   10
What happened to those others who are missing?
Oh, well, to hell with it. If we burn, we burn.

The Jack in this poem is the one who traded the family cow
for a handful of magic beans. You know the story of the
beanstalk well. Jarrell observes that Jack never completed
his quest—that as a hero he failed.

JACK
Randall Jarrell (1914–1965)

The sky darkened watching you
And the year sinking in its journey
Seem to you the slit beanstalk
And the goose crumpled in its pen.

The river, the spilt boats,   5
And the giant like a cloud falling
Are all pieces in your mind
Of a puzzle that, once joined,

Might green again the rotting stack.
Now, the oven's stiff creaking   10

°*Anthropophagi*: cannibals

Vexes you, but lifelessly,
Shameless as someone else's dream;

The harp crying out as you ran
Seems, rustling, your daughters' yellow hair. . . .
As, bound in some terrible wooden charm,   15
You sit here rigid and aghast.

Sometimes, in your good memory,
The strait princess, the giant's simpler wife
Come torn and gazing, begging
The names you could never comprehend,   20

And in the narrowing circle, sitting
With the world's puzzle rusting in your hands,
You know then you can never regain
The land that the harp sang so loudly.

2
THE FALL
FROM INNOCENCE

•

AFTER LONG SILENCE

William Butler Yeats (1865–1939)

Speech after long silence; it is right,
All other lovers being estranged or dead,
Unfriendly lamplight hid under its shade,
The curtains drawn upon unfriendly night,
That we descant and yet again descant   5
Upon the supreme theme of Art and Song:
Bodily decrepitude is wisdom; young
We loved each other and were ignorant.

THE PRIEST'S SOUL

Anonymous

In former days there were great schools in Ireland, where
every sort of learning was taught to the people, and even the poor-
est had more knowledge at that time than many a gentleman has
now. . . .

Now, at this time there was a little boy learning at one of
them who was a wonder to everyone for his cleverness. His parents
were only laboring people, and of course poor; but young as he was,
. . . no king's or lord's son could come up to him in learning. Even
the masters were put to shame. . . . When he grew up his poor father
and mother were so proud of him that they resolved to make him a
priest. . . though they nearly starved themselves to get the money.
Well, such another learned man was not in Ireland, and he was [so]
great in argument. . . that no one could stand before him. Even the
bishops tried to talk to him, but he showed them at once they knew
nothing at all.

Now, there were no schoolmasters in those times, but it was the priests taught the people; and as this man was the cleverest in Ireland, all the foreign kings sent their sons to him. . . . So he grew very proud, and began to forget how low he had been, and worst of all, even to forget God, who had made him what he was. And the pride of arguing got hold of him, so that from one thing to another he went on to prove that there was no Purgatory, . . . no Hell, . . . no Heaven, and then no God; and at last that men had no souls but were no more than a dog or cow, and when they died there was an end of them. "Whoever saw a soul?" he would say. "If you can show me one, I will believe." No one could make any answer to this; and at last they all came to believe that as there was no other world, everyone might do what they like in this; the priest setting the example, for he took a beautiful young girl to wife. . . . It was a great scandal, yet no one dared to say a word, for all the kings' sons were on his side, and would have slaughtered anyone who tried to prevent his wicked goings-on. Poor boys; they all believed in him. . . . In this way notions began to spread about, and the whole world was going to the bad, when one night an angel came down from Heaven, and told the priest he had but twenty-four hours to live. He began to tremble, and asked for a little more time.

But the angel was stiff. . . .

"What do you want time for, you sinner?" he asked.

"Oh, sir, have pity on my poor soul!" urged the priest.

"Oh, no! You have a soul, then," said the angel. "Pray, how did you find that out?"

"It has been fluttering in me ever since you appeared," answered the priest. . . .

"What good was all your learning, when it could not tell you that you had a soul?" [said the angel].

"Ah, my lord," said the priest, "if I am to die, tell me how soon I may be in Heaven?"

"Never," replied the angel. "You denied there was a Heaven."

"Then, my lord, may I go to Purgatory?"

"You denied Purgatory also; you must go straight to Hell," said the angel.

"But, my lord, I denied Hell also," answered the priest, "so you can't send me there either."

The angel was a little puzzled.

"Well," said he, "I'll tell you what I can do for you. You may either live now on earth for a hundred years, enjoying every pleasure, and then be cast into Hell forever; or you may die in twenty-four hours in the most horrible torments, and pass through

Purgatory, there to remain till the Day of Judgment, if only you can find some one person that believes, and through his belief mercy will be vouchsafed to you, and your soul will be saved."

"I will have death in the twenty-four hours," he said, "so that my soul may be saved at last."

On this the angel . . . left him.

Then immediately the priest entered the large room where all the scholars and the kings' sons were seated, and called out to them:

"Now, tell me the truth, and let none fear to contradict me; tell me what is your belief—have men souls?"

"Master," they answered, "once we believed that men had souls; but thanks to your teaching, we believe so no longer. There is no Hell, and no Heaven, and no God. This is our belief, for it is thus you taught us."

Then the priest grew pale with fear, and cried out: "Listen! I taught you a lie. There is a God, and man has an immortal soul. I believe now all I denied before."

But the shouts of laughter that rose up drowned the priest's voice, for they thought he was only trying them for argument.

"Prove it, master," they cried. "Prove it. Who has ever seen God? Who has ever seen the soul?". . .

The priest stood up to answer them. . . . All his eloquence, all his powers of argument had gone from him; and he could do nothing but wring his hands and cry out, "There is a God! . . . Lord have mercy on my soul!"

And they all began to mock him and repeat his own words that he had taught them:

"Show him to us; show your God." And he fled from them groaning with agony, for he saw that none believed; and how, then, could his soul be saved? . . .

Then despair came on him, and he rushed from the house, and began to ask everyone he met if they believed. But the same answer came from one and all: "We believe only what you have taught us," for his doctrine had spread far and wide through the country.

Then he grew half mad with fear, . . . and he flung himself down on the ground in a lonesome spot, and wept and groaned in terror, for the time was coming fast when he must die.

Just then a little child came by. "God save you kindly," said the child to him.

The priest started up.

"Do you believe in God?" he asked.

"I have come from a far country to learn about him," said the child. "Will your honor direct me to the best school they have in these parts?"

"The best school and the best teacher is close by," said the priest, and he named himself.

"Oh, not to that man," answered the child, "for I am told he denies God, and Heaven, and Hell, and even that man has a soul, because he cannot see it; but I would soon put him down."

The priest looked at him earnestly. "How?" he inquired.

"Why," said the child, "I would ask him if he believed he had life to show me his life."

"But he could not do that, my child," said the priest. "Life cannot be seen; we have it, but it is invisible."

"Then if we have life, though we cannot see it, we may also have a soul, though it is invisible," answered the child.

When the priest heard him speak these words, he fell down on his knees before him, weeping for joy, for now he knew his soul was safe; he had met one at last that believed. And he told the child his whole story—all his wickedness, and pride, and blasphemy against the great God; and how the angel had come to him, and told him of the only way in which he could be saved through the faith and prayers of someone that believed.

"Now, then," he said to the child, "take this penknife and strike it into my breast, and go on stabbing the flesh until you see the paleness of death on my face. Then watch—for a living thing will soar up from my body as I die, and you will then know that my soul has ascended to the presence of God. And when you see this thing, . . . call on all my scholars to come and see that the soul of their master has left the body, . . . that there is a God who punishes sin, and a Heaven, and a Hell, and that man has an immortal soul destined for eternal happiness or misery."

"I will pray," said the child, "to have courage to do this work." And he kneeled down and prayed. Then he rose and took the penknife and struck it into the priest's heart, and struck and struck again till all the flesh was lacerated; but still the priest lived, though the agony was horrible, for he could not die until the twenty-four hours had expired.

At last the agony seemed to cease, and the stillness of death settled on his face. Then the child, who was watching, saw a beautiful living creature, with four snow-white wings, mount from the dead man's body into the air and go fluttering round his head.

So he ran to bring the scholars; and when they saw it, they all knew it was the soul of their master; and they watched with wonder and awe until it passed from sight into the clouds.

And this was the first butterfly that was ever seen in Ireland; and now all men know that the butterflies are the souls of the dead, waiting for the moment when they may enter Purgatory, and so pass through torture to purification and peace.

THE CLOD & THE PEBBLE

William Blake (1757–1827)

"Love seeketh not Itself to please,
Nor for itself hath any care;
But for another gives its ease,
And builds a Heaven in Hell's despair."

  So sang a little Clod of Clay,   5
  Trodden with the cattle's feet;
  But a Pebble of the brook,
  Warbled out these metres meet:

"Love seeketh only Self to please,
To bind another to its delight;   10
Joys in another's loss of ease,
And builds a Hell in Heaven's despite."

NURSE'S SONG
from *Songs of Innocence*

William Blake

When the voices of children are heard on the green
And laughing is heard on the hill,
My heart is at rest within my breast
And everything else is still.

"Then come home my children, the sun is gone
  down   5
And the dews of night arise;
Come, come, leave off play, and let us away
Till the morning appears in the skies."

"No, no, let us play, for it is yet day
And we cannot go to sleep;   10

Besides, in the sky, the little birds fly
And the hills are all cover'd with sheep."

"Well, well, go & play till the light fades away
And then go home to bed."
The little ones leapéd & shouted & laugh'd   15
And all the hills echoéd.

NURSE'S SONG
from *Songs of Experience*
William Blake

When the voices of children are heard on the green
And whisp'rings are in the dale,
The days of my youth rise fresh in my mind,
My face turns green and pale.

Then come home my children, the sun is gone down 5
And the dews of night arise;
Your spring & your day are wasted in play,
And your winter and night in disguise.

DOVER BEACH
Matthew Arnold (1822–1888)

The sea is calm tonight,
The tide is full, the moon lies fair
Upon the Straits;—on the French coast, the light
Gleams, and is gone; the cliffs of England° stand,
Glimmering and vast, out in the tranquil bay.   5
Come to the window, sweet is the night air!
Only, from the long line of spray
Where the sea meets the moon-blanched sand,
Listen! you hear the grating roar
Of pebbles which the waves suck back, and fling,   10
At their return, up the high strand,
Begin, and cease, and then again begin,
With tremulous cadence slow, and bring
The eternal note of sadness in.

°*cliffs of England*: the Dover chalk cliffs

Sophocles° long ago   15
Heard it on the Aegean, and it brought
Into his mind the turbid ebb and flow
Of human misery; we
Find also in the sound a thought,
Hearing it by this distant northern sea.   20

The sea of faith
Was once, too, at the full, and round earth's shore
Lay like the folds of a bright girdle° furled;
But now I only hear
Its melancholy, long withdrawing roar,   25
Retreating to the breath
Of the night-wind down the vast edges drear
And naked shingles° of the world.

Ah, love, let us be true
To one another! for the world, which seems   30
To lie before us like a land of dreams,
So various, so beautiful, so new,
Hath really neither joy, nor love, nor light,
Nor certitude, nor peace, nor help for pain;
And we are here as on a darkling plain   35
Swept with confused alarms of struggle and flight,
Where ignorant armies clash by night.

TUMBLING-HAIR

E. E. Cummings (1894–1962)

Tumbling-hair
            picker of buttercups
                        violets

dandelions
And the big bullying daisies
                        through the field wonderful
with eyes a little sorry
Another comes
            also picking flowers

°*Sophocles*: Greek dramatist
°*girdle*: sash
°*shingles*: gravel beaches

3
DUALITIES

A Double-Dyed Deceiver

O. Henry (1862–1910)

The trouble began in Laredo. It was the Llano Kid's fault, for he should have confined his habit of manslaughter to Mexicans. But the Kid was past twenty; and to have only Mexicans to one's credit at twenty is to blush unseen on the Rio Grande border.

It happened in old Justo Valdo's gambling house. There was a poker game at which sat players who were not all friends, as happens often where men ride in from afar to shoot Folly as she gallops. There was a row over so small a matter as a pair of queens; and when the smoke had cleared away it was found that the Kid had committed an indiscretion, and his adversary had been guilty of a blunder. For, the unfortunate combatant, instead of being a Greaser, was a high-blooded youth from the cow ranches, of about the Kid's own age and possessed of friends and champions. His blunder in missing the Kid's right ear only a sixteenth of an inch when he pulled his gun did not lessen the indiscretion of the better marksman.

The Kid, not being equipped with a retinue nor bountifully supplied with personal admirers and supporters—on account of a rather umbrageous reputation, even for the border—considered it not incompatible with indisputable gameness to perform. that judicious tractional act known as "pulling his freight."

Quickly the avengers gathered and sought him. Three of them overtook him within a rod of the station. The Kid turned and showed his teeth in that brilliant but mirthless smile that usually preceded his deeds of insolence and violence, and his pursuers fell back without making it necessary for him even to reach for his weapon.

But in this affair the Kid had not felt the grim thirst for encounter that usually urged him on to battle. It had been a purely chance row, born of the cards and certain epithets impossible for a gentlemen to brook that had passed between the two. The Kid had rather liked the slim, haughty, brown-faced young chap whom his

193

bullet had cut off in the first pride of manhood. And now he wanted no more blood. He wanted to get away and have a good long sleep somewhere in the sun on the mesquite grass with his handkerchief over his face. Even a Mexican might have crossed his path in safety while he was in this mood.

The Kid openly boarded the north-bound passenger train that departed five minutes later. But at Webb, a few miles out, where it was flagged to take on a traveller, he abandoned that manner of escape. There were telegraph stations ahead; and the Kid looked askance at electricity and steam. Saddle and spur were his rocks of safety.

The man whom he had shot was a stranger to him. But the Kid knew that he was of the Coralitos outfit from Hidalgo; and that the punchers from that ranch were more relentless and vengeful than Kentucky feudists when wrong or harm was done to one of them. So, with the wisdom that has characterized many great fighters, the Kid decided to pile up as many leagues as possible of chaparral and pear between himself and the retaliation of the Coralitos bunch.

Near the station was a store; and near the store, scattered among the mesquites and elms, stood the saddled horses of the customers. Most of them waited, half asleep, with sagging limbs and drooping heads. But one, a long-legged roan with a curved neck, snorted and pawed the turf. Him the Kid mounted, gripped with his knees, and slapped gently with the owner's own quirt.

If the slaying of the temerarious card-player had cast a cloud over the Kid's standing as a good and true citizen, this last act of his veiled his figure in the darkest shadows of disrepute. On the Rio Grande border if you take a man's life you sometimes take trash; but if you take his horse, you take a thing the loss of which renders him poor, indeed, and which enriches you not—if you are caught. For the Kid there was no turning back now.

With the springing roan under him he felt little care or uneasiness. After a five-mile gallop he drew in to the plainsman's jogging trot, and rode northeastward toward the Nueces River bottoms. He knew the country well—its most tortuous and obscure trails through the great wilderness of brush and pear, and its camps and lonesome ranches where one might find safe entertainment. Always he bore to the east; for the Kid had never seen the ocean, and he had a fancy to lay his hand upon the mane of the great Gulf, the gamesome colt of the greater waters.

So after three days he stood on the shore at Corpus Christi, and looked out across the gentle ripples of a quiet sea.

Captain Boone, of the schooner *Flyaway*, stood near his

skiff, which one of his crew was guarding in the surf. When ready to sail he had discovered that one of the necessaries of life, in the parallelogrammatic shape of plug tobacco, had been forgotten. A sailor had been dispatched for the missing cargo. Meanwhile the captain paced the sands, chewing profanely at his pocket store.

A slim, wiry youth in high-heeled boots came down to the water's edge. His face was boyish, but with a premature severity that hinted at a man's experience. His complexion was naturally dark; and the sun and wind of an outdoor life had burned it to a coffee brown. His hair was as black and straight as an Indian's; his face had not yet been upturned to the humiliation of a razor; his eyes were a cold and steady blue. He carried his left arm somewhat away from his body, for pearl-handled .45s are frowned upon by town marshals, and are a little bulky when packed in the left arm-hole of one's vest. He looked beyond Captain Boone at the gulf with the impersonal and expressionless dignity of a Chinese emperor.

"Thinkin' of buyin' that'ar gulf, buddy?" asked the captain, made sarcastic by his narrow escape from the tobaccoless voyage.

"Why, no," said the Kid gently, "I reckon not. I never saw it before. I was just looking at it. Not thinking of selling it, are you?"

"Not this trip," said the captain. "I'll send it to you C.O.D. when I get back to Buenas Tierras. Here comes that capstan-footed lubber with the chewin'. I ought to've weighed anchor an hour ago."

"Is that your ship out there?" asked the Kid.

"Why, yes," answered the captain, "if you want to call a schooner a ship, and I don't mind lyin'. But you better say Miller and Gonzales, owners, and ordinary plain, Billy-be-damned old Samuel K. Boone, skipper."

"Where are you going to?" asked the refugee.

"Buenas Tierras, coast of South America—I forgot what they called the country the last time I was there. Cargo—lumber, corrugated iron, and machetes."

"What kind of a country is it?" asked the Kid—"hot or cold?"

"Warmish, buddy," said the captain. "But a regular Paradise Lost for elegance of scenery and be-yooty of geography. Ye're wakened every morning by the sweet singin' of red birds with seven purple tails and the sighin' of breezes in the posies and roses. And the inhabitants never work, for they can reach out and pick steamer baskets of the choicest hothouse fruit without gettin' out of bed. And there's no Sunday and no ice and no rent and no troubles and no use and no nothin'. It's a great country for a man to go to sleep with, and wait for somethin' to turn up. The bananys and oranges and hurricanes and pineapples that ye eat comes from there."

"That sounds to me!" said the Kid, at last betraying interest. "What'll the expressage be to take me out there with you?"

"Twenty-four dollars," said Captain Boone; "grub and transportation. Second cabin. I haven't got a first cabin."

"You've got my company," said the Kid, pulling out a buck-skin bag.

With three hundred dollars he had gone to Laredo for his regular "blowout." The duel in Valdos's had cut short his season of hilarity, but it had left him with nearly $200 for aid in the flight that it had made necessary.

"All right, buddy," said the captain. "I hope your ma won't blame me for this little childish escapade of yours." He beckoned to one of the boat's crew. "Let Sanchez lift you out to the skiff so you won't get your feet wet."

Thacker, the United States consul at Buenas Tierras, was not yet drunk. It was only eleven o'clock; and he never arrived at his desired state of beatitude—a state where he sang ancient maudlin vaudeville songs and pelted his screaming parrot with banana peels—until the middle of the afternoon. So, when he looked up from his hammock at the sound of a slight cough, and saw the Kid standing in the door of the consulate, he was still in a condition to extend the hospitality and courtesy due from the representative of a great nation. "Don't disturb yourself," said the Kid easily. "I just dropped in. They told me it was customary to light at your camp before starting in to round up the town. I just came in on a ship from Texas."

"Glad to see you, Mr.—," said the consul.

The Kid laughed.

"Sprague Dalton," he said. "It sounds funny to me to hear it. I'm called the Llano Kid in the Rio Grande country."

"I'm Thacker," said the consul. "Take that cane-bottom chair. Now if you've come to invest, you want somebody to advise you. These dingies will cheat you out of the gold in your teeth if you don't understand their ways. Try a cigar?"

"Much obliged," said the Kid, "but if it wasn't for my corn shucks and the little bag in my back pocket I couldn't live a minute." He took out his "makings," and rolled a cigarette.

"They speak Spanish here," said the consul. "You'll need an interpreter. If there's anything I can do, why, I'd be delighted. If you're buying fruit lands or looking for a concession of any sort, you'll want somebody who knows the ropes to look out for you."

"I speak Spanish," said the Kid, "about nine times better than I do English. Everybody speaks it on the range where I come from. And I'm not in the market for anything."

"You speak Spanish?" said Thacker thoughtfully. He regarded the Kid absorbedly.

"You look like a Spaniard, too," he continued. "And you're from Texas. And you can't be more than twenty or twenty-one. I wonder if you've got any nerve."

"You got a deal of some kind to put through?" asked the Texan with unexpected shrewdness.

"Are you open to a proposition?" said Thacker.

"What's the use to deny it?" said the Kid. "I got into a little gun frolic down in Laredo and plugged a white man. There wasn't any Mexican handy. And I come down to your parrot-and-monkey range just for to smell the morning-glories and marigolds. Now, do you *sabe?*°"

Thacker got up and closed the door.

"Let me see your hand," he said.

He took the Kid's left hand, and examined the back of it closely.

"I can do it," he said excitedly. "Your flesh is as hard as wood and as healthy as a baby's. It will heal in a week."

"If it's a fist fight you want to back me for," said the Kid, "don't put your money up yet. Make it gun work, and I'll keep you company. But no barehanded scrapping, like ladies at a tea-party, for me."

"It easier than that," said Thacker. "Just step here, will you?"

Through the window he pointed to a two-story white-stuccoed house with wide galleries rising amid the deep-green tropical foliage on a wooded hill that sloped gently from the sea.

"In that house," said Thacker, "a fine old Castilian gentleman and his wife are yearning to gather you into their arms and fill your pockets with money. Old Santos Urique lives there. He owns half the gold-mines in the country."

"You haven't been eating loco weed, have you?" asked the Kid.

"Sit down again," said Thacker, "and I'll tell you. Twelve years ago they lost a kid. No, he didn't die—although most of 'em here do from drinking the surface water. He was a wild little devil,

_____

°*sabe*: understand

even if he wasn't but eight years old. Everybody knows about it.
Some Americans who were through here prospecting for gold had
letters to Señor Urique, and the boy was a favorite with them. They
filled his head with big stories about the States; and about a month
after they left, the kid disappeared, too. He was supposed to have
stowed himself away among the banana bunches on a fruit steamer,
and gone to New Orleans. He was seen once afterward in Texas it
was thought, but they never heard anything more of him. Old
Urique has spent thousands of dollars having him looked for. The
madam was broken up worst of all. The kid was her life. She wears
mourning yet. But they say she believes he'll come back to her some
day, and never gives up hope. On the back of the boy's left hand was
tattooed a flying eagle carrying a spear in his claws. That's old
Urique's coat of arms or something that he inherited in Spain."

The Kid raised his left hand slowly and gazed at it
curiously.

"That's it," said Thacker, reaching behind the official desk
for his bottle of smuggled brandy. "You're not so slow. I can do it.
What was I consul at Sandakan for? I never knew till now. In a
week I'll have the eagle bird with the frog-sticker blended in so
you'd just think you were born with it. I brought a set of the nee-
dles and ink just because I was sure you'd drop in some day, Mr.
Dalton."

"Oh, hell," said the Kid. "I thought I told you my name!"

"All right, 'Kid,' then. It won't be that long. How does
Señorito Urique sound, for a change?"

"I never played son any that I remember of," said the
Kid. "If I had any parents to mention they went over the divide
about the time I gave my first bleat. What is the plan of your
round-up?"

Thacker leaned back against the wall and held his glass
up to the light.

"We've come now," said he, "to the question of how far
you're willing to go in little matter of the sort."

"I told you why I came down here," said the Kid simply.

"A good answer," said the consul. "But you won't have to
go that far. Here's the scheme. After I get the trade-mark tattooed
on your hand I'll notify old Urique. In the meantime I'll furnish you
with all of the family history I can find out, so you can be studying
up points to talk about. You've got the looks, you speak the Spanish,
you know the facts, you can tell about Texas, you've got the tattoo
mark. When I notify them that the rightful heir has returned and is
waiting to know whether he will be received and pardoned, what
will happen? They'll simply rush down here and fall on your neck,

and the curtain goes down for refreshments and a stroll in the lobby."

"I'm waiting," said the Kid. "I haven't had my saddle off in your camp long, pardner, and I never met you before; but if you intend to let it go at a parental blessing, why, I'm mistaken in my man, that's all."

"Thanks," said the consul. "I haven't met anybody in a long time that keeps up with an argument as well as you do. The rest of it is simple. If they take you in only for a while it's long enough. Don't give 'em time to hunt up the strawberry mark on your left shoulder. Old Urique keeps anywhere from $50,000 to $100,000 in his house all the time in a little safe that you could open with a shoe buttoner. Get it. My skill as a tattooer is worth half the boodle. We go halves and catch a tramp steamer for Rio Janeiro. Let the United States go to pieces if it can't get along without my services. ¿Qué dice, señor?"°

"It sounds to me!" said the Kid nodding his head. "I'm out for the dust."

"All right, then," said Thacker. "You'll have to keep close until we get the bird on you. You can live in the back room here. I do my own cooking, and I'll make you as comfortable as a parsimonious Government will allow me."

Thacker had set the time at a week, but it was two weeks before the design that he patiently tattooed upon the Kid's hand was to his notion. And then Thacker called a muchacho,° and dispatched this note to the intended victim:

> El Señor Don Santos Urique,
>   La Casa Blanca,
>
> My Dear Sir:
>   I beg permission to inform you that there is in my house as a temporary guest a young man who arrived in Buenas Tierras from the United States some days ago. Without wishing to excite any hopes that may not be realized, I think there is a possibility of his being your long-absent son. It might be well for you to call and see him. If he is, it is my opinion that his intention was to return to his home, but upon arriving here, his courage failed him from doubts as to how he would be received.
>
>   Your true servant,
>   Thompson Thacker.

° ¿Qué dice, señor?: "What do you say, Sir?"
° muchacho: boy

Half an hour afterward—quick time for Buenas Tierras—
Señor Urique's ancient landau drove to the consul's door, with the
barefooted coachman beating and shouting at the team of fat, awkward horses.

A tall man with a white moustache alighted, and assisted
to the ground a lady who was dressed and veiled in unrelieved
black.

The two hastened inside, and were met by Thacker with
his best diplomatic bow. By his desk stood a slender young man
with clear-cut, sunbrowned features and smoothly brushed black
hair.

Señora Urique threw back her heavy veil with a quick
gesture. She was past middle age, and her hair was beginning to
silver, but her full, proud figure and clear olive skin retained traces
of the beauty peculiar to the Basque province. But, once you had
seen her eyes, and comprehended the great sadness that was
revealed in their deep shadows and hopeless expression, you saw
that the woman lived only in some memory.

She bent upon the young man a long look of the most ago-
nized questioning. Then her great black eyes turned, and her gaze
rested upon his left hand. And then with a sob, not loud, but seeming to shake the room, she cried *"¡Hijo mío!"°* and caught the
Llano Kid to her heart.

A month afterward the Kid came to the consulate in
response to a message sent by Thacker.

He looked the young Spanish *caballero.°* His clothes were
imported, and the wiles of the jewellers had not been spent upon
him in vain. A more than respectable diamond shone on his fingers
as he rolled a shuck cigarette.

"What's doing?" asked Thacker.

"Nothing much," said the Kid calmly. "I eat my first
iguana steak today. They're them big lizards, you *sabe?* I reckon,
though, that frijoles and side bacon would do me about as well. Do
you care for iguanas, Thacker?"

"No, nor for some other kinds of reptiles," said Thacker.

It was three in the afternoon, and in another hour he would
be in his state of beatitude.

"It's time you were making good, sonny," he went on,
with an ugly look on his reddened face. "You're not playing up to
me square. You've been the prodigal son for four weeks now, and
you could have had veal for every meal on a gold dish if you'd
wanted it. Now, Mr. Kid, do you think it's right to leave me out so

---

° *¡ Hijo mío!* : my son
° *caballero* : gentleman

long on a husk diet? What's the trouble? Don't you get your filial eyes on anything that looks like cash in the Casa Blanca? Don't tell me you don't. Everybody knows where old Urique keeps his stuff. It's U.S. currency, too; he don't accept anything else. What's doing? Don't say 'nothing' this time."

"Why, sure," said the Kid, admiring his diamond, "there's plenty of money up there. I'm no judge of collateral in bunches, but I will undertake for to say that I've seen the rise of $50,000 at a time in that tin grub box that my adopted father calls his safe. And he lets me carry the key sometimes just to show me that he knows I'm the real little Francisco that strayed from the herd a long time ago."

"Well, what are you waiting for?" asked Thacker angrily. "Don't you forget that I can upset your apple-cart any day I want to. If old Urique knew you were an impostor, what sort of things would happen to you? Oh, you don't know this country, Mr. Texas Kid. The laws here have got mustard spread between 'em. These people here'd stretch you out like a frog that had been stepped on, and give you about fifty sticks at every corner of the plaza. And they'd wear every stick out, too. What was left of you they'd feed to alligators."

"I might as well tell you now, pardner," said Kid, sliding down low on his steamer chair, "that things are going to stay just as they are. They're about right now."

"What do you mean?" asked Thacker, rattling the bottom of his glass on his desk.

"The scheme's off," said the Kid. "And whenever you have the pleasure of speaking to me address me as Don Francisco Urique. I'll guarantee I'll answer to it. We'll let Colonel Urique keep his money. His little tin safe is as good as the time-locker in the First National Bank of Laredo as far as you and me are concerned."

"You're going to throw me down, then, are you?" said the consul.

"Sure," said the Kid cheerfully. "Throw you down. That's it. And now I'll tell you why. The first night I was up at the colonel's house they introduced me to a bedroom. No blankets on the floor—a real room, with a bed and things in it. And before I was asleep, in comes this artificial mother of mine and tucks in the covers. 'Panchito,' she says, 'my little lost one, God has brought you back to me. I bless His name forever.' It was that, or some truck like that, she said. And down comes a drop or two of rain and hits me on the nose. And all that stuck by me, Mr. Thacker. And it's been that way ever since. And it's got to stay that way. Don't you think that it's for what's in it for me, either, that I say so. If you have any such ideas, keep 'em to yourself. I haven't had much truck with women in my life, and no mothers to speak of, but here's a lady that we've got to keep fooled. Once she stood it; twice she won't. I'm a low-down wolf, and the devil may have sent me on this trail instead of God, but I'll travel it to the end. And now, don't forget that I'm Don Francisco Urique whenever you happen to mention my name."

"I'll expose you to-day, you—you double-dyed traitor," stammered Thacker.

The Kid arose and, without violence, took Thacker by the throat with a hand of steel, and shoved him slowly into a corner. Then he drew from under his left arm his pearl-handled .45 and poked the cold muzzle of it against the consul's mouth.

"I told you why I come here," he said, with his old freezing smile. "If I leave here, you'll be the reason. Never forget it, pardner. Now, what is my name?"

"Er—Don Francisco Urique," gasped Thacker.

From outside came a sound of wheels, and the shouting of some one, and the sharp thwacks of a wooden whipstock upon the backs of fat horses.

The Kid put up his gun, and walked toward the door. But he turned again and came back to the trembling Thacker, and held up his left hand with its back toward the consul.

"There's one more reason," he said slowly, "why things have got to stand as they are. The fellow I killed in Laredo had one of them same pictures on his left hand."

Outside, the ancient landau of Don Santos Urique rattled to the door. The coachman ceased his bellowing. Señora Urique, in a voluminous gay gown of white lace and flying ribbons, leaned forward with a happy look in her great soft eyes.

"Are you within, dear son?" she called, in the rippling Castilian.

"*Madre mia, yo vengo* (mother, I come)," answered the young Don Francisco Urique.

PRINCE LINDWORM

Anonymous

Once upon a time, there was a fine young King who was married to the loveliest of Queens. They were exceedingly happy, all but for one thing—they had no children. And this often made them both sad, because the Queen wanted a dear little child to play with, and the King wanted an heir to the kingdom.

One day the Queen went out for a walk by herself, and she met an ugly old woman. The old woman was just like a witch: but she was a nice kind of a witch, not the cantankerous sort. She said, "Why do you look so doleful, pretty lady?" "It's no use my telling you," answered the Queen, "nobody in the world can help me." "Oh, you never know," said the old woman. "Just you let me hear what your trouble is, and maybe I can put things right."

"My dear woman, how can you?" said the Queen: and she told her, "The King and I have no children: that's why I am so distressed." "Well you needn't be," said the old witch. "I can set that right in a twinkling, if only you will do exactly as I tell you. Listen. Tonight, at sunset, take a little drinking-cup with two ears" (that is, handles), "and put it bottom upwards on the ground in the north-west corner of your garden. Then go and lift it up to-morrow morning at sunrise, and you will find two roses underneath it, one red and one white. If you eat the red rose, a little boy will be born to you: if you eat the white rose, a little girl will be sent. But, whatever you do, you mustn't eat *both* the roses, or you'll be sorry—that I warn you! Only one: remember that!" "Thank you a thousand times," said the Queen, "This is good news indeed!" And she wanted to give the old woman her gold ring; but the old woman wouldn't take it.

So the Queen went home and did as she had been told: and the next morning at sunrise she stole out into the garden and lifted up the little drinking-cup. She *was* surprised for indeed she had hardly expected to see anything. But there were two roses underneath it, one red and one white. And now she was dreadfully puzzled, for she did not know which to choose. . . .

However, at last she decided on the white rose, and she ate it. And it tasted so sweet, that she took and ate the red one too: without ever remembering the old woman's solemn warning.

Some time after this, the King went away to the wars: and while he was still away, the Queen became the mother of twins. One was a lovely baby-boy, and the other was a Lindworm, or Serpent. She was terribly frightened when she saw the Lindworm, but he wriggled away out of the room, and nobody seemed to have seen him but herself: so that she thought it must have been a dream. The baby Prince was so beautiful and so healthy, the Queen was full of joy: and likewise, as you may suppose, was the King when he came home and found his son and heir. Not a word was said by anyone about the Lindworm: only the Queen thought about it now and then.

Many days and years passed by, and the baby grew up into a handsome young Prince, and it was time he got married. The King sent him off to visit foreign kingdoms, in the royal coach, with six white horses, to look for a Princess grand enough to be his wife. But at the very first cross-roads, the way was stopped by an enormous Lindworm, enough to frighten the bravest. He lay in the middle of the road with a great wide open mouth, and cried, "A bride for me before a bride for you!" Then the Prince made the coach turn round and try another road: but it was all no use. For, at the first cross-ways, there lay the Lindworm again, crying out, "A bride for me before a bride for you!" So the Prince had to turn back home again to the Castle, and give up his visits to the foreign kingdoms. And his mother, the Queen had to confess that what the Lindworm said was true. For he was really the eldest of the twins: and so he ought to have a wedding first.

There seemed nothing for it but to find a bride for the Lindworm, if his younger brother, the Prince, were to be married at all. So the King wrote to a distant country, and asked for a Princess to marry his son (but, of course, he didn't say which son), and presently a Princess arrived. But she wasn't allowed to see her bridegroom until he stood by her side in the great hall and was married to her, and then, of course it was too late for her to say she wouldn't have him. But next morning the Princess had disappeared. The Lindworm lay sleeping all alone: and it was quite plain that he had eaten her.

A little while after, the Prince decided that he might now go journeying again in search of a Princess. . . . But at the first cross-ways, there lay the Lindworm, crying with his great wide open mouth, "A bride for me before a bride for you!" So the carriage tried another road, and the same thing happened, and they had to turn back again. . . . And the King wrote to several foreign countries, to know if anyone would marry his son. At last another Princess arrived. . . . And, of course, she was not allowed to see her future husband before the wedding took place,—and then, lo and behold! It was the Lindworm who stood at her side. And next morning the Princess had disappeared: and the Lindworm lay sleeping all alone; and it was quite clear that he had eaten her.

By and by the Prince started on his quest for the third time: and at the first cross-roads . . . lay the Lindworm . . . , demanding a bride as before. And the Prince went straight back to the Castle, and told the King: "You must find another bride for my elder brother."

"I don't know where I am to find her," said the King, "I have already made enemies of two great Kings who sent their daughters here as brides: and I have no notion how I can obtain a third lady. People are beginning to say strange things, and I am sure no Princess will dare to come."

Now, down in a little cottage near a wood, there lived the King's shepherd, an old man with his only daughter. And the King came one day and said to him, "Will you give me your daughter to marry my son the Lindworm? And I will make you rich for the rest of your life."—"No, sire," said the shepherd, "that I cannot do. . . . Besides, if the Lindworm would not spare two beautiful Princesses, he won't spare her either. He will just gobble her up: and she is much too good for such a fate."

But the King wouldn't take "No" for an answer: and at last the old man had to give in.

Well, when the old shepherd told his daughter that she was to be Prince Lindworm's bride, she was utterly in despair. She went out into the woods, crying and wringing her hands. . . . And while she wandered to and fro, an old witch-woman suddenly appeared out of a big hollow oak tree, and asked her, "Why do you look so doleful, pretty lass?" The shepherd-girl said, "It's no use my telling you, for nobody in the world can help me." "Oh, you never know," said the old woman. "Just you let me hear what your trouble is, and maybe I can put things right." —"Ah, how can you?" said the girl, "for I am to be married to the King's eldest son, who is a Lindworm. He has already married two beautiful Princesses, and devoured them: and he will eat me too! No wonder I am distressed."

"Well, you needn't be," said the witch-woman. "All that can be set right in a twinkling: If only you will do exactly as I tell you." So the girl said she would.

"Listen, then," said the old woman. "After the marriage ceremony is over, and when it is time for you to retire to rest, you must ask to be dressed in ten snow-white shifts. And you must then ask for a tub full of lye (that is, washing water prepared with wood-ashes) and a tub full of fresh milk, and as many whips as a boy can carry in his arms, and have all these brought into your bed-chamber. Then, when the Lindworm tells you to shed a shift, do you bid him slough a skin. And when all his skins are off, you must dip the whips in the lye and whip him; next, you must wash him in the fresh milk; and, lastly, you must take him and hold him in your arms, if it's only for one moment."

"The last is the worst notion—ugh!" said the shepherd's daughter, and she shuddered at the thought of holding the cold, slimy, scaly Lindworm.

"Do just as I have said, and all will go well," said the old woman. Then she disappeared again in the oak-tree.

When the wedding-day arrived, the girl was fetched in the royal chariot with the six white horses, and taken to the castle to be decked as a bride. And she asked for ten snow-white shifts to be brought her, and the tub of lye, and the tub of milk, and as many whips as a boy could carry in his arms. The ladies and courtiers in the castle thought, of course, that this was some bit of peasant superstition, all rubbish and nonsense. But the King said, "Let her have whatever she asks for." She was then arrayed in the most wonderful robes and looked the loveliest of brides. She was led to the hall where the wedding ceremony was to take place, and she saw the Lindworm for the first time as he came in and stood by her side. So they were married, and a great wedding-feast was held, a banquet fit for the son of a king.

When the feast was over, the bridegroom and bride were conducted to their apartment, with music, and torches, and a great procession. As soon as the door was shut, the Lindworm turned to her and said, "Fair maiden, shed a shift!" The shepherd's daughter answered him, "Prince Lindworm, slough a skin!" "No one has ever dared tell me to do that before!" said he.—"But I command you to do it now!" said she. Then he began to moan and wriggle: and in a few minutes a long snake-skin lay upon the floor beside him. The girl drew off her first shift, and spread it on top of the skin.

The Lindworm said again to her, "Fair maiden, shed a shift."

The shepherd's daughter answered him, "Prince Lindworm, slough a skin."

"No one has ever dared tell me to do that before," said he and his little eyes rolled furiously. "But I command you to do it now," said she. Then with groans and moans he cast off the second skin: and she covered it with her second shift. . . . But the girl was not afraid, and once more she commanded him to do as she bade.

And so this went on until nine Lindworm skins were lying on the floor, each of them covered with a snow-white shift. And there was nothing left of the Lindworm, but a huge thick mass, most horrible to see. Then the girl seized the whips, dipped them in the lye, and whipped him as hard as ever she could. Next, she bathed him all over in the fresh milk. Lastly, she dragged him on the bed and put her arms round him. And she fell fast asleep that very moment.

Next morning very early, the King and the courtiers came and peeped in through the keyhole. They wanted to know what had become of the girl, but none of them dared enter the room. However, in the end, growing bolder, they opened the door a tiny bit. And there they saw the girl, all fresh and rosy, and beside her lay— no Lindworm, but the handsomest prince that anyone could wish to see.

The King ran out and fetched the Queen: and after that, there were such rejoicings in the castle as never were known before or since. The wedding took place all over again, much finer than the first, with festivals and banquets and merrymakings for days and weeks. No bride was ever so beloved by a King and Queen as this peasant maid from the shepherd's cottage. There was no end to their love and their kindness towards her: she had saved their son, Prince Lindworm.

Genesis, CHAPTER 4

And Adam knew Eve his wife; and she conceived, and bare Cain, and said, I have gotten a man from the Lord. And she again bare his brother Abel. And Abel was a keeper of sheep, but Cain was a tiller of the ground.

And in process of time it came to pass, that Cain brought of the fruit of the ground an offering unto the Lord. And Abel, he also brought of the firstlings of his flock and of the fat thereof. And the Lord had respect unto Abel and to his offering: But unto Cain and to his offering he had not respect. And Cain was very wroth, and his countenance fell.

And the Lord said unto Cain, Why art thou wroth? and why is thy countenance fallen? If thou doest well, shalt thou not be accepted? and if thou doest not well, sin lieth at the door: and unto thee shall be his desire, and thou shalt rule over him.

And Cain talked to Abel his brother: and it came to pass, when they were in the field, that Cain rose up against Abel his brother, and slew him.

And the Lord said unto Cain, Where is Abel thy brother? And he said, I know not: Am I my brother's keeper?

And he said, What hast thou done? the voice of thy brother's blood crieth unto me from the ground. And now art thou cursed from the earth, which hath opened her mouth to receive thy brother's blood from thy hand. When thou tillest the ground, it shall not henceforth yield unto thee her strength; a fugitive and a vagabond shalt thou be in the earth.

And Cain said unto the Lord, My punishment is greater than I can bear. Behold, thou hast driven me out this day from the face of the earth; and from thy face shall I be hid; and I shall be a fugitive and a vagabond in the earth; and it shall come to pass, that every one that findeth me shall slay me.

And the Lord said unto him, Therefore whosoever slayeth Cain, vengeance shall be taken on him sevenfold. And the Lord set a mark upon Cain, lest any finding him should kill him.

And Cain went out from the presence of the Lord, and dwelt in the land of Nod, on the east of Eden.

4
FERTILITY:
CYCLES OF NATURE

•

THESE ARE THE DAYS WHEN BIRDS COME BACK
Emily Dickinson (1830–1886)

These are the days when birds come back,
A very few, a bird or two,
To take a backward look.

These are the days when skies put on
The old, old sophistries of June,—   5
A blue and gold mistake.

Oh, fraud that cannot cheat the bee,
Almost thy plausibility
Induces my belief,

Till ranks of seeds their witness bear,   10
And softly through the altered air
Hurries a timid leaf!

Oh, sacrament of summer days,
Oh, last communion in the haze,
Permit a child to join,   15

Thy sacred emblems to partake,
Thy consecrated bread to break,
Taste thine immortal wine!

HE WAS
Richard Wilbur (1921–   )

a brown old man with a green thumb:
I can remember the screak on stones of his hoe,

208

The chug, choke, and high madrigal wheeze
Of the spray-cart bumping below
The sputtery leaves of the apple trees,   5
But he was all but dumb

Who filled some quarter of the day with sound
All of my childhood long. For all I heard
Of all his labors, I can now recall
Never a single word   10
Until he went in the dead of fall
To the drowsy underground,

Having planted a young orchard with so great care
In that last year that none was lost, and May
Aroused them all, the leaves saying the land's   15
Praise for the livening clay,
And the found voice of his buried hands
Rose in the sparrowy air.

I Wandered Lonely As a Cloud

William Wordsworth (1770–1850)

I wandered lonely as a cloud
That floats on high o'er vales and hills,
When all at once I saw a crowd,
A host, of golden daffodils;
Beside the lake, beneath the trees,   5
Fluttering and dancing in the breeze.

Continuous as the stars that shine
And twinkle on the milky way,
They stretched in never-ending line
Along the margin of a bay: 10
Ten thousand saw I at a glance,
Tossing their heads in sprightly dance.

The waves beside them danced; but they
Outdid the sparkling waves in glee;
A poet could not but be gay,   15
In such a jocund company;
I gazed—and gazed—but little thought
What wealth the show to me had brought:

For oft, when on my couch I lie
In vacant or in pensive mood,   20
They flash upon that inward eye
Which is the bliss of solitude;
And then my heart with pleasure fills,
And dances with the daffodils.

MY HEART LEAPS UP

William Wordsworth

My heart leaps up when I behold
    A rainbow in the sky:
So was it when my life began;
So is it now I am a man;
So be it when I shall grow old,   5
    Or let me die!
The Child is father of the Man;
And I could wish my days to be
Bound each to each by natural piety.

FROM THE SONG OF SOLOMON

Rise up, my love, my fair one, and come away.
For, lo, the winter is past,
The rain is over and gone;
The flowers appear on the earth;
The time of the singing of birds is come,   5
And the voice of the turtle is heard in our land;
The fig tree putteth forth her green figs,
And the vines with the tender grape give a good
    smell.
Arise, my love, my fair one, and come away.

THE DARKLING° THRUSH

Thomas Hardy (1840–1928)

I leant upon a coppice gate°
    When Frost was specter-gray,

°*Darkling*: in the dark
°*coppice gate*: gate leading to a wooded area

And Winter's dregs made desolate
    The weakening eye of day.
The tangled bine-stems° scored the sky   5
    Like strings of broken lyres,
And all mankind that haunted nigh
    Had sought their household fires.

The land's sharp features seemed to be
    The Century's corpse° outleant,   10
His crypt the cloudy canopy,
    The wind his death-lament.
The ancient pulse of germ and birth
    Was shrunken hard and dry,
And every spirit upon earth   15
    Seemed fervorless as I.

At once a voice arose among
    The bleak twigs overhead
In a fullhearted evensong
    Of joy illimited;   20
An aged thrush, frail, gaunt, and small,
    In blast-beruffled plume,
Had chosen thus to fling his soul
    Upon the growing gloom.

MY HEART

Anonymous

My heart is all happy,
My heart takes wing in singing,
Under the trees of the forest,
The forest our dwelling and our mother.
On my thread I have taken,   5
A little, a very little bird.
My heart is caught on the thread,
On the thread with the bird.

°*bine-stems*: twining stems
°*Century's corpse*: This poem was written on December 31, 1900, the last
    day of the 19th century

ACKNOWLEDGMENTS (Cont'd)

E. E. CUMMINGS. "in Just–" Copyright © 1923, 1951, by E. E. Cummings. Reprinted from his volume, *Complete Poems 1913–1962*, by permission of Harcourt Brace Jovanovich, Inc.

A. E. HOUSMAN. "When I Was One-and-Twenty" from "A Shropshire Lad," Authorized Edition, from *The Collected Poems of A. E. Housman.* Copyright 1939, 1940, © 1965 by Holt, Rinehart and Winston. Copyright © 1967, 1968 by Robert E. Symons. Reprinted by permission of Holt, Rinehart and Winston, Publishers.

JOHN STEINBECK. From *Tortilla Flat* by John Steinbeck. Copyright 1935, Copyright © renewed 1963 by John Steinbeck. All rights reserved. Reprinted by permission of Viking Penguin, Inc.

HAZEL W. HERTZBERG. "Iroquois Creation Myth" reprinted with permission of Macmillan Publishing Co., Inc., from *The Great Tree and the Longhouse* by Hazel W. Hertzberg. Copyright © American Anthropological Association 1966.

WILLIAM CARLOS WILLIAMS. "The Use of Force" from *The Farmer's Daughters* by William Carlos Williams. Copyright 1938 by William Carlos Williams. Reprinted by permission of New Directions Publishing Corporation.

WOVOKA. "The Ghost Dance" from *Bury My Heart at Wounded Knee* by Dee Brown. Copyright © 1970 by Dee Brown. Reprinted by permission of Holt, Rinehart and Winston, Publishers.

E. E. CUMMINGS. "La Guerre." Copyright, 1923, 1951, by E. E. Cummings. Reprinted from his volume, *Complete Poems 1913–1962*, by permission of Harcourt Brace Jovanovich, Inc

"Oisin in Tír na nÓg." From *Old Celtic Romances*, P. W. Joyce, ed., published by The Devin-Adair Company, Old Greenwich, Conn. Reprinted by permission of The Devin-Adair Company.

GEORGE GARRETT. "The Quest" reprinted by permission of Charles Scribner's Sons from *The Reverend Ghost: Poems from Poets of Today IV* by George Garrett. Copyright © 1956, 1957 by George Garrett.

"Blood Clot Boy." Clark Wissler and D. C. Duvall, *Mythology of the Blackfeet Indians* (Anthropological papers of the American Museum of Natural History, vol. II, part I; New York, 1909), pp. 55–57. Reprinted in Joseph Campbell, *The Hero with a Thousand Faces*, Bollingen Series XVII (copyright © 1949 by Bollingen Foundation), pp. 338–340, published by Princeton University Press.

JUDITH WRIGHT. "Legend" from *The Gateway* by Judith Wright. Reprinted by permission of Angus & Robertson (UK) Ltd.

WILLIAM DICKEY. "Exploration over the Rim" from *Of the Festivity* by William Dickey, published by Yale University Press. Reprinted by permission of the author.

RANDALL JARRELL. "Jack" reprinted with the permission of Farrar, Straus & Giroux, Inc., from *The Complete Poems* by Randall Jarrell. Copyright © 1942 by Randall Jarrell, copyright renewed 1970 by Mary von Schrader Jarrell.

WILLIAM BUTLER YEATS. "After Long Silence" reprinted with permission of Macmillan Publishing Co., Inc., from *Collected Poems* by William Butler Yeats. Copyright 1933 by Macmillan Publishing Co., Inc., renewed 1961 by Bertha Georgie Yeats.

E. E. CUMMINGS. "tumbling-hair." Copyright 1923, 1951, by E. E. Cummings. Reprinted from his volume, *Complete Poems 1913–1962*, by permission of Harcourt Brace Jovanovich, Inc.

O. HENRY. "A Double-Dyed Deceiver" reprinted by permission of Doubleday & Company, Inc.

EMILY DICKINSON. "These Are the Days When Birds Come Back" reprinted by permission of the publishers and the trustees of Amherst College from

BIBLIOGRAPHY

It might be observed that any stab at constructing a bibliography here is paradoxical. Throughout the text I have tried to establish that all literature grows from mythological seed. Hence, any brief listing of myth collections, novels, plays, poems and short stories can do little more than reflect this editor's tastes, at the exclusion of countless other works that are equally applicable to the theme of this text. What follows, then, is a compilation of materials that have worked for me and some colleagues in the classroom. The reference works are mainly for the instructor's use and should serve well enough. Some of them are suitable for students who have expressed a deep interest in the subject of mythology.

Myths and Closely Related Readings

Allen, J. (ed.). *Hero's Way* (Prentice Hall). This is an excellent collection of poems, gathered under headings that signify the various progressive stages of the quest. Each section is introduced with a useful essay. Highly recommended.

Asimov, I. *Words from Myths* (Houghton Mifflin).

———. *Beowulf.*

Bullfinch, T. *The Age of Fable* (Airmont).

Campbell, J. *Myths to Live By* (Bantam).

Conrad, J. "The Secret Sharer."

Coolidge, O. *Greek Myths* (Macmillan).

———. *Legends of the North* (Houghton Mifflin).

———. *Hercules and Other Tales* (Scholastic).

Crane, M. (ed.). *Fifty Great Short Stories* (Bantam).

Crane, S. *The Red Badge of Courage*. This is a particularly good novel for use in demonstrating modern applications of mythological truths. Henry Fleming's journey is reflective of countless quests, and his fear is the stuff of mortality, without which no character in literature can be considered a hero.

Davidson, H. *Gods and Myths of Northern Europe* (Penguin).

Evslin, B. *Heroes, Gods, and Monsters of Greek Myths* (Bantam).

Feldman, S. *African Myths and Tales* (Dell).

Frazer, J. *The New Golden Bough* (New American Library).

Graves, R. *Greek Gods and Heroes* (Doubleday).
————. *Greek Myths, Vols, I, II* (Penguin).
Hamilton, E. *Mythology* (Mentor).
Homer. *The Iliad* (Rouse translation, Mentor).
————. *The Odyssey* (Rouse translation, Mentor).
Hosford, D. *Thunder of the Gods* (Holt).
Isherwood, C. (ed.). *Great English Short Stories* (Dell). This includes Conrad's "The Secret Sharer" and twelve other excellent short works.
Joyce, P., ed. *Old Celtic Romances* (Devon-Adair).
Malory, T. *Le Morte D'Arthur.*
————. **"The Phoenix."**
Rouse, H. *Gods, Heroes, and Men of Ancient Greece* (Signet).
Sabin, F. *Classical Myths That Live Today* (Silver Burdett).
Shelley, M. *Frankenstein.*
Stevenson, R. *The Strange Case of Dr. Jekyll and Mr. Hyde.*
Tolkien, J. *The Lord of the Rings* (Ballantine). A conscious imitation of the classic quest tale, this novel is nonetheless both entertaining and instructive.
Tripp, E. *Handbook of Classical Mythology* (T. Y. Crowell). This is a highly useful, witty, and inclusive source work for students and teachers alike.
Vergil. *The Aeneid* (Dickinson translation, Mentor).

Reference Works

Campbell, J. *The Hero with a Thousand Faces* (World).
————. *The Masks of God*, vols. I, II, III, and IV (Viking).
Eliade, M. *Cosmos and History: The Myth of the Eternal Return* (Harper & Row).
————. *Images and Symbols* (Sheed & Ward).
————. *Myths, Dreams, and Mysteries: The Encounter Between Contemporary Faiths and Archaic Realities* (Harper & Row).
Frye, N. *The Anatomy of Criticism: Four Essays* (Atheneum).
Gayley, C. *The Classical Myths in English Literature and in Art* (Blaisdell).
Guirand, F. (ed.) *Larousse Encyclopedia of Mythology* (Prometheus Press).
Henderson, J., and M. Oakes. *The Wisdom of the Serpent: The Myths of Death, Rebirth, and Resurrection* (George Braziller, Inc.).
Jung, C. *Man and His Symbols* (Doubleday).
Littleton, C. *The New Comparative Mythology* (U. of California Press).
Watts, A. *The Two Hands of God: Myths of Polarity* (Macmillan).
Zimmerman, J. *Dictionary of Classical Mythology* (Harper).